Anonymous

Speeches, letters, articles on the Gold Coinage Controversy of 1869

Anonymous

Speeches, letters, articles on the Gold Coinage Controversy of 1869

ISBN/EAN: 9783337108762

Printed in Europe, USA, Canada, Australia, Japan

Cover: Foto ©ninafisch / pixelio.de

More available books at **www.hansebooks.com**

SPEECHES,

LETTERS, ARTICLES, &c.

ON THE

GOLD COINAGE CONTROVERSY

OF

1869.

LONDON:
PRINTED AT THE BANK OF ENGLAND;
JOHN COE, SUPERINTENDENT.

1870.

INTRODUCTION.

ON the 6th August, 1869, Mr. J. B. SMITH, the Member for Stockport, invited the CHANCELLOR of the EXCHEQUER to state to the House of Commons his opinions upon the questions of an International Gold Coinage, and the expediency of establishing a charge for the conversion of Gold Bullion into Coin at the Mint.

The CHANCELLOR of the EXCHEQUER, in reply, dealt very fully with both of these questions, concluding his Speech with these words :—

" These are the remarks I had to make to the House.
" They are not given with any great confidence in my own
" opinion. All I am anxious to do before we separate
" is to give to hon. Gentlemen and the country at large a
" subject for consideration. It appears to me that the
" subject is not so difficult as might be supposed; and that
" by a single measure we may secure to ourselves the great
" benefit of saving all the expense incurred on our own gold

"coinage, without imposing those expenses on anyone else, "and at the same time of striking a coin which would have "the advantage of an international circulation."

The Gold Coinage Controversy is the answer to this invitation, and the purpose of the following pages is to preserve, in a commodious form, what has been said and written upon the important subjects in question, under the many differing points of view from which they have been regarded and discussed by so many different persons.

The specific proposition of the CHANCELLOR of the EXCHEQUER, to the support or refutation of which the various speakers and writers on the question have addressed themselves, is a reduction in the weight of the sovereign, to the extent of one grain ($\cdot$993 exactly) in the $123\frac{1}{4}$ grains of standard gold, now contained in the sovereign.

Out of this charge, or deduction so retained, it is proposed that the Mint shall repay itself the cost of the conversion of the Bullion into Coin, and provide for the renewal of the Coinage by founding and maintaining an endowment fund towards securing the State against the depreciation of the coin in time to come by wear and tear.

Another purpose of the proposed depreciation of the sovereign is to produce a coin exactly equivalent to a new French coin of 25 francs, and thus to facilitate, so far as this country is concerned, the establishment of an International Coinage.

The Collection is prefaced by the Speech of the CHANCELLOR of the EXCHEQUER on the occasion referred to, and the Report, under the joint signatures of the late Mr. GRAHAM, Master of the Mint in London, and Colonel J. T. SMITH, formerly Master of the Mint at Calcutta, in which the proposition for the establishment of a Mintage Charge on the Coinage of Gold is put forward for the first time under official responsibility.

These are followed by an Extract from the Evidence of Major HYDE, the Master of the Mint at Calcutta, in 1866, before a Commission appointed to examine into the Currency Laws of India, inasmuch as it contains the germ of the proposition, afterwards so elaborately worked out in Colonel SMITH's "Remarks on a Gold Currency for India,"—

"That the value of Coins *within the Currency* may be "increased without altering the weight of pure metal "contained in them, by alterations of the rules and practice "of Mints."

A very valuable Paper on "The British Coinage," printed under the signature of Mr. GRAHAM, as Appendix No. XI. to the Report of the Royal Commission on International Coinage, is added to the Collection.

The literature of the Controversy includes, amongst other papers well worthy of reference, the Report of the Royal Commissioners on "International Coinage;" Mr. W. STANLEY JEVONS's Paper on the "Condition of the

Metallic Currency of the United Kingdom, with reference to the question of International Coinage," reprinted from the Journal of the Statistical Society of London, and Mr. ERNEST SEYD'S Pamphlet on "Seigniorage and a Charge for Coining," as well as his work on "Bullion and the Foreign Exchanges."

The subject was discussed, on the reading of a Paper by Dr. FARR, at the Meeting of the British Association held at Exeter on the 25th August, 1869.

R. W. CRAWFORD,
Governor.

BANK OF ENGLAND,
    December, 1869.

INDEX.

LETTERS ON THE GOLD COINAGE.

Page.	Signature.	Date of Newspaper.	Newspaper.
207	"Aliquis".........	22nd September, 1869	Times.
230	Do.	28th ,, ,,	,,
36	Aytoun, Mr. J......	14th August ,,	Morning Advertiser.
52	Do.	17th ,, ,,	,,
77	Do.	23rd ,, ,,	,,
220	Bruton, Mr. L.	25th September ,,	Daily Telegraph.
243	Do.	5th October ,,	,,
247	Do.	7th ,, ,,	,,
250	Do.	13th ,, ,,	,,
171	"Bullionist"	14th September ,,	Times.
25	Hankey, Mr. T.	10th August ,,	,,
93	Do.	26th ,, ,,	,,
261	Hendriks, Mr. F. ...	9th October ,,	Economist.
280	Do.	13th November ,,	,,
294	Do.	20th ,, ,,	,,
116	Herschel, Sir J. F. W.	2nd September ,,	Times.
248	"H. M. H."	9th October ,,	Daily Telegraph.
29	Hubbard, Mr. J. G...	16th August ,,	Times.
48	Do.	17th ,, ,,	,,
54	Do.	20th ,, ,,	,,
71	Do.	21st ,, ,,	,,
111	Do.	1st September ,,	,,
123	Do.	3rd ,, ,,	,,
129	Do.	4th ,, ,,	,,
150	Do.	11th ,, ,,	,,
253	Do.	7th October ,,	,,

Page.	Signature.	Date of Newspaper.			Newspaper.
182	Hunt, Mr. T. N.	18th September, 1869			Economist.
81	Jevons, Mr. W. S.	24th August	,,		Times.
145	Do.	10th September	,,		,,
196	Levi, Mr. L.	20th	,,	,,	Daily Telegraph.
237	Do.	29th	,,	,,	,,
173	Lubbock, Sir J.	16th	,,	,,	Times.
209	Do.	22nd	,,	,,	,,
273	Do.	20th October		,,	,,
85	"Monetarius"	24th August	,,		,,
211	Nicholson, Mr. N. A..	22nd September	,,		,,
192	Overstone, Lord	20th	,,	,,	,,
213	Do.	25th	,,	,,	,,
87	"P."	25th August	,,		Morning Post.
154	"Par"	13th September	,,		Times.
162	Do.	14th	,,	,,	,,
176	Do.	16th	,,	,,	,,
185	Do.	20th	,,	,,	,,
217	Do.	25th	,,	,,	,,
232	Do.	28th	,,	,,	,,
266	Do.	19th October	,,		,,
59	Seyd, Mr. E.	20th August	,,		,,
73	Do.	21st	,,	,,	,,
106	Do.	30th	,,	,,	,,
167	Do.	14th September	,,		,,
96	Smith, Col. J. T.	26th August	,,		,,
102	Do.	28th	,,	,,	,,
135	Do.	8th September	,,		,,
139	Do.	9th	,,	,,	,,
282	Smith, Mr. J. B.	26th October	,,		,,
27	"W."	10th August	,,		,,

ARTICLES.

Page.	Newspaper.	Date of Newspaper.
40	Bullionist	14th August, 1869.
223	Do.	25th September ,,
278	Do.	23rd October ,,
202	Daily Telegraph	21st September ,,
238	Echo	30th ,, ,,
67	Economist	21st August ,,
151	Observer	12th September ,,
226	Do.	26th ,, ,,
19	Times	9th August ,,
43	Do.	16th ,, ,,
63	Do.	20th ,, ,,
274	Do.	19th October ,,

PARLIAMENTARY REPORTS, ETC.

Page.	Title.	Date.
18	Extract from the Evidence of Major Hyde, the Mint Master at Calcutta, given before the Commission to inquire into the operation of Act XIX. of 1861, at its first sitting, held at Calcutta on the 6th Feb., 1866.	
308	Half a dozen Propositions respecting the Gold Coinage, by J. F. W. H.	
33	Proceedings in Parliament	13th August, 1869.
12	Report of the Master of the Mint and Colonel Smith	6th April, 1869.
1	Speech delivered in the House of Commons, by the Rt. Hon. Robert Lowe, Chancellor of the Exchequer	6th August, 1869.
301	The British Coinage. (Appendix No. XI. to the Report of the Royal Commission on International Coinage.)	

THE GOLD COINAGE CONTROVERSY.

1869.

EXTRACT FROM A

SPEECH Delivered in the House of Commons, by the Right Honourable Robert Lowe, Chancellor of the Exchequer, on Friday, August 6, 1869.—(Hansard.)

THE CHANCELLOR OF THE EXCHEQUER:— I now turn to my hon. friend the Member for Stockport (Mr. J. B. Smith), who has introduced to us a very interesting subject, and one which might very well, at a time of less pressure, occupy the attention of the House—namely, the subject of our coinage. The coinage of this country is in a most unsatisfactory state; there is no doubt of that. The waste with which it is carried on is enormous. The possession of a gold and silver coinage I do not look upon myself as a necessity, but rather as a luxury, and as an indulgence to a popular taste—which, by the way, is a very expensive taste—but as it is the taste of the people of the country, I suppose it will continue to be gratified. It is quite necessary that the coinage of this country should correspond with gold and silver; but I am not aware there is any necessity it should actually consist of those metals. Since the year 1850, according to the calculations of Professor Jevons, who has looked deeply into the subject and has brought great ability to bear upon it, and whose conclusions are adopted by the Master of the Mint, Colonel Smith, and other authorities, we have coined 98,000,000 of sovereigns, and of these 98,000,000 about 44,000,000 have disappeared altogether. Either they have been exported from the country and have not returned to it, or they have been melted down. We have thus had the satisfaction of bestowing a great deal of labour and ingenuity and cost in the manufacture of an article of great merit and neatness in our gold coinage, which has formed a sort of quarry out of which other countries make gold coinage for their own use. The reason of this is not far to seek. As my hon. friend has said, we, almost alone of the nations of the world who make coin, give to the person who brings us gold the same weight of gold in coin, upon which we have bestowed labour, as we receive from him in a rude unwrought state. We give him our coinage at less than its cost; we give back weight for weight a manufactured article in exchange for the raw material out of which that article is made. It necessarily follows that, as we choose to circulate our coinage at less than its value, so, as coin, it commands less than its value, and is worth less than it really ought to be. It is impossible to make all sovereigns of the same weight; at least, if possible, it can only be done by a minuteness of machinery and a carefulness of labour which make it not a paying thing to do; the consequence is that, within certain limits, sovereigns are heavier one than the other. These sovereigns having no value given to them in respect of the manufacture, the material coin is so much bullion, and is treated as such; and persons take out the heaviest sovereigns and melt them down—a process by which they make a halfpenny for each. London was for many years the seat of this manufacture, which was carried on close to the Mint, where the sovereigns were made, so that the two establishments were side by side, one coining money, and the other melting it down. Then the manufacture went to Paris,

Chancellor of the Exchequer.

where it flourished many years; and now it is carried on at Brussels. While this goes on upon the Continent, there is another cause for the sovereign being put into circulation at the price or value of so much bullion. From the fact that the State charges nothing for the labour expended in the manufacture of it, and that it has no more exchangeable value than the bullion out of which it is made, the sovereign is liable to be exported as bullion, and there are great inducements to export it, because it is bullion already assayed and the weight of which is ascertained. All persons know pretty nearly what the weight of the sovereign is, and therefore it is bullion in the most convenient form for export. The consequence is that, whenever the rate of exchange is against us, and there is an export of bullion from this country, it is very convenient, besides exporting bullion in the unmanufactured state, to export it in the manufactured state, in sovereigns, and by that means to cause a violent and sudden contraction of our currency, which would not otherwise occur. Those are some of the evils that arise from our present system, but they are not all the evils. Although we give our currency to the public for nothing, the Government undertaking the business of an unremunerative manufacture, we take not the slightest precaution, when we have issued that currency, that it shall maintain its value. The original weight of the sovereign ought to be about 123·274 grains of gold, and when the sovereign is so worn that it has lost three-fourths of a grain in value—when it has got below $122\frac{1}{2}$ grains in value, it ceases to be a legal tender. The legal life of a sovereign is about eighteen years, it having in that time, from wear and tear, fallen below its original value. We take no trouble to call in this coin, and do nothing to save the public from the accident of taking light coin; and the consequence is that, after all our expense and trouble, $31\frac{1}{2}$ per cent. of our sovereigns and 47 per cent. of our half-sovereigns are not a legal tender, because they are light weight; and that, for a country which prides itself above all things upon keeping up its gold standard, and upon having a circulation above all doubt and suspicion, is not only a very great and serious evil, but a great reproach and discredit. I must add that it is an evil which will assume a practical form, because, under these circumstances, a re-coinage will be speedily called for. Something must be done to call in this light coin, and it is assumed that somewhere about £400,000 will be required to re-coin the loss in the weight of our coinage. We are going upon the plan at present of giving out a sovereign, which passes from hand to hand until some unfortunate person finds that it is not a legal tender, and is obliged to sell it for what it is worth for bullion. While we are very liberal in respect of giving our labour for nothing, we seem to be very careless and remiss in taking steps to keep up the integrity and standard of our money.

That is as nearly as I can state it the condition of things with regard to the currency of this country. Well, what is the remedy for this grievance? It is perfectly obvious that it is to be remedied by a natural, simple, and ordinary proceeding; in short, that in manufacturing money we should do as other manufacturers do and take pay for our labour. In effect we sell money to those who bring us gold; for an ounce of gold we give in exchange £3 17s. 10½d., and that is the exact weight of an ounce of gold. It appears to me that, while as manufacturers we are absurdly liberal in this respect, we should be much more wise to follow the example of all other countries and impose a mintage, brassage, or seigniorage, or whatever it might be called, so as to indemnify ourselves for the expense of maintaining our currency. The practice of this country has been the contrary ever since the reign of Charles II. The opinion that it is right there should be a mintage for the coining of money has been held by almost every considerable writer on political economy. And I will cite one or two instances. Sir Dudley North says—

"The free coinage is a perpetual motion found out, whereby to melt and coin without ceasing, and so to feed goldsmiths and coiners at the public charge."

Chancellor of the Exchequer.

Adam Smith says—

"When the tax upon a commodity is so moderate as not to encourage smuggling, the merchant who deals in it, though he advances, does not properly pay the tax, as he gets it back in the price of the commodity. The tax is finally paid by the last purchaser or consumer. But money is a commodity with regard to which every man is a merchant. Nobody buys it but in order to sell it again, and with regard to it there is in ordinary cases no last purchaser or consumer. When the tax upon coinage, therefore, is so moderate as not to encourage false coining, though everybody advances the tax, nobody finally pays it, because everybody gets it back in the advanced value of the coin."

Therefore, according to Adam Smith, we actually throw away this money we pay for coinage, because it is quite possible for us to get it back at nobody's expense. Another passage to the same effect from Adam Smith is as follows :—

"The Government, when it defrays the expense of coinage, not only incurs some small expense, but loses some small revenue, which it might get by a proper duty; and neither the Bank nor any other private persons are in the smallest degree benefited by this useless piece of public generosity."

That is the highest authority, and his arguments are of force sufficient to convince anyone that the course we are taking is no more warranted by abstract principles than it is successful in the results that it produces. The same opinion is held by M'Culloch. He says—

"Coins charged with a seigniorage equal to the expense of coinage do not pass at a higher value than what naturally belongs to them, but at that precise value; whereas, if the expense of coinage be defrayed by the State, coins pass at less than their real value. A sovereign is of greater utility and value than a piece of pure unfashioned gold bullion of the same weight; because, while it is as well fitted as bullion for being used in the arts, it is, owing to the coinage, better adapted for being used as money, or in the exchange of commodities. On what principle, then, should Government decline to charge a seigniorage or duty on coins, equal to the expense of coinage—that is, to the value which it adds to the coins?"

That being the case, then, I think the authorities fairly establish for us that there ought to be some seigniorage charged upon coin.

But the question still remains—what seigniorage? This question is answered in a Paper which some time ago I laid on the table of the House, and which I dare say has

attracted the attention of hon. Members—a Paper signed by the Master of the Mint and Colonel Smith, the former Master of the Mint at Calcutta—two of the highest authorities that could give an opinion on the subject. In that Paper they say that it is the duty of the State to require such a seigniorage as would indemnify it for the expense of coinage in the first place, for re-coinage when worn out, and also for the wear and tear, or for the bullion that would be required in restoring the coin to the state in which it was when first issued. They argue this matter in the most clear and conclusive manner, and the conclusion they come to is that a charge of £1 8s. 1½d. for every 100 sovereigns would be sufficient not only to indemnify the State for coining and re-coining, but also for the wear and tear the coin might undergo. They propose that every year the sovereigns coined eighteen years before should be called in and re-coined, and they prove that by a moderate charge of this kind, amounting to about 1 2-5ths per cent., the coinage of the country could be maintained in its integrity. The question of mintage at this time I shall not push further; though it seems to me that the arguments in favour of the course I have explained are exceedingly strong and convincing. But I am bound to say that there is an argument against it which must be considered, though I have never seen it brought forward in any essay. It has been assumed that if the State gives the coinage for nothing, or manufactures the bullion that is brought to the Mint, making a charge for the labour, the result is exactly the same and the coin is of the same value. No one is more opposed than I am to any attempt to tamper with the current value of the sovereign. Anything which would alter the current value of the sovereign—that is, the value of the sovereign wherever it is legal tender—and oblige a man to make calculations how much more he should pay or receive for the sovereign than he is accustomed to pay or receive, would be impossible to enforce in this country. Now, if you charge a mintage for the sovereign, you raise its current value. At
Chancellor of the Exchequer.

present we sell the sovereign as a manufactured article for bullion of the same weight, and a certain number of sovereigns for a fixed amount of bullion having just the weight of these sovereigns. But suppose we ask more for the sovereign than we do now—suppose we require 1 or 2 per cent. more, it is quite evident that nobody will come to exchange bullion for sovereigns until the sovereigns have risen to a value that will make it worth his while to do so—that is, till they have risen to the value of the extra percentage demanded. It must be remembered that sovereigns are perpetually being destroyed. They are lost in ships, they are melted down, they cease to circulate, and if the supply of them by Government be arrested by an impediment placed in their way, such as an extra price, of course no more sovereigns will be coined until they become so raised in value as to come up to the price that the Government demands for them. The effect of a seigniorage in raising the value of the coin is thus described by Adam Smith—

"Were the private people who carry their gold and silver to the Mint to pay themselves for the coinage, it would add to the value of those metals in the same manner as the fashion does to that of plate. Coined gold and silver would be more valuable than uncoined. The seigniorage, if it was not exorbitant, would add to the bullion the whole value of the duty; because the Government having everywhere the exclusive privilege of coining, no coin can come to market cheaper than they think proper to afford it."

Ricardo expresses a similar opinion, as follows:—

"It appears, then, that although a given weight of bullion can never exceed in value a given weight of coin, a given weight of coin may exceed in value a given weight of bullion by the whole expense of seigniorage, however great that seigniorage may be, provided that there was effectual security against the increase of money through the imitation of the coins by illegal means."

And the following passage occurs in Mr. Mill's *Principles of Political Economy*:—

"If Government, however, throws the expense of coinage, as is reasonable, upon the holder, by making a charge to cover the expense (which is done by giving back rather less in coin than has been received in bullion, and is called levying a seigniorage), the coin will rise to the extent of the seigniorage above the value of the bullion. If the Mint kept back 1 per cent. to pay the expense of coinage, it would be against the interest of the holders of bullion to have it coined until the coin was more valuable than the bullion by at least that fraction. The coin, therefore, would be kept 1 per cent. higher in value, which could only be by keeping it 1 per cent. less in quantity, than if its coinage were gratuitous."

And Mr. M'Culloch says—

"A small seigniorage or duty upon the coinage of both gold and silver would probably increase still more the superiority of those metals in coin above an equal quantity of either of them in bullion. The coinage would, in this case, increase the value of the metal coined in proportion to the extent of this small duty; for the same reason that the fashion increases the value of plate in proportion to the price of that fashion. The superiority of coin above bullion would prevent the melting down of the coin, and would discourage its exportation. If upon any public exigency it should become necessary to export the coin the greater part of it would soon return again of its own accord. Abroad it could sell only for its weight in bullion. At home it would buy more than that weight. There would be a profit, therefore, in bringing it home again."

Therefore, if the Government were to demand a seigniorage of 1 per cent., it would really raise the sovereign to a value of 1 per cent. beyond its present value; and everybody who owed money would pay 1 per cent. more than he bargained for, and everyone who received money would receive 1 per cent. more than he had a right to expect. That is the conclusion which Mr. M'Culloch has come to, and he states it as an argument against the imposition of a mintage. I think the difficulty might be perfectly well met by deducting the payment from the sovereign, instead of requiring 1 per cent. to be paid in money at the Mint; for it is no matter how you take it, whether by a money payment of 1 per cent., or 2d. for one sovereign, or by giving 122$\frac{1}{4}$ grains of gold instead of 123$\frac{1}{4}$. Whether you take it from the sovereign or take it in the shape of money payment, it does not matter to the State; but the difference is that, in the first case, the sovereign will be worth 2d. more than it is now; in the second case, the 2d. will be deducted from the metal of which the sovereign is made, and it will retain its present value. If there be a seigniorage, we must make up our minds to a deduction from the value of the sovereign to the amount of the seigniorage we charge, and that not with the

Chancellor of the Exchequer.

view of altering but retaining the value of the sovereign.
Unless you take something from its value the effect must
necessarily be to raise the coin beyond the value of the
bullion for which it is given in exchange. I apologize for
going into these matters, but really they are of great practical
interest. I am not even proposing anything to the House
now, but I merely wish to ventilate the subject, and give
hon. Gentlemen and the public at large the means of thinking
over this matter, and forming a judgment on a very curious
question, and one of great interest. There is another side
to the transaction, and that relates to the question of an international coinage, to which the hon. Gentleman has called
my attention. Well, the French Government have put
themselves into communication with us. They have written
to me on the subject of international coinage, and wish to
know what steps the Government of England are willing to
take in the matter. I was in no condition to give any
definite answer. The Chancellor of the Exchequer can
speak with no other breath than that of the House of
Commons, and until I knew the feeling of the House of
Commons I could not venture to give any opinion; but in
my answer I ventured to go thus far. There are two things
perfectly plain—the one that, under any circumstances, we
could not have any hope of establishing an international
coinage—on the chance of which I do not wish to dilate
now—with a country that has two standards. France has a
gold and a silver standard. A gold and a silver standard is
not a double, but an alternate standard. The two metals
are always fluctuating in their relations to each other; it is
in the nature of things for the cheaper metal for the time
being to drive out the dearer. Therefore, when the silver
standard drives the gold coin out of circulation, it leaves us
nothing to compare our international coin with except the
silver standard, to which it would have no exact relation.
And so I ventured to say, in answer to the question, that it
would be impossible to hold out hopes of assimilation until
France made up her mind to give up the silver standard and

have only a gold standard; and I am happy to say that France is favourable to the abandonment of her silver standard, as I gather from the Report of a Commission on the subject which I have received. Again, it seems to me, on abstract principles, that we should never have an international coinage, unless the coin were identical in weight and fineness, and unless the seigniorage charged on it were identical in both countries; because, if I am right in my view, that the value of coin is affected by the terms on which it is put into circulation—that is, the amount of mintage charged for it—then, on the supposition of having different mintages, we should have coin put into circulation having different values. People would take their gold to be coined where the thing could be done most cheaply, and thus the coin for which the higher mintage was paid would be reduced in value by the more abundant produce of the cheaper mint. That is all I have ventured to say in reference to the matter to the French Government, and I trust that I have not gone beyond the proper limit in saying it. The conditions which I have mentioned are really elementary conditions of the whole question. But I wish here to point out that I believe it is possible for England and France, if they can make up their minds to give up a little of their prejudices for the sake of the great advantage of having an international coinage, to obtain that object, and I will just show the House how that could be done. The French are proposing to coin a 25-franc gold piece, 5 francs more than the Napoleon. That would be less in value than the sovereign by 22 centimes, or about 2d. If we were about to impose a seigniorage of about 1 per cent., or ·993 of a grain, and take gold to that amount from the coin, our sovereign would be identical with the 25-franc piece. It would still remain as a current coin in this country of exactly the same value as now, and it would have the additional advantage that it would be identical in value with the 25-franc piece. But, in order that that might be done, France would have to make a sacrifice on her part. I forget the mintage she

Chancellor of the Exchequer.

charges; I believe it is between a fifth and a quarter per cent. If she could be prevailed upon to make it 1 per cent., we should have solved the problem as far as England and France are concerned, of an international coinage. The operation would be performed by modifications of the same principle—France would, as now, take the payment in money, England would deduct from her coin, and thus equality would be obtained. It is singular to remark what a number of coins in the world approach one another in value. The Spanish doubloon, the Prussian Frederick, the half-eagle of America, approach exceedingly near in value to each other, and I think it very possible, if France would meet us in this way—should Parliament be induced to look at the matter from the point of view I have put it—we might come to some arrangement by which we should get the blessing of one coinage throughout Europe, a great step in civilization. These are the remarks I had to make to the House. They are not given with any great confidence in my own opinion. All I am anxious to do before we separate is to give to hon. Gentlemen and the country at large a subject for consideration. It appears to me that the subject is not so difficult as might be supposed; and that by a single measure we may secure to ourselves the great benefit of saving all the expense incurred on our own gold coinage, without imposing those expenses on anyone else, and at the same time of striking a coin which would have the advantage of an international circulation.

GOLD CURRENCY.

Return to an Order of the Honourable The House of Commons, dated 28 June 1869;—*for*,

COPY " of REPORT addressed to the Chancellor of the Exchequer by the Master of the Mint and Colonel *Smith*, late Master of the Calcutta Mint, on the MINTAGE necessary to cover the Expenses of Establishing and Maintaining the GOLD CURRENCY."

Treasury Chambers,
28 June 1869.
ACTON S. AYRTON.

REPORT addressed to the Chancellor of the Exchequer by the Master of the Mint and Colonel *Smith*, late Master of the Calcutta Mint, on the MINTAGE necessary to cover the Expenses of Establishing and Maintaining the GOLD CURRENCY.

1. WHAT would it cost, first to manufacture a sovereign, and afterwards to keep it in good condition for all time? The coin is always losing weight by wear, while it passes from hand to hand, and ends by becoming light (after three quarters of a grain of gold have been lost), and is no longer legally current. The individual piece has thus a limited existence, and must be withdrawn and replaced by a new sovereign of full weight; that again by another in due time; and so on. Now, for what present payment could this succession be maintained? What is the contract price

to cover the first construction, and all future restoration? To this interesting question the answer to be given is that 100 sovereigns could be put into circulation and kept always in proper condition for the sum of one pound eight shillings and a penny halfpenny (1*l*. 8*s*. 1½*d*.) paid when the coin was first issued.

2. It will be seen at once how important this datum becomes, if the project be entertained of making the gold coinage of the country self-supporting. It defines the amount of an endowment that would have to be provided, in some way or other, for the permanent maintenance of the coin.

3. The charge stated of 1*l*. 8*s*. 1½*d*. on 100 sovereigns is deduced from several considerations; the cost of producing a single sovereign at the Mint, the total number of gold coins that are believed to be in circulation within the United Kingdom, and the length of time that the sovereigns and half-sovereigns last, before becoming light and legally uncurrent. The first cost, the number, and the durability of the coins have therefore to be considered.

4. The cost at which a sovereign is produced varies considerably with the number turned out from the Mint in the course of the year. Taking the present annual average production of 5 million sovereigns, the cost of each sovereign is found to be 0·72 of a penny, or nearly three farthings; while for a production of 25 millions in a year the cost is found to fall to 0·31 penny. For an annual production approaching to 10 millions, the amount which we have particularly to consider, the cost may be safely taken at about 0·5 penny, or one halfpenny on each sovereign. This will come, on the amount of gold coinage (5 millions) at present required to be issued, to 10,416*l*. 13*s*. 4*d*.

5. This estimate, taken from the experience of the British Mint, of one halfpenny per pound sterling, is almost identical with 2·1 per mille, which is the charge fixed for coining gold in the Mints of France.

6. The expense of an annual renewal of coins that have become light by wear, and have ceased to be legally current, has also to be taken into account. This will depend on the number that annually become light. The quantity of gold coin at present circulating in the United Kingdom is generally estimated at about 80 millions, an estimate which has lately received a valuable confirmation from the researches of Professor Jevons. The observations also recorded by Mr. Jevons respecting the loss by wear on sovereigns of various ages, indicate considerable regularity in wear, and that sovereigns fall below the legal weight, on an average, after a circulation of 18 years, and half-sovereigns in 10 years. It is to be presumed, then, that a sovereign which appears by its date to be 18 years old, ought to be withdrawn as being light. If such a regulation was carried into effect, one-eighteenth part of the whole gold currency would be withdrawn annually. On a coinage amounting to 80 millions, the proportion in question would amount to 4,444,444 sovereigns.

7. It must, however, be observed here, that the coinage of 80 millions is made up of 68 millions of whole sovereigns, of which 1-18th part have to be renewed annually, and 24 millions of half-sovereigns, 1-10th part of which have also to be renewed. The annual coinage thus due to renewal would amount to 3,777,777 sovereigns and 2,400,000 half-sovereigns, which would cost, at a halfpenny each, 12,870 *l.* 7 *s.* 5 *d.*

8. The loss of metal by wear, which would require to be replaced on re-coining old pieces, is the heaviest item of expenditure. The preceding two charges apply only to the mechanical work of coining.

9. Mr. Jevons's experiments and observations furnish the best data we possess for estimating the annual loss by wear on 100 sovereigns. It is 8·371 pence. This is a loss of 0·08371 penny on each sovereign. The number in circulation being again taken at 80 millions, this gives an

Mint Report.

annual loss on the whole gold currency, amounting to 27,903 *l.* 6 *s.* 8 *d.*

10. The above is calculated upon the assumption that the whole 80 millions consists of sovereigns; but if the additional wear upon the half-sovereigns is allowed for, the annual loss would be increased, according to Mr. Jevons, to 35,000 *l.*

11. These three items are the principal, if not the only, grounds upon which a Mint charge can be properly based. They are—

						£.	*s.*	*d.*
I. First coinage,	say 4,000,000	bullion at ½ *d.*	or 0·21 per cent.			8,400	0	0
II. Annual renewal,	3,777,777	at ½ *d.*	- - -	£.	7,870 7 4·88			
	2,400,000	ditto	- - -		5,000 0 0	12,870	7	4·88
III. Loss by wear	- - -	of sovereigns	- - -		22,000 0 0			
		of half ditto	- - -		13,000 0 0	35,000	0	0
	10,177,777	- - · -	- - -	£.		56,270	7	5

12. What does this amount to on our estimated annual coinage of about 10 millions, made up of 4 millions of first coinage, and 6 millions of renewal? It is 1·40676 (1 *l.* 8 *s.* 1½ *d.*) per cent.

13. The amount of mintage charge which the calculations appear to justify is not far short of 1½ per cent. on the value of the gold coined, and it will be observed that the estimate here made is somewhat lower than the one subjoined which is founded on abstract mathematical calculation. It may be explained that the latter assumes that coins once sent into circulation never leave it, which may be more or less true with a protected currency; but there will never cease to be coins which drop out of circulation annually, owing to shipwrecks, fires, melting, losses, &c., and which thereby tend to reduce the number to be renewed.

14. On the other hand, there is a circumstance which, if allowance be made for it, would increase the charge, namely, the number of sovereigns, estimated at about 30 millions, which circulate in foreign countries, and part of

which, when they become light, are likely to return again to the United Kingdom, and occasion loss in their renewal.

15. Treating the question rigorously as an actuary's problem in assurance, it becomes necessary to ascertain what sum of money set aside to-day will be sufficient, part to pay the immediate expense of first coinage at 0·21 per cent., and the remainder, invested at 3 per cent. interest, to provide a like sum of 0·21 to pay for re-coinage at the end of every 18 years, besides the requisite sum to make good the intervening 18 years' abrasion of the coins, reckoned at 4·3 grains of gold per 100 sovereigns per annum, and thus amounting to 0·62787 l. per cent. at the end of that time.

The immediate payment, then, is 0·21 l., and the further payment at the end of every 18 years perpetually (0·62787 + 0·21 =) 0·83787 l. per cent.; and to calculate the sum proper to be invested to meet the regular periodical payment of 0·83787 l., it must be observed that, by the well-known formula $\frac{1}{(1 + rx)^n - 1}$ (where n represents the years of interval, viz., 18 for sovereigns, and 10 years for half-sovereigns, and $r = $ ·03, or 3 per cent. interest) the sum of money requisite at 3 per cent. to meet payments of 1 l. every 18 years is 1·4236231 l.; consequently the sum necessary to provide for the periodical payments of 0·83787 l. must be (1·4236231 × 0·83787 =) 1·192811 l., which, added to the immediate expense in *first* coinage (0·21 l. per cent.), makes the total charge to the Government 1·402811 l. per cent. for bullion coined into sovereigns only.

In like manner, with respect to the half-sovereigns, the sum of money requisite at 3 per cent. to meet payments of 1 l. every 10 years is 2·90765 l., and the loss by wear of each half-sovereign allowed for by Mr. Jevons is ·512 grains gold in 10 years, or ·8306698 l. on the 100 l. value; consequently, in order to ascertain the sum to be set aside to meet this loss, and also the re-coinage at the end of every tenth year, we must add the ·8306698 l. to 0·21 l., making 1·0406698 l., and multiply by 2·90765, thus making

Mint Report.

$3 \cdot 02589354\, l.$, the sum to be set aside for every $100\, l.$ value; again, adding to this the expense of *first* coinage at $0\cdot 21\, l.$ per cent., the total expense to be incurred becomes $3\cdot 2358935\, l.$ per cent. for half-sovereigns only.

From the above it appears that the endowment necessary to be provided for the first coinage and permanent maintenance of—

Sovereigns is - $1\, l.$ $8\, s.$ $1\tfrac{1}{2}d.$, or $1\cdot 402811\, l.$ per cent.; and
Half-sovereigns $3\, l.$ $4\, s.$ $8\, d.$ or $3\cdot 2358935\, l.$ per cent.

But the proportions of the sovereigns and half-sovereigns in our currency being as 68-80ths and 12-80ths, it follows that 68-80ths of $1\cdot 402811\, l.$ added to 12-80ths of $3\cdot 2358935\, l.$ will be the whole sum required to be set aside to meet the future expenses of our mixed currency.

Now 68-80ths of $1\cdot 402811\, l. = 1\cdot 192390\, l.$
and 12-80ths of $3\cdot 235893\, l. = 0\cdot 485384\, l.$

Total - - $1\cdot 677774\, l.$ per cent., or $1\, l.$ $13\, s.$ $6\, d.$ for every $100\, l.$

These results are based upon the mere bullion by itself, and are quite independent of all other considerations.

Thomas Graham, Master of the Mint.

6 April 1869. *J. T. Smith*, late Master of the Calcutta Mint.

EXTRACT from the Evidence of Major HYDE, the Mint Master at Calcutta, given before the Commission to inquire into the operation of Act XIX. of 1861, at its first sitting, held at Calcutta on the 6th February, 1866.

(Questions 106 to 110.)

THE PRESIDENT:—

106. Have you ever considered the expediency of having a Gold Currency?—I have considered the question, but I cannot attach any value to such opinions as I have formed, and I should give them with hesitation.

107. Have you ever heard the natives of India express a wish for a Gold Currency?—Yes; I know that gold is popular with natives. Gold is found in small quantities all over India. It was the earliest known coinage. It was the currency of the South of India up to a comparatively late period, and has been traditionally connected with the times of the greatness of its people. Gold was largely paid by natives of India as tributes, and even now forms a portion of every nuzzur. It was imported into India by the Romans during the first century at the rate of £450,000 per annum in exchange for cotton and indigo. No silver is found in India, which fact, coupled with the probability that the wealth of India was formerly comparatively with foreign countries much greater than it is now, and such as to enable its people to use gold as a currency, may account for its previous use and its present traditional popularity.

108. Do natives anticipate that gold coin would be taken more freely than rupees?—All that I have ever heard has been a vague desire for a gold coinage. I have never heard from a native a single practical suggestion on the subject.

109. What coin would you prefer to see introduced?— The sovereign.

110. Why do you prefer a sovereign to any Indian coin? —I look to the Australian sovereign being made identical with the English sovereign, in which case it would be the most economical arrangement, as saving the country the cost of re-coining a gold currency. It would enable merchants, in time of emergency and large influxes of bullion, to lay down their money in India quicker and with certainty. A sovereign worth rs. 10 gives a decimal valuation, which is easier in accounts than that of 1 to 15 in the mohur. If the English sovereign be made a legal tender at rs. 10, the cost of the rupee could be adjusted to that rate by an increase of Mint charges on silver, and until by re-action of foreign markets the effect of those charges was nullified, the sovereign would pass current at rs. 10 to a sovereign. The present rate of rs. 10·132 per sovereign would seem to shew that an increase in Mint charges on silver by 2 per cent., or up to 4·1 per cent. total charges, would effect the object. A slight alteration in the copper coinage changed to bronze would make a very good decimal currency that would, when the time arrived to change the standard to gold, require only the depreciation of the rupee, or 2-shilling piece, to assimilate it to the currency of the mother country.

THE TIMES.

(August 9, 1869.)

The Chancellor of the Exchequer has, at the end of the Session, given the public a subject to think over between this time and the re-assembling of Parliament next year. "All I am anxious to do before we separate," he said on Friday night, "is to give to honourable members and the country at large a subject for consideration." In other words, Mr. Lowe has, like a schoolmaster, favoured his young friends with a holyday task to get up in the vacation. We hope they will undertake it, and, we dare say, the indefatigable persons who spend their autumn in the Economic Section of the British Association, the pursuit of Social Science, and kindred pleasures, will have something to say about the matter; but we fear the mass of politicians will return Mr. Lowe his problem just as they received it. He encourages us with the soothing declaration that it is very simple; but it does not look so. The embarrassing word " value"—most absurd of economic terms—occurs much too often in his exposition, while "currency," " seigniorage," "double standard," " balance of exchanges," and other well-known occasions of despair chase one another through the columns devoted to the report of his speech.

The best way to make Mr. Lowe's desires intelligible is to plunge at once *in medias res*. At present the brand-new sovereign is a piece of gold weighing 123·274 grains, and if merchants take uncoined bullion·to the Mint they receive back exactly the same weight of gold in exchange, but transformed from uncoined metal into sovereigns. These are the two facts from which to start. The Mint makes no charge for coining, and the weight of the sovereign is 123·274 grains, or, as it may be expressed otherwise, the Mint receives gold from those who bring it, and gratuitously returns the same weight of metal to them in stamped pieces, each weighing 123·274 grains. Mr. Lowe proposes that in future the sovereign shall weigh 122·274 grains, or, perhaps, more accurately, 122·25 grains; but that those who wish to have bullion coined into sovereigns shall be compelled to bring, as heretofore, gold at the rate of 123·274 for each pound, the difference of a grain being retained by the Mint. Mr. Lowe thus desires to impose a Mint-charge, or seigniorage, to make it rather less than 1 per cent., and to levy it by reducing the weight of the sovereign, while maintaining the standard weight of the gold to be delivered at the Mint in exchange for sovereigns. What are the reasons for advocating such a change? In the first place, it is alleged that all other nations enforce a seigniorage in coining. This of
The Times.

itself would not greatly affect our judgment, as the mere fact that we are singular in pursuing a special course would not materially shake our confidence in its wisdom; nay, if it turns out on inquiry that we have defied the example of the rest of the world for 200 years, as we have done in this matter of minting, we are apt to think we must be right. But, secondly, if the sovereign only weighed 122¼ grains, it would correspond almost exactly with the weight of 25 francs in gold—that is to say, four sovereigns would be absolutely equal to five napoleons, and the Imperial Government is, moreover, prepared to issue at the Hôtel des Monnaies pieces of gold, new louis d'or, equivalent to 25 francs. The reduction in the weight of the sovereign would thus make it and this new French coin interchangeable; nay, the napoleon itself would be admissible in our currency as equal to 16s., and a great step in advance would have been made towards the establishment of an international coinage. We have not, however, yet stated the great argument Mr. Lowe relies upon as at least most influencing his own mind—that the change would produce an annual saving to the nation. We give away for nothing the labour of assaying, partitioning, and stamping the gold which the bullion merchants bring to the Mint. It will be readily seen that the cost of this labour might be exacted from those who wished to have gold coined without running the danger attendant on an excessive seigniorage. We doubt, however, whether 1 per cent. is not a charge dangerously exceeding the actual outlay, as it cannot—and, indeed, it is allowed that it does not—cost a pound to coin a hundred sovereigns; but it may be said that, although it costs the Mint less than this, it would probably cost a private coiner more. In effect, the charge recommended by Mr. Lowe might probably be safely demanded, and the Exchequer would be relieved of the cost of coinage. This is not all. As we coin for nothing we coin much more bullion than the necessities of commerce require, for while a man wishing to export bullion gets it coined simply as a certificate of weight and purity, another proportion—and, considering the subject, a large proportion—of our coinage is, for other reasons, melted down again almost as soon as it is coined. The standard weight of the sovereign is 123·274 grains, but the sovereign remains a legal tender as long as it is 122·5 grains in weight, and in spite of all the delicate machinery at the Mint, it is impossible to secure an exact equality in the weight of sovereigns when issued. It has been authoritatively declared that " there is reason to believe that large " masses of new British sovereigns are occasionally treated " so as to separate out the heavy pieces, and these are dis- " posed of as bullion; while the lighter pieces, which may " still be all of legal weight, are preserved and put into " circulation." Mr. Lowe told the House on Friday that this process of sifting and melting was formerly carried on next to the Mint, " so that the two establishments were side " by side, one coining money, the other melting it down; " but the prejudices of insular legislation have driven the manufactory to Brussels. A last reason for imposing a seigniorage is that ever since the outcry against light sovereigns—now more than a quarter of a century since—we have taken no pains to insure the full weight of our coin, and it has fallen terribly below the standard. Mr. Jevons, who read an elaborate paper on the subject before the Statistical Society last November, and to whom the Chancellor of the Exchequer on Friday acknowledged himself indebted for calling his attention to it, has shown that about 31 per cent. of the current coinage consists of light money, the proportion varying from 22 per cent. at Manchester to 44 per cent. in the eastern and west midland counties. The cost of re-coining the currency as it now exists, due to the deficiency of weight of sovereigns to be withdrawn, is estimated at 300,000*l.*, irrespective of the expenses of the Mint, which will amount to more than 40,000*l.* The seigniorage Mr. Lowe proposes would reduce the amount of money coined in future, pay the working expenses of the Mint, and provide for the replacement of

The Times.

light coin from time to time; and this last object Mr. Lowe would secure by demonetizing coins more than 18 years old, the age it is calculated a coin with proper wear will remain of good weight.

It rarely happens that all the reasons are on one side, and there are arguments against the imposition of a seigniorage in the way suggested by the Chancellor of the Exchequer which induced the International Monetary Commission to reject the proposal. What is a pound? The answer has hitherto been—a piece of gold weighing 123·274 grains, and upon this footing contracts have been based. Mr. Lowe recommends that it shall weigh only 122·274 grains in future, and it is argued that the adoption of the proposal would diminish the obligations of debtors and detract from the lawful claims of creditors by one per cent. Mr. Lowe denies this conclusion. His reasoning is somewhat refined, and his conclusion, that a gain may be secured to the State without a loss to anybody, is so paradoxical that the argument deserves the title of a financial puzzle much more than the simple devices which have been so named. The way in which we understand the Chancellor of the Exchequer, following Adam Smith, to put the case, is this—that, although a sovereign will weigh but 122·274 grains, no person can buy one except by giving 123·274 grains of gold to the Mint for it, and the cost of the production of the sovereign remains, therefore, unchanged, although its weight is diminished. Hence we may deduce, if we confine our attention to the United Kingdom, that the sovereign will maintain an undiminished value in exchange. But how can this reasoning be applied when we remember the existence of other nations? The sovereign is abroad 123·274 grains of gold of certified quality, and its value is measured by reference to the demand for pure bullion. The Chancellor of the Exchequer and Mr. Jevons suggest a reply. The change in the weight of the sovereign will make it a coin in France as much as in England, and, as has been pointed out, lays the basis of a universal currency, so that if the reasoning be admitted to be sound which declared that the sovereign would maintain its full value if the United Kingdom alone were to be regarded, it must be admitted to be universally sound, for by United Kingdom is simply meant the sphere of circulation of the sovereign as a coin. The result is anomalous, and we might, perhaps with advantage, leave it in this condition to excite the speculative faculties of the country; but it may nevertheless be as well to suggest a consideration which seems to have been omitted. The grain of gold which would be reserved by the Mint out of the 123·274 bought for a sovereign would not be lost, but would in due course be coined by the Mint itself for the remuneration of the Exchequer, so that the number of sovereigns poured upon the world would be increased reciprocally as the weight of each diminishes. The purchasing power of each sovereign would be diminished precisely as the number added to the circulation would be increased,—that is, precisely as the weight of each would be diminished. This reasoning appears to turn the flank of Mr. Jevons and the Chancellor of the Exchequer, and without following steps any one can trace for himself, it would lead to this result—that the future gain to the Exchequer would be felt by the loss of purchasing power of the product of the Australian and Californian digger, and in the process there would occur that benefit to the debtor and loss to the creditor which has been deprecated. We do not, however, press this as an invincible obstacle to the proposal; on the contrary, we hold it is right that the Australian digger should be called upon to pay for the labour hitherto gratuitously added to the commodity he produces, and the derangement of the relations of debtor and creditor may possibly, as Mr. Jevons suggests, be adjusted as easily as a derangement due to an increase of income tax; but it is a necessary addition to the complexity of the problem Mr. Lowe has sent forth for autumnal reflection, and we send it forth to fructify in the minds of those who care to understand it.

The Times.

THE SOVEREIGN.

(The Times, August 10, 1869.—To the Editor.)

Sir,—The able article in *The Times* of this morning induces me to hope that you will be kind enough to allow me to add a few remarks on the same subject. Mr. Lowe proposes to reduce the weight of the sovereign from 123·274 grains of gold to 122·274 grains, and he believes that the new smaller sovereign will have the same purchasing power as the present sovereign, weighing 123·274 grains, and his argument is based on the supposition that no one will be able to obtain the new small sovereign without giving the Mint gold of the weight of 123·274 grains. This is Colonel Smith's argument, who goes still further, for he contends that a sovereign of only half its present weight may possess the same purchasing power in this country, provided it can be obtained only at the Mint, and only by giving 123·274 grains of fine gold in exchange for it. Colonel Smith never contended that the smaller or lighter sovereign would command the same value out of the country, but he would secure its exportable value by obliging the Mint to give to anybody 123·274 grains of gold for every one of these new sovereigns, and thus the exportable value would be obtained, while the value for home use would equally be obtained, because no one would take gold to the Mint to be turned into coin, unless it was found that in consequence of the necessity for having gold coin for use, the new sovereign would purchase as much as the old sovereign of greater weight; but without such a power of exchange at the Mint, to which Mr. Lowe made no allusion in his speech on Friday last, he surely will not contend that 122·274 grains of gold will have the same purchasing power out of this country as 123·274 grains would command, although it might be inferred from his speech that if an artificial value were given by the creation of our international coinage such would be the result.

A holder of English stock living in France, and desiring
Mr. Thomson Hankey.

to have his dividend, say of 100*l.*, transmitted to him, now knows that he can at all times receive in France for his 100*l.*, 100 times 123·274 grains, or 12327·4 grains of gold *minus* the expense of transmission. Will Mr. Lowe be able to satisfy this person that he will be as well off by receiving 12227·4 grains of gold, provided there is an international system of coinage, which could hardly, however, be rendered compulsory, or made a legal tender throughout Europe ? Mr. Lowe has doubtless read the evidence given before the Commission last year on International Coinage, but, if so, he has certainly arrived at a different conclusion from that of the Commissioners.

I am not prepared to assert positively that a reduction of the weight of gold in a sovereign, so as to make it exactly equal, when coined, to a 25-franc gold piece, would even, without compensation as between debtors and creditors, inflict any very serious evil; but I do not believe that any really international coinage would be of the smallest benefit to commerce, although I admit it would be very convenient to travellers. But I feel convinced that Mr. Lowe is mistaken in the idea that a very large number of sovereigns are coined annually beyond what are wanted for use as British coin in some part of the world. That a certain number are annually melted to be re-coined in other countries is doubtless the case, and a certain number are melted by jewellers as a convenient mode of giving out an easily ascertained value of gold to workmen for use; but the latter would probably continue to be the custom for convenience even if there were a seigniorage on the coin; nor do I believe that any seigniorage would prevent a certain amount of gold coin being melted, for melting coin for conversion into other coin is, I believe, very frequent in countries where a seigniorage exists; but if I am right that the quantity of gold coined at our Mint and melted for re-coinage abroad is not very great, then the loss from wear and tear would not be to any considerable degree diminished by the charge of seigniorage at our Mint.

Mr. Thomson Hankey.

If this country, in consequence of the general adoption of an international coinage (to which England was a party), were required to coin gold for very general circulation elsewhere than in British dominions, then a charge for mintage, or a seigniorage, might become a matter of serious importance; but so long as our coinage is mainly in use by our own countrymen, and even among them mainly by British tax-payers, then the charge on the country is a very unimportant one, considering the almost universal advantage of having our gold and silver readily coined at any moment, and to any extent that may be required, for the use of the country at large. A mintage charge, or a seigniorage, or by whatever name it may be called, differs very little from a small tax on the importation of gold. I believe that Mr. Lowe is mistaken in thinking that sovereigns are frequently exported when the exchanges are favourable for such operation in lieu of bar gold. The contrary is, I believe, the fact. No exporter, unless for some peculiar operation, would ship sovereigns if he could purchase bar gold.

I am, Sir, your most obedient servant,

THOMSON HANKEY.

45, PORTLAND PLACE,
Aug. 9, 1869.

THE SOVEREIGN.

(The Times, August 10, 1869.—To the Editor.)

SIR,—The proposal of the Chancellor of the Exchequer, as explained in your leading article to-day, appears to be to issue a sovereign containing one grain less gold than the present sovereign, and to retain the one grain as a charge for coining.

Now, this is but a proposal pure and simple for the debasement of the standard for the benefit of the State.

W.

The history of our currency shows the inevitable consequences of such a proceeding to be a rise of prices and a fraud on creditors under the existing standard.

However, from the report of the speech of the Chancellor of the Exchequer in the House of Commons, as given in *The Times*, I understand the proposal to be slightly different as to the mode of procedure, but, as I shall endeavour to show, the same as to its effects. It appears to be proposed to issue a sovereign containing one grain less gold, and to levy a charge to be paid in money equal in value to this grain as the charge for making the sovereign. The argument in support of this proposal is, that a charge for coining the sovereign will appreciate its value by the amount of the charge. Therefore, to reduce the proposed sovereign to the value of the present one, it will be necessary to take out of the coin gold equal in value to the charge for coining it.

It may be said in the first place that a charge for coining will not maintain the value of the sovereign at the price of the gold *plus* the charge for coining it. The value at any one time will depend on the demand for it whatever it may have cost to make it. This elementary principle, however, does not enter into the argument, as what the Chancellor of the Exchequer appears to maintain is that by transferring the charge for coining from the State to the public the sovereign will be appreciated in value to the extent of the charge.

Suppose A wants 113 grains of pure gold coined into a sovereign and B agrees to bear the cost of coining it, a sovereign will be produced.

Suppose, at another time, A gets 113 grains of gold made into a sovereign at his own cost, a sovereign will be produced of the same value as the first.

The first of these examples represents the existing regulations of the country, the second the proposed regulations.

At present one of the public, represented by A, wants
W.

a sovereign and supplies the gold, and the State (B) makes it for him. It is proposed that in future the public shall pay for the coining of their gold, but obviously, the alteration cannot affect the value of the sovereign.

From this it also follows that, even under this arrangement, the amount of gold in the sovereign cannot be reduced without at the same time producing all the evils consequent on a debasement of the standard.

W.

August 9, 1869.

THE GOLD COINAGE.

(The Times, August 16, 1869.—To the Editor.)

SIR,—There can be no doubt of the great practical interest of the speech delivered by the Chancellor of the Exchequer on the gold coinage on the 6th instant, and as he commends the subjects then ventilated to public consideration, I venture to ask your insertion of the following remarks.

A scheme of " international coinage " meets with Mr. Lowe's sympathy, but to reconcile himself to its adoption, he apparently relies upon the arguments and conclusions propounded by Professor Jevons, Mr. J. B. Smith, Member for Stockport, and Colonel Smith, lately Master of the Calcutta Mint. As connected with their advocacy of an international coinage it will be my duty to show that Mr. Lowe's reliance has been misplaced; but the inquiry raises many other points open to discussion, upon which I will touch with all possible conciseness.

The pound sterling is at once the unit of our money of account, the medium of exchange, and the standard of value; and its legal embodiment is a coin containing 113 grains of fine gold (123·274 grains of standard gold 11-12ths fine).

Mr. J. G. Hubbard.

That the coin should be 11-12ths fine is not essential, but as the standard of value it is essential that the coin representing the pound sterling contain 113 grains of fine gold, neither more nor less, and it could not be varied without entailing mischief far exceeding any possible advantage.

Our gold coinage is conducted gratuitously at the Mint, and it has been recommended that it should be in future subject to Seigniorage or Mintage. These terms express, however, very different ideas.

Seigniorage is the current value which the *seigneur* (or State), in virtue of his prerogative, attested by his stamp, adds to the intrinsic value of the coin. The seigniorage on English silver coin is equal to 10 per cent.; on copper coin it is equal to 100 per cent. Coins circulating with a seigniorage are tokens, and cannot be a standard of value.

Mintage, or "*Brassage*," as the French term it, is a charge for the conversion of the metal into coin. It has been levied by most countries, but not by England in this century. Mr. Lowe disapproves a " Free Mint." I agree in that disapproval. So long since as 1843, in my pamphlet *The Currency and the Country*, which preceded the Bank Charter Act of 1844, I recommended a mintage charge of $1\frac{1}{2}d$. per ounce, and in 1853, when Deputy-Governor of the Bank, I supported, in correspondence with the Treasury, an identical proposition made by Sir J. Herschel, then Master of the Mint.

The enactment which I then suggested was a very brief one:—That the Mint should charge $1\frac{1}{2}d$. per ounce for coinage, or, in other words, buy gold at $3l.$ $17s.$ $9d.$, and that the Bank should buy gold at $3l.$ $17s.$ $7\frac{1}{2}d.$, instead of $3l.$ $17s.$ $9d.$, as at present. (Your readers will understand that the importer of bullion may take his gold to the Mint if he pleases, but that practically he always takes it to the Bank, whose immediate payment at the rate of $3l.$ $17s.$ $9d.$ is preferable to the deferred receipt of $3l.$ $17s.$ $10\frac{1}{2}d.$ at the Mint.)

Mr. J. G. Hubbard.

As a consequence of their diminished buying price for bullion, the selling price of the Bank would also be diminished, and by selling bar gold at 3*l*. 17*s*. 9*d*. the export of coin for any purpose but that of currency would be precluded.

This change of action would avert the wasteful destruction of English gold coins, but it would leave intact the standard of value, and its only disturbing effect would be an unimportant change in the conditions under which the import and export of bullion occur. If New York now exports bullion to London when the exchange is above 110, and imports gold when the exchange is under $107\frac{1}{2}$, she would thereafter export when the exchange was above 110·20 and import when the exchange was under 107·70, but the range of the effective par of exchange would remain unaltered. The foreigner having a payment to make to this country would no longer enjoy the exceptional and unreasonable advantage of having his raw commodity manufactured into legal coin at the cost of the English nation, and he alone could lament the alteration. The charge of $1\frac{1}{2}d$. per ounce proposed as mintage by Sir John Herschel in 1853 was equivalent to the 1-6th per cent. at which the cost of coinage had been computed, and by the cost of coinage the mintage should be rigidly limited. In whatever degree that limit be exceeded, in the same degree you obstruct the free circulation of gold acting as the adjustor of international balances of trade, you enlarge the scale of the variation of exchange, and, by increasing the uncertainties of commerce, you enhance the price of commodities.

If the mintage be sensibly increased beyond the cost of coinage, you provoke private coinage, not of base money, but of standard though illegal coin, undistinguishable from genuine coin, but winning for its author a portion of the profit sought for the State through an unwise exercise of power.

Seigniorage is an entirely different matter. In this country it cannot be applied to the gold coin, for the gold coin is not only a medium of exchange, it is also the standard or measure of value, and no legislation can affect its intrinsic efficacy. The standard may be enlarged, or it may be reduced; the grains of gold (the elements of the pound) may be diminished in number or they may be multiplied; but the grain of gold retains its immaculate virtue in defiance of all external assaults.

Parliament is omnipotent to legislate, but legislation is not omnipotent. Parliament might be persuaded by the Member for Stockport to enact that a sovereign with 112 grains of gold should be equivalent to a sovereign with 113 grains, but such legislation would be as futile as that which earlier in the century affirmed that the shilling and the 1*l*. Bank-note, then at 20 per cent. discount, were equivalent to a guinea. A circulation of the diminished sovereign might undoubtedly be forced upon the country, and then every debtor would profit and every creditor would suffer by the difference of 1 per cent. in the value of the new currency. The great mass of the people might never be aware of the transition; but our foreign trade would at once disclose the fact. Abroad our coins are appreciated, not by what we call them, but by what they are, and so we should need to send 113 new sovereigns to pay for goods which we could have bought with 112 old sovereigns; while, on the other hand, our foreign debtors might take us at our word, and save 1 per cent. by discharging in our new standard obligations contracted in the old.

The reasoners in favour of combining material depreciation and statutable appreciation of the sovereign fail to see that an abstraction of a portion of the standard coin must be a contraction of the measure of value, but that a charge for coinage can be only a charge upon the importer, and cannot enhance the value or power of the coin.

In this conclusion the Commissioners on international coinage were nearly unanimous. Mr. J. B. Smith, the Member for Stockport, and Colonel Smith, late Master of the Calcutta Mint, seem, however, to be of a contrary con-

Mr. J. G. Hubbard.

viction. I do not know that argument can go further. Shall we try an experiment?

They hold that a coinage charge enhances the value of a coin. English sovereigns are coined free, Australian sovereigns are coined at a charge of 1 per cent. for coinage.

They value, therefore, 100 Australian at 101 English sovereigns.

I propose to meet Australia half-way, and deliver to Mr. Smith or Colonel Smith, at Madras or Bombay, 100,000 Australian sovereigns for 100,500 English. We shall each hope to gain 500 sovereigns. The operation, if satisfactory, can be repeated, and the result shall be duly reported to the Chancellor of the Exchequer.

Permit me to resume the subject in another letter, and to remain,

Sir, your obedient servant,

J. G. HUBBARD.

PRINCE'S GATE,
Aug. 10, 1869.

THE GOLD COINAGE.

(House of Commons, August 13, 1869.)

MR. ALDERMAN LAWRENCE wished to ask the Chancellor of the Exchequer a question of which he had privately given him notice. The right hon. Gentleman had put to hon. Members a conundrum compounded of coinage, circulation, and the currency, and so much doubt prevailed with regard to his meaning that he desired, if possible, to elucidate it. He begged accordingly to ask the Chancellor of the Exchequer, in his suggestion the other evening respecting the gold coinage, whether he proposed that a person sending to the Mint a bar of gold for which he now received 100 sovereigns, without any charge or deduction being made for coinage, should in future receive only 99 sovereigns of the same weight and quality as at present, and that one sovereign should be retained, being the amount of the expenditure upon coinage; or whether he proposed that the said bar of gold should in future be coined into 101 sovereigns, of less weight or quality than at present, and that the person sending such bar of gold should receive back 100 of such sovereigns, the remaining one being retained by the Mint for expenses of coining; and also, if the latter proposition were carried into effect, whether it would necessarily involve the reduction of the intrinsic value of the pound sterling to be paid under existing deeds, mortgages, contracts, and other engagements, public and private, at home or abroad.

The CHANCELLOR of the EXCHEQUER:— The conundrum which I proposed to the House does not involve either of the propositions. My suggestion was this: that a man—taking the words of the question—who brought to the Mint a bar of gold for which he would now receive 100 sovereigns should receive 100 sovereigns still, but that each of these sovereigns should be lighter than the present sovereign by one grain, value somewhere about 2*d*., approximating nearly to 1 per cent. on the value of the sovereign. The proposal was—at least the idea was, for there was no proposal—that if this one grain were deducted from the value of each of the sovereigns issued, there would remain over and above the bar of gold brought to the Mint, after the issue of the 100 sovereigns forming its equivalent, 100 grains of gold, which the Mint would pay into the Exchequer under the head of miscellaneous expenses, to be applied to the general purposes of revenue. I need not, therefore, enter into the question as to the effect of the proposal in either of the hypothetical cases put by the hon: Gentleman upon contracts, mortgages, engagements, and all the other things. But as regards the practical proposition which I did make I may say one word. The hon. Gentleman asks about the intrinsic value. I do not know what "intrinsic value" means; it is an ambiguous phrase. As far as I know there is no such thing as intrinsic value. It is not an inherent quality in the substance itself which gives to it its pecuniary value; the intrinsic value, in the sense which the hon. Gentleman means, is, as I conceive, relative; that is to say, measuring the value of the thing in question by the amount of labour and capital which it would take to produce it. But if the hon. Gentleman means by intrinsic value the amount of gold which the sovereign will contain, then my proposition certainly involves the reduction of the intrinsic value to the extent of one grain in 123¼ grains. I will answer his question in this way :—If the sovereign be treated, not as gold, but as bullion, it will have one grain less of producing power; but if the sovereign be viewed not as bullion, but as gold, its producing power will remain just the same as at present. And the reason is obvious. The only seller of new sovereigns is the Government; and if new sovereigns could only be acquired upon the condition of paying 1 per cent. more for them than is now paid, that 1 per cent. would necessarily limit the demand for sovereigns till they attained the value put upon them. As sovereigns, therefore, they would be as valuable as at present, while as bullion they would be less valuable. And that attains precisely the object I have in view, which is that the sovereign should be circulated in this country, but should not be melted abroad.

Mr. Alderman LAWRENCE wished to understand whether the person bringing the bar of gold to be coined would pay anything for coining it.

The CHANCELLOR of the EXCHEQUER:— I think I have answered the question before. The person bringing the bar of gold to be coined—assuming it to be worth 100 sovereigns—would have deducted from the value 100 grains of gold; and to that extent he would pay.

THE CHANCELLOR OF THE EXCHEQUER MUST BE TAUGHT POLITICAL ECONOMY.

(The Morning Advertiser, August 14, 1869.)

MR. LOWE is a chartered Libertine; he has made himself feared by Mr. Gladstone and Mr. Bright, and they dare not interfere with him or prevent him from doing as he pleases. There is no doubt that they both bear him a grudge for his conduct in 1866, and would pay him off for it if they could; but this they dare not do. It is really too bad that the whole trade and commerce of the country should be exposed to injury by the freaks and vanity of a man who, on account of the mere interests of party, has been placed in a situation for which he is totally unfitted, and that from the want of the necessary training and education. If Mr. Lowe had even a smattering of acquaintance with the Bank Act of 1844, he would never fall into the gross blunders which every speech he makes evinces. What greater absurdity could have been brought forward than the announcement made by him on Friday of the existence of a manufactory at Brussels for the melting down of sovereigns, and of which announcement we are convinced he is now heartily ashamed. The temper which Mr. Lowe manifested on Tuesday last, in his answer to Mr. Sinclair Aytoun's questions upon this subject, shows that he is now aware that he has been humbugged and imposed upon by his informant in the most ridiculous manner. Why does not Mr. Lowe put himself under the tuition of his colleague Mr. Göschen, who was once a Bank director, and who is perfectly acquainted with the principles of currency, and with all our currency acts and regulations?

Mr. Göschen should commence the education of Mr. Lowe by reading over to him the Bank Act of 1844, explaining the different clauses, and especially that one which

Mr. J. Aytoun.

obliges the Bank to give notes to every person who brings standard gold to the establishment. It is his ignorance of the existence of this enactment which has been the chief cause of the blunders of the Chancellor of the Exchequer.

In the absence of Mr. Göschen, we shall explain to Mr. Lowe the nature of this clause. Gold is manufactured into sovereigns by the Mint in the proportion of 3 l. 17 s. 10½d. for every ounce, and every person who brings any amount of standard gold to the establishment receives it all back in sovereigns, and that without any charge. The gold, however, brought to the Mint must be regularly assayed and reduced to standard or sovereign gold of 22 carats. Notwithstanding the facility of converting gold into sovereigns, it is very seldom that a private individual takes bullion to the Mint to be converted into sovereigns. He takes it to the Bank, which undertakes this operation for him, and which, upon the deposit of the standard assayed bullion, gives the party bringing it Bank notes created for that express purpose, and which notes may be exchanged immediately for sovereigns. But the Bank gives notes at the rate of 3 l. 17 s. 9d. per ounce, thus gaining 1½d. per ounce upon the transaction, which is, in fact, a seigniory paid to the Bank for undertaking with the Mint the conversion of the gold into sovereigns. The possessor of the bullion gives this in order to have it converted into money at once, which could not be done if he went directly himself to the Mint, which would keep him waiting perhaps six months.

In this way almost all the gold which enters England finds its way to the Bank, and is immediately converted into circulation by the creation and issue of Bank of England notes over and above the 15,000,000l. of fixed issue of the Bank, the Bank retaining the bullion as a security for the cashing of the notes issued. The Bank at this moment has in its cellars above 19,500,000l. in coin and bullion, for which that amount of Bank of England notes has been issued. The Bank sends from time to time its bullion to the Mint to be coined into sovereigns, according as sovereigns are needed to cash the notes which have been issued. When gold, therefore, is required to be sent abroad for any purpose whatever, that is always taken from the store in the Bank cellars, for obtaining which notes must be paid in and cancelled. Bullion assayed and of the standard weight is generally sent abroad. It sometimes happens, however, that for particular objects sovereigns are preferred, but never with the intention of melting them down; for the bullion in the Bank is in every respect the same as the bullion which would be obtained by melting the sovereign.

One observation we shall make as to the operation of this clause. It is that at the present time the possessor of gold pays a seigniory to the Bank for its conversion into sovereigns. He pays in gold $1\frac{1}{2}d.$ more per ounce than he receives; that is to say, he receives in Bank notes $3l.$ $17s.$ $9d.$ for $3l.$ $17s.$ $10\frac{1}{2}d.$ deposited with the Bank in gold. The sovereign, however, is kept at its full weight. Now, what would be the case if Mr. Lowe's plan were carried out? The Bank would be stripped of its gains by acting as the intermediary betwixt the bullionist and the Mint. The possessor of gold would be obliged to go directly to the Mint. He would pay, as in his dealings with the Bank, a larger amount than he received. But this would be in a debased sovereign, instead of a less value in notes. The bullionists would not lose by the transaction, and they would continue to send their gold to be coined as before into sovereigns—only sending it directly to the Mint instead of to the Bank. The consequence of this would inevitably be a debasement in the value of the sovereign, not only in the foreign but in the home market; for it is self-evident that an increase in the amount of sovereigns in circulation would take place in exact proportion to the diminution in the amount of gold in each.

To meet the objection to Mr. Lowe's proposal, as stated in our article of Thursday, Colonel Smith, the Master of

Mr. J. Aytoun.

the Mint, has, we perceive, published a letter in *The Times* of yesterday. He writes:—

" It has been remarked that if one per cent. were taken out of the coins, the several grains thus withdrawn being coined into new pieces and added to the circulation, the number of sovereigns poured upon the world would be increased reciprocally as the weight of each diminishes, and hence the purchasing power of each sovereign would be diminished precisely as the number added to the circulation is increased—that is, precisely as the weight of each would be diminished."

This is a very fair statement of our argument. Now, how does he meet it:—" The results here mentioned could not occur in the ordinary course of commerce. It might happen if the whole 80 millions of our present currency were suddenly re-coined into nearly 81 millions, and thrown into trade. But this is not practicable. It would take four or five years to re-coin our sovereigns; so that the compulsory addition to the circulation would not exceed 200,000*l*. per annum. In the meantime, it is found that our coins require to be replenished to the extent of five millions annually, and it is obvious that the intrusion of 200,000 or 300,000 coins by the action of the State, as a partial supplement to the losses sustained by the currency, would only diminish *pro tanto* the quantity of bullion taken to the Mint from outside."

This is a somewhat confused and obscure passage. The only thing which is perfectly clear is that Colonel Smith proposes that the debasement of the sovereign should only take place piecemeal, at the rate of five millions annually; so that, during the interval, we are to have two sets of sovereigns circulating together—a full weight coin and a light one. A very pretty proposal to be made by a Master of the Mint!

JAMES AYTOUN.

THE BULLIONIST.

(August 14, 1869.)

THE Chancellor of the Exchequer has at length succeeded in mooting a question of large scope and import—that of the Gold Coinage of this country; he has with sufficient explicitness indicated his opinion to be against the maintenance of our gold coins at their present weight or fineness for various reasons assigned, and as Mr. Lowe has received a character for tenacity of purpose, and is likely therefore to omit no means of enforcing his ideas practically, the nation has seriously to consider whether those ideas are sound and just, or the reverse.

Mr. Lowe is not a believer in the expediency of retaining a gold currency in this country at all. The waste, he says, with which it is carried on is enormous. " The possession of a gold and silver coinage I do not look upon as a necessity, but rather as a luxury, and indulgence of the popular taste." This was not the opinion of a statesman who is generally regarded as a much higher authority than our present Chancellor of the Exchequer. The latter, however, may consider Sir Robert Peel's principles respecting the currency to be antiquated. What did that great minister say on this point of the question ? " There is," he declared, " no doubt some expense in the maintenance of a metallic circulation, but none in my opinion sufficient to countervail the advantage of having gold coin generally distributed throughout the country, accessible to all, and the foundation of paper credit and currency." We confess adherence to Sir Robert Peel's opinion, and to sharing in the popular taste ; and as Mr Lowe supposes (with a sigh) that this taste must be gratified, we conclude that he shrinks from the effort of imposing his own. The Chancellor of the Exchequer resigns himself; and England may keep its gold currency.

He is dissatisfied on two points, however, on which he

invites consideration with a view to change. The first is that the Mint makes no charge for coining bullion, the cost of which is, therefore, borne by the public instead of being defrayed, as it ought to be, by the persons bringing the gold to have it minted; nor is any provision made for meeting the loss by wear and tear of the coins, which he estimates would amount on the light pieces now in circulation to 400,000*l*. To cure this double defect of our law, Mr. Lowe would propose the levying of a seigniorage, say of 1 per cent., of the nature of which we shall have a word to offer presently. The other object which the Chancellor of the Exchequer couples with this proposal is the establishment of an international coinage, by assimilating the intrinsic values of English and French gold coins.

Now, without at present minutely discussing the question whether it be consistent or not with sound policy and substantial justice for the State to coin the legal money of the nation at the public expense, we may observe that Mr. Lowe's argument on behalf of exacting a seigniorage when considered in connection with the means suggested by him for bringing about an international coinage is obscure, if not contradictory, and suggests suspicion that it is an afterthought. There are obviously two ways in which payment may be taken by the Mint for the work it performs; either by diminishing the weight or the fineness of the coins, or keeping these at the full standard, by receiving the amount in the shape of a separate payment. Combating an argument of Mr. McCulloch's against the first-named mode, Mr. Lowe declares that the difficulty may be met, no matter how it is taken, " Whether you give for one sovereign $122\frac{1}{4}$ grains of gold instead of $123\frac{1}{4}$—whether you take it from the sovereign or in the shape of a payment, does not matter a bit." But is this option reconcilable with having an international coinage; if the English sovereign is to be left of full weight and fineness, how can it possibly exchange for the proposed French 25f. piece? To establish the exact correlation between the values of the two coins, Mr. Lowe himself argues that the intrinsic value—that is, the quantity of pure gold in the sovereign—must be reduced by about 1 per cent., or ·999, and that at the same time France would have to raise her charge for mintage to one per cent., which is at present only ·0193 per cent.

The international coinage project therefore implies of necessity a degradation of the English standard. An international coinage would doubtless be a desirable thing to accomplish, chiefly however as regards the convenience of travellers, because in commercial and exchange transactions no inconvenience whatever is now felt. But the maintenance of our standard of money is a sacred obligation. That standard has subsisted untouched for 250 years, and has been affirmed as a fundamental principle by every statesman of repute during that period. To induce Parliament to tamper with it for any purpose whatever, is, we trust, immeasurably beyond the power of Mr. Lowe's logic, or the cogency of any arguments whatever. The Chancellor of the Exchequer has no better name to give to that principle than the term "crotchet." Are we wrong in suggesting that there exist grounds of suspicion that this question of imposing a seigniorage at the Mint would scarcely have arisen, if the international coinage scheme had not been entertained?

We confess we see no other reason for proposing to make a charge at the Mint. The law is, that that establishment is bound to give coin in exchange for standard bullion, weight for weight—which is, 3*l.* 17*s.* 10½*d.* an ounce; but in point of fact, bullion is never taken to the Mint by private persons or dealers to be coined. That work is done practically altogether through the agency of the Bank of England. There would be a delay of some weeks, after the bullion was deposited, before the coin could be received, occasioning a loss of interest which, to the holder, would be equivalent to a seigniorage or payment. The difference between 3*l.* 17*s.* 10½*d.*, at which the Bank must pay its notes in coin, and 3*l.* 17*s.* 9*d.*, at which it is

The Bullionist.

bound to give notes for bullion, "is sufficient" as estimated by Sir Robert Peel, in 1844, "to cover the expense of mintage." It also protects the public from being charged with a constant expense of coinage, which might arise if a person were at liberty one day to deposit bullion and the next to demand coin. The questions involved, however, in this great subject are too numerous and important to be dealt with in a single article, and we therefore propose to recur to the subject on an early occasion.

THE TIMES.
(August 16, 1869.)

THE Chancellor of the Exchequer has much to answer for in having thrown down that problem of the gold coinage for the consideration of public men during the vacation. We do not know whether it will, as a medical correspondent complained on Friday, prolong the sleepless habit of the Session to the indefinite postponement of that serene and dreamless sleep the overtasked brain demands after the hard work of legislation, but it has plainly excited a vast amount of speculation. Our columns have been enriched with contributions of many degrees of merit towards the solution of the difficulty, and the flood still continues. We print to-day a letter from Mr. Hubbard, which he promises to follow up with another, which we hope will take the heart out of the mystery. He is, as our readers know, not the only Bank Director who has given us his assistance, although, indeed, the subject is one on which every man apparently thinks himself as well qualified as his neighbour to express an opinion. If some of the letters we have published betray by their free phraseology unpractised and untrained students, what are they to the many more which have perished without seeing the sun? It would be a terrible but a retributive punishment to condemn the Chancellor of the Exchequer in his first days of holyday by the unarithmetical sea to read the rejected effusions his theories have provoked.

The main, and we may say the sole, question for practical investigators is whether the reduction of the weight of the sovereign from 123·274 grains of gold to 122·274 grains, subject to the condition that the person seeking to have bullion converted into coin at the Mint shall be required to bring 123·274 grains as before for each sovereign, will reduce the value of the sovereign in exchange. At present the possessor of bullion who takes it to the Mint receives back the same weight coined into sovereigns, each weighing 123·274 grains. According to the suggestion of the Chancellor of the Exchequer he would get the same number of sovereigns, but each sovereign would weigh 122·274 grains only, and the weight of sovereigns received back would be less than the weight of bullion brought for coinage by as many grains as there might be sovereigns returned, the difference being retained by the Mint as a recompense for the charge for coinage, and, of course, duly converted into money by the Exchequer. This is the simple statement of the proposition as we understand it to have been thrown out by Mr. Lowe, and his apparent hesitation in enlightening Mr. Alderman Lawrence was probably due to a failure to understand the difficulty propounded.

Before attacking anew the special question involved in Mr. Lowe's scheme, it may be useful to apprehend some of the general consequences of imposing a Mint charge. In the first place, let us understand that the value of a coin is to be measured by the quantity of any commodity it will buy, and in the same way the value of bullion is to be ascertained. If, for instance, a piece of gold will exchange for a certain quantity of corn at one time, and for double the quantity at another, the value of the piece relatively to corn has doubled, and although a change like this, taken alone, might be due to a change in the value of corn, yet if we found that the same variation in the purchasing power

The Times.

of the piece was universally apparent, we should declare absolutely that the piece had doubled in value. With this explanation we may go on to say that a coin can never be less in value than the gold it contains, for if a coin had less purchasing power than the gold in it the possessor of the coin would at once melt it down to have the advantage of the difference. In the same way it may be seen that a coin can never be greater in value than the gold required to be given for it, for if it were, the possessors of bullion would at once have their gold converted into coin. In England these limits—the gold in a coin and the gold to be given for a coin—have hitherto been practically identical, and the value of the coin has therefore always been identical with the value of the gold in it. In a country where, on the other hand, a seigniorage or mintage is exacted the value of a coin may vary between the limits we have specified; it may rise so high as the gold to be given for it, or it may fall so low as the gold in it; it can never pass outside those bounds on either side.

It may now be possible to understand the actual operation of the Coinage Laws of England and of other nations. The Australian and Californian miners commonly send their gold to London in the first place, as an *entrepôt*, and it is open to them to dispose of it in bulk in the market, or to send it to one or other of the European Mints. As we have seen, the gold in bulk and the minted gold of England are always of the same value; but in France and wherever a mintage is charged the gold in bulk, though never less in value than the coin the Mint would give in exchange for it, may exceed that coin in value by the percentage of the mintage. The gold brought to Europe in bulk would, therefore, commonly be thrown by preference into the English Mint, and added in the first place to our currency. This action would not be without its consequences. The equilibrium of our currency would be disturbed by the addition. The supply of gold brought into it would diminish the value of gold or raise prices, and the inequality of prices thus created would in turn cause an importation of commodities and an efflux of gold until equilibrium was once more restored. The natural action, therefore, of the absence of a seigniorage thus confirms to the full Mr. Lowe's complaint that it threw a burden of coinage upon the English Mint for no other purpose than to be followed by a speedy melting down again of much of the bullion just coined, and the establishment of a Mint charge is not merely justified, but required in defence of the English taxpayer. It is, of course, another question whether that Mint charge shall be levied by reducing the weight of the sovereign, as Mr. Lowe suggests, maintaining the weight of the gold to be rendered at the Mint for a sovereign, or by imposing a seigniorage *eo nomine*, keeping the weight of the sovereign unaffected.

The English sovereign can never, under existing regulations, differ in value from the gold in it, but when a Mint charge is exacted a coin may vary in value from the value of the gold in it up to the value of the gold to be given for it. The English sovereign now is of the value of 123·274 grains of gold. Were the suggestion of the Chancellor of the Exchequer adopted it would oscillate between the value of 123·274 grains, when importers would pour gold into the Mint, down to the value of 122·274 grains, when a temptation to melt down would begin to arise. But suppose the alternative form of mintage adopted, and the weight of the sovereign being kept 123·274, the owner of bullion wishing to have it minted were required to bring an additional grain to defray the charge. We are forced to the conclusion that the value of the coin would then vary also, but its limits would only be the value of 123·274 grains (its weight) and of 124·274 grains (the weight given for it). It may be at once suggested that under these circumstances the judicious plan would be to diminish the weight of the sovereign by half a grain, and increase the weight to be delivered at the Mint by the same amount, in which case the mean value of the sovereign would remain unaltered, the modification

The Times.

which is confessed to be necessary in the French mintage being accomplished by a similar reduction in the 25-franc piece; but the considerations we have so far pursued do not exhaust this pretty problem. To complete it, it would be necessary to bear in mind the point to which we drew attention in first considering the question,—the effect of the change in altering the value of gold itself. At present the producer of gold finds one of his principal vents at the English Mint, but the imposition of a seigniorage there would have an effect on his production precisely the same in character as that of an import duty. In fact, the seigniorage would be an import or *octroi* duty attached to a particular market. The producer will naturally desire to get the same for his product as before; but as it will suffer a deduction of 1 per cent. in passing through the Mint, he will be tempted to send his bullion to other markets until an equilibrium is established between its purchasing power there and the purchasing power of the "sweated" sovereign. The general effect would be a reduction in some proportion —probably slight—of the purchasing power of gold everywhere, which would in theory react upon its production on the other side of the globe. The profits of the digger would thus feel the effects of the remission of the burden of the English taxpayer; but, although this pursuit of consequences is scientifically valuable, it would, perhaps, be thought unnecessary to attend to them in legislation, and for practical purposes we may fall back on the suggestion that the value of the sovereign should be preserved as far as is consistent with the imposition of a seigniorage by the diminution in weight and increase in cost in equal proportions.

THE GOLD COINAGE.

(The Times, August 17, 1869.—To the Editor.)

Sir,—Since I addressed my first letter to you on this subject, the Chancellor of the Exchequer has, in reply to Mr. Alderman Lawrence, again ventilated "his idea" that "if you deduct one grain from every sovereign, and that the sovereign so curtailed be viewed, not as bullion, but as Gold, its producing power will remain the same as at present," and "the reason (he continues) is obvious,—the only seller of new sovereigns is the Government, and if new sovereigns could only be acquired upon the condition of paying 1 per cent. more for them, that 1 per cent. would necessarily limit the demand for sovereigns till they obtained the value put upon them." Here, at least, we have a theory; how would practice and experience justify it?

The importer of bullion has but one customer here—the Mint—upon whom he can certainly rely; and he will send his bullion to the Mint or sell it to the Bank upon the new regulations, and in either case he will receive for his merchandise 1 per cent. less than he would have got last year. But Mr. Lowe affirms "that the new charge of 1 per cent. will limit the demand for new sovereigns till they have attained the value put upon them." (?) It will do no such thing. The suggestion implies that a holder of 80,000*l.* in bullion wishing to convert his bars into money, either to meet his obligations or to make an investment, would be stayed in the transaction by the Mint charge of 1 per cent., and wait until the retention of his gold from the currency of the country raise the value of some hundred millions in coin and bank-notes now in circulation, by 1 per cent.; so that he might then exchange his bullion for coin worth 1 per cent. less in fine gold, but 1 per cent. more in " power." How long would the importer have to wait? and how would the concurrent circulation of the old and new coin be reconciled? It is essential to the completeness of Mr. Lowe's

Mr. J. G. Hubbard.

argument that these questions be distinctly answered. It may be argued that until this appreciation of the existing coinage were obtained bullion would not be imported. I reply, that the appreciation would never come, and certainly the importers of bullion would not wait for it. Why is bullion imported? A foreign country or colony buys largely of our manufactures, and, after setting off against their cost the value of its exports, finds itself still indebted to this country. The balance must be settled by credits on other countries, by a loan, or by a remittance in gold.

As the medium of adjusting international balances, from 20 to 30 millions in precious metals are annually imported into and exported from this country. The operations leading to these movements of bullion are dealings in commodities necessary for the countries buying them. The price of these commodities varies widely from time to time without materially checking their use, and the imposition of a seigniorage of 1 per cent. would neither paralyze commerce nor arrest the transmission of bullion required for the purposes of trade. Mr. Lowe thinks he can "raise the producing power of the sovereign as gold," but that would be a feat baffling even his ingenuity. Gold is cosmopolitan: within the zone of civilization it asserts its superiority to all arbitrary interference, and, subject to the slight variations attending local causes, it everywhere exhibits the same intrinsic value.

Mr. Lowe, indeed, affirms " that, as far as he knows, there is no such thing as intrinsic value." The phrase in some sense may be, as he says, " ambiguous," and I do not question that a clever casuist may apparently demonstrate that there is no such thing as either " truth," or " matter," or " value." To a dying man, " intrinsic value " cannot exist in any sublunary object; but we must regard our subject as men in the world, using a phrase in general acceptance, usefully embodying, therefore, some definite idea, and gold, proverbially quoted to illustrate the expression, may naturally afford its best interpretation. Gold,

E

then, an article beyond all others in universal demand, as being everywhere exchangeable for other commodities, has become the almost universal standard or measure of value, an office for which it is peculiarly fitted by its rarity, its durability, and its capacity for being easily transported.

Gold, whether as dust, bars, or coin, is commercially estimated not by the shape, size, or stamp of the bar or coin, or by the conditions under which it received that form or stamp, but solely by the purity of the metal; and this purchasing power, which the world of commerce recognizes in the pure metal, constitutes the "intrinsic value" of gold.

Colonel Smith, whose argument thus far is identical with that of Mr. Lowe, affirms with him that " if a Mint charge of 1 per cent. were established, 100*l*. would purchase as much as 101*l*. would have done previously;" but he frankly admits " that this additional value would only attach to the coins during currency and within the limits of the kingdom, and that, if exported, the holder would lose 1 per cent. of their value." This result would be a conclusive evidence of a depreciated standard. Colonel Smith is quite correct in his admission, and only wrong when he dreams that the same coin, worth only 25f. at Calais can be worth 25f. 20c. at Dover. If, indeed, the ocean, which constitutes our great highway of commerce, were an impassable gulf, and if our industry and transactions were confined to the United Kingdom, Colonel Smith's ambition might be satisfied, and he might see an economical Finance Minister, without raising a revolution, gradually and almost imperceptibly contract the elements of value in the standard coin until it sank to half its normal worth ; but commerce is the corrector of all such frauds, and its touch explodes the most ingenious theory if unsustained by practical knowledge, and those little words "if exported," which Colonel Smith reluctantly admits, are in truth the crucial test which declares the unsoundness of the doctrine he has so valiantly maintained.

Mr. J. G. Hubbard.

Colonel Smith's idea on this subject is echoed by Mr. Lowe when he says—

"As sovereigns they would be as valuable as at present, while as bullion they would be less valuable, and that attains precisely the object I have in view, which is, that the sovereign should be circulated in this country, but should not be melted abroad."

I sympathize with Mr. Lowe's object, and I have shown that his object would be effectively attained by the Bank selling bar gold at three-halfpence an ounce under the price of sovereigns, and that it would not be attained by depreciating the sovereign. Were the gold coin debased to half its value, it would still be melted and exported if the country needed an unusual supply of corn or cotton, and had no other immediate means of paying for it. Mr. Lowe proposes to create a metallic monster—a coin which would be neither a token nor a standard of value. It would not be a token, for a token is a domestic coin, and it is limited in its legal exchangeability; nor would it be a standard of value, for a standard coin, while unlimited as a legal tender, is, at the same time, exchangeable within the area of civilized commerce at its professed value. The pound sterling has hitherto been a truth; let it not become a sham.

I rejoice in Mr. Lowe's disapproval of a double standard of value. He did well to insist upon its incompatibility with our system; but I trust he has not permitted the French Government to regard the double standard as the only or the chief obstacle to our adopting a 25-franc piece as our standard coin. Mr. Lowe has accepted the opinions of men eminent for their knowledge in engineering, in mathematics, and in chymistry; would that he had also consulted his colleague, Mr. Göschen—a man distinguished for his perfect mastery of the science of exchanges, which embraces every question regarding coinage and the natural laws which regulate the movements of the precious metals.

In my next I hope to discuss the wear and tear of our coinage; and remain,

Your obedient servant,

PRINCE'S GATE, J. G. HUBBARD.
Aug. 16, 1869.

MR. HUBBARD ON MR. LOWE'S SCHEME.

(The Morning Advertiser, August 17, 1869.)

IT is refreshing, after all the irrelevancies which—*à propos* of Mr. Lowe's conundrum—have been published in *The Times*, both in leading articles and letters from correspondents, to have at last the opinion of one man of high reputation as a financier. Mr. Hubbard, like ourselves, pronounces himself out-and-out against the plan of the Chancellor of the Exchequer. He states, as we have already done, that to take a grain from the weight of the sovereign would be to lower the standard of value upon which all contracts and commercial operations have been carried on, and would be a direct fraud, by which the rights of the creditor would be sacrificed to the advantage of the debtor.

So far we heartily concur with Mr. Hubbard. But in one point we differ from him. Although determinately opposed to Mr. Lowe's proposal to debase the sovereign, he is against the bullionist having his gold converted into sovereigns for nothing, and would make him pay 1½*d*. for every ounce of gold converted into coin. Mr. Hubbard informs us in his letter in *The Times* that in 1843, the year before the passing of the Bank Act, he—at that time a Director of the Bank of England—published a pamphlet, in which he recommended this. Sir Robert Peel, Lord Overstone, and the other financiers who acted with Sir Robert Peel were, however, of a different opinion, and it was decided that the State should undertake the expense of converting gold into sovereigns.

By the Act of 1844 a sovereign is nothing more than a piece of bullion weighing 123·274 grains, and of 22 carats of fineness; for every person possessing gold can get it converted, without cost, into sovereigns, and can again, without traversing any law, have it melted down again into bullion. Such being its nature, a sovereign is not only an

Mr. J. Aytoun.

English coin, it is a universal one, which enables us to trade in every part of the civilized world without an exchange. A sovereign is just as useful to us for the purchase of wine at Bordeaux as for the purchase of hams at York.

Another immense advantage arises from our free coinage—it places our currency completely upon the footing of a purely metallic one. When gold comes into the country it is either taken directly to the Mint and converted into sovereigns, or it is taken to the Bank and deposited there, and bank notes given out and circulated precisely in the same way as would have taken place with the sovereigns, the currency being thus increased by paper instead of by gold. We have thus by the operation of Sir Robert Peel's Act—and to which Mr. Gladstone was a party, being then a Member of the Cabinet—a most admirable system of currency, increasing and diminishing precisely in the same way as a purely metallic currency, and with every bank note perfectly secured against the possibility of loss to the holder; and all this system is to be upset because Mr. Lowe wishes to have the credit of saving the expense of the Mint. We should like to know what those expenses amount to. We do not believe they are above 200,000*l.* or 300,000*l.* a-year, and for such a *bagatelle* as this has all this uproar been made; and in order to prove what a zealous, economical, far-seeing Chancellor of the Exchequer Mr. Lowe is, and how superior to Mr. Gladstone, who, during the many years he was Chancellor of the Exchequer, never imagined any such absurd alterations as those proposed by Mr. Lowe, under the suggestions of his allies, the two Smiths—the one the Member for Stockport, and the other the *ci-devant* Master of the Calcutta Mint.

JAMES AYTOUN.

THE GOLD COINAGE.

(The Times, August 20, 1869.—To the Editor.)

SIR,—One reason, if it be a good one, is generally considered to be a sufficient justification; but the Chancellor of the Exchequer alleges two reasons for his scheme concurrently to contract by clipping, and to expand by statute, the gold coin of the realm. His first reason—the advantage of identifying our pound sterling with 25f. in gold—I have already noticed. The second is the expediency of imposing a coinage charge which shall cover the cost of establishing and maintaining the gold currency in its integrity.

I postpone for the moment the consideration of the amount of our gold currency and of the proportion which is now light, in order to deal at once with the main proposition, and trace its consequences if carried into effect.

It is assumed that every sovereign becomes light in eighteen years, and every half-sovereign in ten years, and that to withdraw the sovereigns and half-sovereigns when light and replace them would require a "mintage charge not far short of $1\frac{1}{2}$ per cent. on the value of the gold coined."

This charge, if made, would operate in the reduction of the price paid to the importer of bullion, and so the price given by the Bank would be not 3l. 17s. 9d. per oz., as now, but 3l. 16s. 7d. As to the reason for this charge the importer would be thoroughly indifferent, and he would soon adjust his operations to the change. The scale of variation in foreign exchanges would be enlarged, there would be more uncertainty in commercial transactions, and there would be the possibility of a Mint being put in action beyond the reach of Her Majesty's Government, where sovereigns, unimpeachable in everything but their origin, would be produced for private advantage, and to the relief of Her Majesty's Mint. In any case there would be no lack of gold coin bearing the Queen's effigy, and discharging all the purposes of a gold coinage.

Mr. J. G. Hubbard.

The Government will have made their profit upon the original coinage, and be prepared to exchange, piece for piece, heavy coin for light. Would they receive all the light sovereigns brought to them, or all the sovereigns 18 years old? If the former, there will be constant occupation for the Mint, for, with so good a customer awaiting them, the "sweating" fraternity of whom Mr. Lowe complains will extend their industry, remove at their own discretion a portion of every sovereign passing into their hands, and return the attenuated coin to the Light Gold Office, to be exchanged for an equal number of full-bodied pieces. The process of "sweating" must be applied with discretion and delicate adjustment to the human frame, but the gold coin may in four-and-twenty hours be reduced from its normal dimensions to such a bulk as the moderation of the operator may determine; and the pecuniary return will be so satisfactory as to attract a crowd of competitors into the new field of industry. Is any limit to be assigned to the degree of tenuity in which Her Majesty's coin may be returned to the Mint for re-construction? I suppose not, for obviously the lighter the coin the greater its claim on the compassion of the Chancellor of the Exchequer, and yet I fear that the coin which may be renewed within each financial year may involve a very serious deficiency in the balance-sheet of the Mint.

But possibly I over-estimate the proposed indulgence. It may be intended to redeem the light gold coin, but only when it has done at least 18 years of active service. Very good; 18 years is the briefest period which should qualify the dilapidated money to renew its youth, and this rule postpones the more serious " sweating " process, which will fall only upon the superannuated sovereigns, and they, whatever their condition, could be further fraudulently reduced before they are finally consigned to the crucible of the Master of the Mint. There is, however, *one* disadvantage attending this postponed retirement. Sovereigns, like men, have varied destinies. Some enter upon an existence so tranquil that a whole generation may pass away without their encountering a scratch, while others, from their infancy, are exposed to the rough jostlings of a restless and revolutionary age, and before they reach maturity are thoroughly worn out, and hardly to be recognized as their former selves; and thus to renew light sovereigns only when 18 years old would be to leave a large number of them in circulation. The Report of the Mint Masters informs us that 30 millions of sovereigns circulate in foreign countries, and these will all the more readily, when the "heavy for light Bureau" is opened, return hither for renewal at the cost of this country. Whether, therefore, the rule be to accept all light coin, or only light coin of a stipulated age, the plan in either sense appears seriously objectionable, as tending to encourage the maltreatment of the Queen's coin.

The Chancellor of the Exchequer, it must be remarked, does not claim the credit of originality. He enunciates, with a view to its ventilation, a scheme founded upon a Report of Mr. Graham, Master of the Mint in Tower-hill, and of Colonel Smith, late Master of the Mint at Calcutta, and one cannot but ask why this conjunction of great authorities? Was Mr. Graham uncertain in his convictions? Was his name alone inadequate to recommend so novel a proposition? Or has Mr. Lowe taken a hint from the Episcopate, and, following the example of a Bishop who cannot work without two Archdeacons, whom he designates his "eyes," has he appointed two Mint Masters to be "eyes" to the Chancellor of the Exchequer?

On examining the Report of the Mint Masters, I find that the real author of the scheme is Mr. Jevons. The Report speaks of the general estimate of the coins in circulation "having received a valuable confirmation from the researches of Professor Jevons," and remarks that "Mr. Jevons's experiments and observations furnish the best *data* we possess for estimating the annual loss by wear."

I turn, therefore, to Professor Jevons's paper "On the Metallic Condition of the Metallic Currency," and I not
Mr. J. G. Hubbard.

only find Mr. Jevons (p. 430) anticipating Mr. Lowe by a declaration "that there is no such thing as value intrinsic in a thing," but I find him (p. 436) distinctly enunciating Mr. Lowe's scheme thus:—" In imposing a Mint charge the Government might most properly undertake to prevent the coinage falling again into its present discreditable state by *constantly* withdrawing at its own cost a certain amount of light gold." At page 440 Mr. Jevons gives a table showing in parallel columns the number of sovereigns coined in each year from 1817 to 1867, and the number of each year's coinage found now to be in circulation upon an aggregate of 100,000.

Upon this table Mr. Jevons founds his calculations, thus :—

The coinages of 1863 and 1864 were	14,578,000
But of these the Bank held unissued, say ..	578,000
Remain as affecting the general circulation	14,000,000

Of 100,000 sovereigns now in circulation, those dated 1863 and 1864 amount to 18,671. "We may say, therefore, *with confidence*" (Mr. Jevons *loqr.*) " that the whole circulation of sovereigns is $\frac{100000}{18671}$, or 5,356 times (5 1-3) as great as the number of *sovereigns* now in the hands of the people." And so 14,000,000 × 5 1-3 gives 75,000,000 as the extreme limit of sovereign circulation.

This amount of 75,000,000 Mr. Jevons subsequently modifies by deductions for coin undistributed or exported, but I am only concerned with the process by which he reaches it, and the features which strike me in that process are the arbitrary selection of dates and an apparent want of congruity, the formula adopted being simply stated thus :— As 18,671 (examined sovereigns dated 1863 and 1864) : 100,000 (the aggregate of the examined sovereigns) : : 14,000,000 (the issued coins of 1863 and 1864) : the whole circulation. The resulting quotient is 75,000,000; but, applying the same formula to the coinage of 1865 and 1866 (with the deduction as before of 2,800,000 in store at the Bank from the combined coinage—viz., 5,497,000), the figures run thus:—As 4,211 : 100,000 : : 2,697,000 : 64,026,000; giving, therefore, a result considerably below the previous one. Taking again the earlier dates 1852 and 1853, we have—As 10,618 : 100,000 : : 18,651,000 : 175,655,000. This last result supplies the somewhat needless information that out of a total coinage of 171,563,000 *not more* than 175,655,000 are now circulating in the country.

Perhaps it may be said that arbitrary selections of particular years are unreliable, but that the formula applied to a general aggregate average must yield a correct result. Let it be tried. Then—As (the sum of tested coins) 100,000 : (the aggregate of tested coins) 100,000 : : (the sum of various coinages) 171,563,000 : (the coin in circulation) 171,563,000. As it is upon the formula eventuating in these meaningless results that Mr. Jevons depends when he announces *with confidence* the amount " of the gold in circulation" (p. 441), as it is, " by this method of calculation he *demonstrates* " the limit of that circulation (p. 444), I have thought it my duty to examine it closely; and, if I may presume to criticise the calculations of a Professor of Political Economy, I would say that his formula is essentially defective, inasmuch as his first and third terms are not of one kind.

The fallacy of Mr. Jevons's method can be accurately illustrated by imagining him to apply it in 1861 to a census of England and Wales. He selects for his test the county of Rutland, and discovers a total population of 20,000, of whom 2,000 are between the ages of 10 and 15. He ascertains that the registered births within the five corresponding years 1846-1851 were 3,000,000, and he then applies his formula:—As 2,000 : 20,000 : : 3,000,000 : 30,000,000. Thirty millions would thus be ascertained to be the extreme limit of the population, a perfectly safe conclusion, seeing that it is only 20,500,000. In this illustration, as in Mr. Jevons's computation of the coinage, no account is taken of emigrations and deaths, of exports and meltings. But it is

Mr. J. G. Hubbard.

obvious that no necessary proportion exists between the number of births of either coins or men 20 years since, and the number of the individuals then born and now existing in a given area.

Mr. Jevons's treatise contains much interesting matter, and facts industriously collected, the accuracy of which I am at present unprepared either to corroborate or deny. But as the Chancellor of the Exchequer has challenged public opinion (among other points) upon a scheme for a coinage sustentation fund, prepared by his Mint Masters, but by them avowedly founded upon the authority of Mr. Jevons, I must distinctly declare that Mr. Jevons's method of calculation in connection with the subject is fallacious, and the conclusions derived from it utterly worthless.

I trust at no distant day to offer you some remarks upon the mode hitherto pursued with reference to the light gold coin; and remain, Sir,
Your obedient servant,
J. G. HUBBARD.

GOLD COINAGE.

(The Times, August 20, 1869.—To the Editor.)

Sir,—The Chancellor of the Exchequer and others insist upon saying that we in England coin gold free of charge to the importer. This is right in theory, but wrong in practice—*i.e.*, we certainly profess to coin free of charge, but our Mint regulations, on the other hand, compel the bullion holder to sell gold to the Bank of England. He may go to the Mint, if he brings 10,000*l.*, and will wait a certain time, otherwise it is more profitable to go to the Bank. The Bank pays 77*s.* 9*d.* per oz. for standard gold, the importer must submit to the computation of assays to ⅛th grain fine, to a deduction of 12 grains for weight, and to a charge of 4*s.* 6*d.* for assays. The whole of these deductions amount to 0·2828 per cent., but it is better to

Mr. Ernest Seyd.

submit to the loss; the delay, &c., at the Mint is generally considered the excuse for the proceeding. In France a direct charge of 6f. 70c. for 3,100f. is made, their assays are to 1-10,000th part fine, there is no deduction for weight, and assays cost 1f. 50c.; the whole of their charges amounting to 0·2296 per cent. If the delay of seven days, at 3 per cent. per annum, be added to this, the whole charge is 0·3091 per cent., but the French Mint, through the Bank of France, now pays cash for all fine gold, so that the delay falls away. These statements can be verified in the bullion market; they are clearly proven in a pamphlet entitled *The Question of Seigniorage and Charge for Coining*, published by Effingham Wilson.

England, therefore, while professing to charge nothing for coining gold, by a kind of legerdemain exacts more than the French, who have a minting charge established by law. The conclusion that English gold is thus exported because it is actually coined free of charge is wrong. It is the more wrong because it is well known that the allowance for fineness and weight (Mint remedy) enjoyed by the English Mint is larger than that of France, and English gold coin on the average is less fine than French and American gold,—that is to say, it is less fine from the respective legal standard. Proper inquiry will confirm this, and will also confirm the fact that French and American gold coin is far more liable to exportation and to melting down than English sovereigns. The want of information which Mr. Lowe's advisers display in reference to this matter is pitiable, and these assertions, coming through his authority, are calculated to mislead the British public.

The proposal to exact a seigniorage of 1 per cent. on sovereigns, so as to reduce them from their present gold value of 25·2215f. to 25f., amounts, as Alderman Lawrence thinks, to a conundrum; in reality it is a little bit of *hocus pocus*, the secret of which England, as well as France, will not fail to discover. Two proposals may be made,—France must either raise the gold value of her napoleons to 16s., or

Mr. Ernest Seyd.

England must reduce its sovereigns to 25f., by coining them with less gold; this can only be done in a direct and open manner, and we must submit to the inconveniences of the change. Colonel Smith and his party propose, however, that we should charge a seigniorage of 1 per cent.,—*i.e.*, deduct 1 per cent. of gold from the coin, and replace it by 1 per cent. seigniorage.

This necessitates that France on her part should deduct 1 per cent. seigniorage from bullion without changing her coin. The *hocus pocus* of the matter is this:—Bullion in England will be raised 1 per cent., but the 1 per cent. will be deducted again, leaving its Mint price at 77s. 10½d. per oz.; but this 77s. 10½d. consists of the new shillings—namely, the 1-20th part of the pound worth 25f., which now is worth 25·2215f.

In France, however, the coin will remain as it is, the price of bullion will be 1 per cent. less; so that, apparently, as far as the disturbance of bullion value is concerned, the whole inconvenience will fall on France. Are the French likely to submit to this? The effect of the proposed arrangement is this:—

England lowers the value of her sovereign.

France lowers the value of her bullion.

England and France introduce the charge of seigniorage.

But if the direct and open way of squaring the difference between 25·2215f. and 25f. be adopted, the effort is simply that England lowers the value of her sovereign.

The tutors of Mr. Lowe pretend, in their arrangement, to have effected a compromise, but in both cases England is obliged to reduce her sovereign, so that England gains nothing by this pretended compromise. And if this is the case, why should we call upon the French to make a far more serious disturbance of their monetary arrangements, and why should we, to cover all, introduce the seigniorage?

The question of seigniorage is one that Englishmen should understand well: it has been frequently discussed in English financial literature, and in regard to its standard coin, England has always maintained that the value of the sovereign rests solely upon gold. If Mr. Lowe is right in saying that a coin made of 99 parts of gold and one part of seigniorage is worth 100, he means that 1 per cent. of seigniorage is equal in value to 1 per cent. of gold; consequently, 2, or 5, or 50 per cent. of seigniorage are worth 2, or 5, or 50 per cent. of gold,—why, indeed, should we not substitute seigniorage altogether, and do without gold? Doctrines of this kind have been held by would-be financiers from time immemorial, and from time immemorial they have always been wrecked without leaving a vestige behind. The intrinsic value of gold, if not recognized by Mr. Lowe, has always been recognized by the world at large, and the common sense of the English nation especially has known how to make the best practical use of it. It is to be feared that our Chancellor of the Exchequer will make a complete *fiasco* with these very old and yet, to us, new theories.

Colonel Smith maintains that the value of a thing is what it costs to produce; other people think that the test of value depends upon what a thing will fetch. The former conception produces the most extraordinary results, and Colonel Smith goes so far as to say that if the State chooses to charge 50 per cent. import duty or seigniorage on gold—if it actually deducts this from the sovereign—the value of the 10s. remaining will, nevertheless, be equal to the 20s.

In conclusion, I beg to say that, according to my opinion, a small Mint charge sufficient to cover the first coinage, not exceeding one-third per cent., is a fair and legitimate charge which can be borne, but anything above this first charge takes the character of a seigniorage, and in that character it is nothing but a sham, against which logic, commerce, and the common sense of the people will rebel, and this rebellion, in spite of political authority, will be successful in the end.

I remain, Sir, your obedient servant,

1 A, Princes St., Bank, E.C.   ERNEST SEYD, F.S.S.
Aug. 13, 1869.

THE TIMES.

(August 20, 1869.)

WE have received another letter from Mr. Hubbard on the problem of the Gold Coinage, and he promises us some more remarks "at no distant day." It is evident that though the Bank Court may have been worsted in their contest with the Chancellor of the Exchequer on the payment of the dividends, there is at least one Bank Director —and, if we may credit report, there are many more to back him—prepared to fight to the uttermost the proposal to reduce the weight of the sovereign.

We have expressed at length on former occasions our views of the nature and effect of Mr. Lowe's proposition, and we do not find it necessary to modify our conclusions. We hold the propriety and justice of exacting a seigniorage sufficient to cover the expense of coining to be fully established, and Mr. Hubbard so far coincides in opinion with the Chancellor of the Exchequer. It is a practical question, upon which we offer no opinion, whether it is possible to demand a seigniorage so high as one per cent. without incurring the consequences of private coinage. It cannot be denied that one per cent. is a considerable charge, but it is to be remembered that the making of spurious coins of the same weight and fineness as the authentic sovereign would be an enterprise undertaken in a surreptitious fashion, and it would probably require a larger margin than one per cent. to become profitable. Mr. Hubbard cautiously says " there would be the possibility of " a mint being put in action beyond the reach of Her " Majesty's Government, where sovereigns unimpeachable " in everything but their origin would be produced for " private advantage and to the relief of Her Majesty's " Mint," but we shall doubtless be not far wrong in holding that Mr. Hubbard himself looks upon this possibility as remote, if not fanciful. Assuming that a mintage of one per cent. is exacted, and that it is not sufficient to stimulate private coinage, we endeavoured to trace its effects on the value of the sovereign, and we arrived at the conclusion, which we supported by reasoning, that its value would vary from time to time between the value of the gold it contained and the value of the gold given for it, and that the imposition of a mintage would be followed by a secondary effect on the value of gold itself, slightly reducing its purchasable power all over the world. Hence if Mr. Lowe's suggestion were adopted, and the sovereign reduced in weight from 123·274 to 122·274 grains, but 123·274 grains were required as at present to be delivered at the Mint in exchange for every sovereign issued, the value of the pound would vary between its present value (that of 123·274 grains) and the value of its new weight (that of 122·274 grains), and it would suffer an average depreciation which might, perhaps, be taken at one-half per cent. On the other hand, if the weight of the coin were kept unchanged and mintage exacted by requiring 124·274 grains to be delivered at the Mint for every sovereign issued, the value of the sovereign would be increased on an average about one-half per cent. It was an obvious practical conclusion that, in order to keep the mean value of the sovereign unaltered after the imposition of a seigniorage, the weight of the sovereign should be reduced, and the weight of gold delivered at the Mint for it should be increased in equal proportion.

What is the bearing of Mr. Hubbard's present letter upon these speculations? It has no bearing upon them. It leaves them altogether unaffected. Mr. Hubbard's letter is divisible into two parts. In the first he hits a blot, or, as we should prefer to say, points out an omission in Mr. Lowe's expository statement at the end of the Session. One object of the Chancellor of the Exchequer is to provide out of the margin of mintage the cost of re-coinage. Sovereigns under ordinary wear and tear lose a portion of their weight, and to call them in and re-coin them would entail a considerable loss on the Mint. Mr. Lowe's rate of
The Times.

seigniorage would be sufficient to cover the depreciation of the coinage as shown by past experience; and he proposed that, for the future, all coin over eighteen years of age should cease to be legal tender, and should then be withdrawn from the currency. It is plain that this is not enough. The depreciation coin undergoes now from fair usage, when it is known that a light coin ceases to be receivable at the Bank, is very different from the deterioration it would undergo if it were proclaimed that all light coins under eighteen years of age, and having just attained that age, would be exchanged for coins of full weight on presentation at the Mint. But it is not to be supposed that the Chancellor of the Exchequer was unconscious of this truth. Mr. Lowe would never allow a person to bring to the Mint a bit of gold once a sovereign, but "sweated" down to half its bulk, and demand a full sovereign for it, because it was not more than 18 years old. In his brief explanation of the suggestion he recommended to the attention of the public, he dwelt only on the leading points, without going into the lesser details of the plan. We apprehend that while coins over eighteen years old would be thrown out of circulation entirely, and be only receivable at the Mint as so much bullion, coins under that age would be exchanged under strict conditions limiting the diminution of their weight to what is the ordinary wear as proved by past experience. Mr. Lowe, if challenged, would undoubtedly have entered upon a further explanation of this character, and with this supplementary statement that half of Mr. Hubbard's letter which deals with the operation of re-coinage would fall to the ground.

 The first half of Mr. Hubbard's present communication is pertinent and just, but it is concerned with an omission in Mr. Lowe's statement, and when that omission is supplied its value ceases. The second half has the faintest possible relevancy to the proposal of the Chancellor of the Exchequer, and is, moreover, vitiated by an essential misconception. It is sufficiently known that the method

now in agitation of dealing with the gold currency was first broached by Professor Jevons, in a paper he read before the Statistical Society. The Professor had endeavoured, among other things, to discover the amount of gold in actual circulation in the kingdom, and for that purpose pursued the following method:—With the assistance of bankers in different parts of the country, he caused a large number of sovereigns in use to be sorted under the years of their coinage, and he found that out of 100,000 sovereigns in circulation those dated 1863 and 1864 amounted to 18,671. He knew from the records of the Mint and the Bank that just 14 millions of sovereigns of the years 1863 and 1864 had been put into circulation, and therefore no more than that amount could be in circulation. If the full amount had remained in circulation, he argued, we should be able to reason thus:—Since we find that for every 18,671 sovereigns of 1863 and 1864 in circulation a gross number of 100,000 is in circulation, we may deduce by the Rule of Three that for 14 millions of 1863 and 1864 in circulation the gross circulation is 75 millions. It is mere Proportion,— as $18{,}671 : 100{,}000 : : 14{,}000{,}000 :$ answer $= 75$ millions nearly; and the result is that we may affirm with confidence that 75 millions is the *extreme limit* of sovereign circulation. Mr. Hubbard has entirely lost sight of the force the words "extreme limit" possess, and misunderstood Mr. Jevons to conclude that 75 millions is the actual amount in circulation. Hence it unfortunately happens that all Mr. Hubbard has written in the second part of his letter is due to a misconception of his own which makes it worthless. The point would in any case be of small importance. Mr. Jevons having formed an estimate, by processes such as we have indicated, of the gold coinage in use in the kingdom, compared it with the gold coinage that had been issued, and concluded that a large proportion of our sovereigns are melted down, exported, lost, or otherwise go out of circulation. Mr. Hubbard will probably not deny this conclusion, and we doubt not on re-examination
The Times.

he will allow the accuracy of the reasoning on which it is founded.

If we might venture to offer a word of advice to the large number of persons in the commercial world now agitated by the proposed reformation of the gold coinage, we should recommend them to beware of being lost in a multiplicity of details. Let them consider the recent correspondence between the Bank and the Chancellor of the Exchequer. Mr. Lowe made a proposal to which the Court replied with an elaborate analysis of the existing plan of paying dividends. They might as well have told him of the number of stones in Sir John Soane's building. He brushed aside this cloud of verbiage, and called the attention of the Directors to the simple point before them, whereupon, though they had the means of a very good fight at hand, their opposition at once collapsed. A similar experience may be imminent in the matter of the gold coinage; and it is necessary for those who deny the wisdom of a change to confine their attention to the following questions :—(1) Is a seigniorage desirable at all? (2) What is the limit to which it may safely be carried? (3) Shall it be obtained by reducing the weight of the sovereign, or by requiring more uncoined gold to be brought for sovereigns of the present weight, or by combining these two changes? Everything else mixed up with the arguments on these queries will only serve to weaken the influence of those who reason upon the subject.

THE ECONOMIST.
(August 21, 1869.)

Mr. Lowe's idea as to the gold coinage has been much discussed as it well deserved to be, but as yet he cannot be complimented on the result. That idea, as our readers will remember, is to take two pennyworth of bullion out of every sovereign and to charge twopence for making every sovereign, and then to say that these two changes counterbalance one another—that the charge made for coining adds as much to the value of the sovereign as the amount of bullion taken from it tends to diminish the value. In other words, the light sovereign will be worth as much as a heavy one if something is paid for making the light one and nothing is paid for making the heavy one.

The first difficulty of this is to make common people understand it. An ordinary person will hardly be induced to believe that the coin which weighs less is as valuable as the coin which weighs more. Only a complete concurrence of authorities could convince him that such was the fact, and it would be difficult for any accumulation of concurrent authorities really to convince people. But in fact there is no such concurrence of authorities. Mr. Hubbard, for example, who has had so much experience as a Bank Director, and who has for so many years given so much attention to the currency, denies Mr. Lowe's doctrine altogether. He says that the light sovereign on which the charge is made will not be as valuable as the heavy sovereign, on making which no charge is levied. He says—

"The reasoners in favour of combining material depreciation and statutable appreciation of the sovereign fail to see that an abstraction of a portion of the standard coin must be a contraction of the measure of value, but that a charge for coinage can be only a charge upon the importer, and cannot enhance the value or power of the coin."

But if great authorities thus disagree, how will common persons, who must take a change like this upon authority, ever be satisfied?

We cannot indeed assent to all Mr. Hubbard's reasoning. He seems to us to go as much too far in one direction as Mr. Lowe goes in the other. He considers, if we understand him, that the imposition of a Mint charge for making a coin has no *tendency* to augment the value of such coin. Mr. Lowe, on the other hand, reasons as if the imposition of such a charge would with mathematical certainty and complete accuracy, at all times and in all places, raise the value of such coin. As we last week explained, we hold that the

The Economist.

truth lies between these two extreme notions. As a rule and upon an average of years, the imposition of a Mint charge upon a coin will augment its exchangeable value. But it will not augment that value always and equally, and you never could at any one time be sure that it had so augmented it. The value of coin, like the value of everything else, is determined at each particular moment by the supply and demand of the moment. In the long run, no doubt, that value is regulated by the cost of production, because the supply is so regulated. People will not work at a loss, and, therefore, they will not produce coin or any other article unless they think they shall have a profit for doing so. But at any one moment people may have produced too much of any commodity, and in that case its price will fall. The cost of production is not a momentary regulator of price—it only regulates for a most part and on an average. A slight increase in the cost of production will have a tendency to raise the price of the article produced, but it will not do so instantly or certainly.

That the Bank Directors, or some of them, should not agree with Mr. Lowe, will not, perhaps, after what has happened, surprise many people; but what may surprise them is that all the members of the Cabinet do not agree with him. At least, last year Mr. Göschen gave elaborate evidence before the International Coinage Commissioners exactly in opposition to Mr. Lowe. He was asked:—

"2328. Some of the witnesses who have appeared before us have thought that although the quantity of fine gold in the sovereign was reduced, and its intrinsic value therefore reduced, its value might nevertheless be maintained by levying a seigniorage of about the same per-centage value; have you ever considered at all whether that would be so ?—I think it would not be so.

"2329. Supposing that the value of the sovereign was reduced by the amount of 2d., would it not be necessary, in order to discharge in the new currency any debt which had been contracted in the old, that the payment for the future should be 1l. 0s. 2d. ?—It would.

"2330. Do you think that by levying a seigniorage upon the new coin to the extent of one per cent., which is about the same value as 2d. in the 1l., it would be possible to avoid making that compensation with any regard to justice to the creditor ?—I do not think it would remove the injustice."

And he goes on to show that at various times coin is subjected to special causes which tend sometimes to lower, sometimes to raise, its value. In like manner, gold bullion is subject also to a whole set of causes tending sometimes to raise its value, as compared with coin, and sometimes to diminish it. For some purposes, coin is more convenient than bullion; and for some, bullion is more convenient than coin.

"I think," says Mr. Göschen, "it is conceivable that there are many cases in which the export of bar gold is more convenient than that of coin; for instance, it packs much better, and avoids a certain amount of loss of weight which, if I have been correctly informed, arises from the transmission of coin. For all purposes of long journeys bar gold is more valuable than coin. An export of coin might take place not only in order to pay for balances due upon the trade of different countries, but there might be a sensible alteration in the amount of coin circulating in a country by the introduction of new banking expedients in some of the countries in the Monetary Convention, where the system of bank notes has not been greatly developed. If in those countries that system were to have greater development, or if in countries where banking was still in its infancy the system of Clearing-houses were to be adopted, either of those changes would evidently reduce the quantity of coin requisite. Such changes would, in my opinion, have this effect—that there would be less demand for coin, and, therefore, if there is less demand for coin the price that you have paid for turning bar gold into coin would lose a portion of its value, because there would be more coin in the country than would be wanted, and a portion of that coin would evidently have to be turned back again into bar gold. If there is a redundancy of coin in the country from any circumstance, the additional value given to that coin arbitrarily, that is to say, not by the amount of gold contained in it, but by the amount of seigniorage charged, would in my opinion be considerably diminished, if not entirely lost."

In these ways and in other ways the value of coin is daily fluctuating, sometimes one way and sometimes another, and the value of bullion is similarly changing, sometimes upwards and sometimes downwards, but you cannot be sure at any given moment that there will be between the value of the coin and the value of the bullion that precise amount of difference which the amount of the Mint charge imposed on making the coin would induce us at first sight to expect.

But we need not dwell on this now. The present point is that Mr. Lowe's scheme fails in intelligibility. It is a puzzle as he states it, and when the highest authorities are asked whether what he says about it is true or false, they are not agreed. Some say he is right, and some say he is wrong. We own this seems to us a fatal flaw. A plan in England can only be adopted either because everybody understands the reason of it, or because the most respected persons say it is right. But here nobody understands the reason, and the most respected persons do not agree.

THE GOLD COINAGE.

(The Times, August 21, 1869.—To the Editor.)

Sir,—Any one who embarks in this discussion should do so only for the sake of establishing sound principles, and should be ready to retract any erroneous statement either of fact or argument; and I certainly shall cheerfully confess any mistake or misconception of which I may be convicted.

I should be sincerely grieved if I had misconceived and so misrepresented Mr. Jevons. It is quite true that Mr. Jevons presents 75,000,000 as the amount which the sovereigns in circulation cannot exceed, but so far from supposing that he gave this amount as the *actual circulation*, and commenting upon it in that light, I describe it as Mr. Jevons's extreme limit of "sovereign circulation," and as one "which he subsequently modifies by deductions for coin undistributed or exported." I beg, therefore, to be acquitted of this, the only misconception imputed to me.

It was to the process by which Mr. Jevons attained these 75,000,000 that I objected and do object. The formula adopted can lead not even to an estimate. It ends, as I have shown, if honestly applied, only in proving this—that the coin in circulation cannot exceed the coin minted, a fact which is self-evident. Arbitrarily to select two years out of fifty as the basis of the formula may enable the Professor to hit off in his quotient a probable result, but the formula or method which he adopts I faithfully illustrated by its sup-

Mr. J. G. Hubbard.

posed application to a census of population; and I do not think it a matter of small importance that a scheme for the regulation of the Imperial coinage should be avowedly based upon computations illogical in their construction, and therefore worthless in their results.

To the three questions with which your article to-day concludes, I could reply in terms which would leave few differences between us, but that I feel bound to substitute the word *mintage* for *seigniorage*, as regards our gold coin. The distinction is not one of my making, nor unreal.

In the *Dictionnaire de l'Economie Politique*, Paris, 1853, I find, under the title " Seigneuriage,"—

"Droit que le seigneur percevait à titre d'impôt sur les matières d'or et d'argent destinées à la fabrication des monnaies. Ce droit était distinct de celui de Brassage, qui avait pour objet de couvrir les frais de fabrication."

Substituting, therefore, the word which expresses my own meaning, I reply,—

1. A mintage is desirable.

2. A mintage cannot be safely carried beyond the cost of coining.

3. It should be levied as a charge upon the owner of the bullion, whether by deduction from the gold when coined or by a corresponding payment from himself is, of course, unimportant.

It is essential to bear in mind that the legal medium of payment—that, for instance, in which the Bank must redeem a 5*l.* note—is so many grains of gold, not in dust or in a bit of a bar, but in a *coin*, and the question in contention is, " Can you by statute give to that coin an increase of value which would be effective in making a legal payment; and, if you can, are there any and what limits to that increase?"

I have the honour to be,
    Sir, your obedient servant,
      J. G. HUBBARD.

PRINCE'S GATE,
 Aug. 20, 1869.

THE GOLD COINAGE.

(The Times, August 21, 1869.—To the Editor.)

Sir,—In my previous letter I asserted that English gold coin, being proportionately less fine than French or American gold coin, and consequently less identical with bullion, is less liable to exportation. It may be advisable that you should be furnished with clear and decisive data establishing the fact.

The Mint remedy in England is fixed by law at 12 grains for 1lb. troy weight of gold coin—*i.e.*, for every 5,760 grains, 12 grains may be short; this allowance is equal to 2*l*. 2*s*. for every 1,000*l*., or 0·21 per cent. The remedy for the quality of the sovereign is 1-16th carat in the 22 carats —*i.e.*, the coin may be only 21 15-16ths carats fine. This is equal to 2*l*. 17*s*. in the 1,000*l*., or 0·285 per cent. The joint allowance for weight and quality of the pieces is, therefore, nearly 5*l*. per 1,000*l*., or ½ per cent.; in other words, the Mint may issue 1,000*l*. in coin worth only 995*l*. 1*s*. without infringing upon the Mint Laws.

The Mint remedy in France consists of 0·2 per cent. for weight and 0·2 per cent. for standard, together 0·4 per cent., and 1,000 napoleons may be issued worth only 996. This shows the theory of the remedies, according to which the English coin may diverge from its standards by 1 per mille more than French gold coin. (The French Government intends to reduce the remedy to 1 per mille.)

In practice, however, as far as the weight of new coin is concerned, no advantage accrues to the Mints on account of the remedy for weight, which is intended as a provision for irregularities in single pieces, and if a number—say 1,000 sovereigns or 1,000 napoleons, new from the Mints—are weighed they will be found correct, or nearly correct, in the aggregate. The bullion scale, in fact, exercises an immediate control over the operation of the Mint Masters in respect of weight.

Mr. E. Seyd.

In regard to fineness or standard quality it is not so easy to control the Mints. The British public are under the impression that English sovereigns stand highest as far as correctness in quality is concerned. In reality, the British gold coin falls much more below its standard fineness than French, American, and Russian coin. Jewellers in this country, when making articles from sovereign gold, run the danger of a refusal on the part of Goldsmiths' Hall to mark their manufactures as 22 carats fine; they are therefore obliged, although they use the standard coin of the realm, to re-melt the same first with a certain number of grains of fine gold, so as to satisfy the assayer—in other words, they must first make it standard gold, which it is not in the form of coin. But the best proof of the greater inferiority of the British gold coin is given by the action of the Bank of England. The Bank of England cuts light gold coin, and so renders it unfit for further circulation; the holder of such coin thus loses, in the first place, the value of the gold worn away by abrasion, and the cut sovereigns are handed back to him as being now only bullion. (The loss so far amounts from 1d. to 4d. per sovereign.) The bullion now remaining is the metal of which the coin had been made, presumably at the rate of 77s. 10½d. per oz., and worth that much, or, at the Bank price for buying gold, at least 77s. 9d. per oz. Yet the Bank of England will not give more than 77s. 6½d. for it. Worth at Mint price 934½d., the Bank pays but 930½d. per oz., a deduction of 0·43 per cent.

At the same time the Bank of England buys Russian half Imperials, which are of precisely the same legal standard (22 carats fine) as sovereigns, at 77s. 7½d. an ounce—1d. more than British metal. Why should this be so? For French gold coin the Bank pays 76s. 2d. per oz., which, calculated at the fineness of French coin of 900 as against 916 2-3rds (22 carat, or British standard), is equal to 77s. 7d.; and for American gold coin, 76s. 2¾d. is paid, equal to 77s. 7¾d. per oz. In paying these prices for Russian, French, and American gold, the Bank, as a matter

Mr. E. Seyd.

of course, has regard to certain irregularities which may occur in the quality, and therefore offers a price low enough to make their purchases safe; besides this, the Bank must make a profit. And if these coins were melted down, and assayed according to the millième process (which is more exact than our British system of carats), it would be found that they were worth from $\frac{1}{2}d.$ to $1\frac{1}{2}d.$ more than the Bank gives for them. It must further be remarked that French and American coin, if taken to the Mint, requires alloying, which is not necessary, or should not be necessary, for British metal, which has already been coined. Yet, with all this, the Bank of England pays much less for British gold than for the coinage metal of other nations—it holds, in fact, the coin of the realm itself as standing lowest in regard to accuracy. And this difference, as a permanent one, exceeds 1*l.* in the 1,000*l.*, while it is equal to 4*l.* 3*s.* in the 1,000*l.* as far as departure below the Mint value is concerned. It cannot surely be supposed that the Bank of England has any grudge against our gold. The truth is this. The Bank knows that English gold coin is always much below the standard, and it cannot afford to pay more. The Bank holds no monopoly in regard to light coin; parties may go elsewhere to sell it, or they may melt it down into bars, when they will find that the majority of such bars are one-eighth of a grain, and a vast proportion one-fourth of a grain, below standard. They may also offer the light coin to the Mint, and the experience will be made that the Bank is right in not giving more than 77*s.* $6\frac{1}{2}d.$

That the figures here given are correct is the direct result of the prices offered at the Bank for the various descriptions of gold coin. They prove clearly that British gold coin is less "identical" with bullion than other coinages, and that consequently it is less liable to be exported. Mr. Lowe tries to make out the contrary, but it will be evident that our supposed free and superior coinage, together with the whole edifice of argument which Mr. Lowe has built upon it, is a huge fallacy. It is time that the

British public should be made aware of these facts; the British public is one that understands figures, and holds figures as superior even to familiar boasts and prejudices.

Mr. Lowe has stated that a manufactory for melting sovereigns had formerly existed close to the Mint; that it is now removed to Brussels. The public is likely to attach credit to such a statement. It is, nevertheless—and what I have said here will bear out the assertion—an utterly unfounded and even ridiculous piece of clap-trap, at which all the houses in the bullion trade are indignant because of its utter folly. The Master of the British Mint knows well that he issues very few heavy pieces. His weighing machines reject from 18 to 20 per cent. of imperfect coins. The light ones are re-melted; the heavy pieces set aside. He should not allow the slur of issuing heavy pieces to rest upon him. The picking out of such heavy pieces, even if by chance a few of them should slip, does not pay; it does not pay even to pick out Australian sovereigns, which contain about 45 per mille of silver as alloy.

I have ventured to bring the matter before you in this manner, believing that it is important enough to deserve consideration in connection with the statements made and the conclusions drawn by those who advocate the imposition of a seigniorage of 1 per cent. In the face of these facts many may agree with me that Mr. Lowe's first proposition upon which he recommends the charge—namely, that it will keep gold coin in the country, which is now liable to exportation—is quite wrong. Mr. Hubbard, in his letter of the 20th, effectually disposes of the second proposition—that of creating, by means of the seigniorage, a redemption fund for light coin; the third, that of making the seigniorage available for an equalization of the English with the French coinage, and which, after all, is that which moves Colonel Smith's party in the question, remains to be disposed of.

I am, Sir, your obedient servant,

1A, PRINCES STREET, BANK, E.C.   ERNEST SEYD.
Aug. 20, 1869.

MR. LOWE'S SEIGNIORAGE SCHEME.

(The Morning Advertiser, August 23, 1869.)

THE *Morning Advertiser* was the first to denounce and expose the Chancellor of the Exchequer's financial crotchet. We pointed out, the very day after his celebrated speech in answer to Mr. J. B. Smith's question, that Mr. Lowe's plan was nothing more nor less than an alteration of the standard of value, a debasement of the currency, and a repudiation, to a certain degree, of our obligation as a nation to the public creditor. The Chancellor of the Exchequer based his proposal upon the most absurd grounds. He stated as one of the chief reasons why his plan should be adopted, the continual withdrawal from the circulation of sovereigns, in order to have them melted down in a certain manufactory at Brussels. We denounced this from the very first as a piece of rhapsodical balderdash, and we now quote from a correspondent in Mr. Lowe's own organ—*The Times*—a full confirmation of our assertion of the non-existence of any such melting manufactories as those referred to by Mr. Lowe. A letter from Mr. Ernest Seyd, a great bullion merchant, published in *The Times* of last Saturday, contains the following passage :—

" Mr. Lowe has stated that a manufactory for melting sovereigns had formerly existed close to the Mint; that it is now removed to Brussels. The public is likely to attach credit to such a statement. It is, nevertheless—and what I have said here will bear out the assertion—an utterly unfounded and even ridiculous piece of clap-trap, at which all the houses in the bullion trade are indignant because of its utter folly. The Master of the British Mint knows well that he issues very few heavy pieces. His weighing machines reject from 18 to 20 per cent. of imperfect coins. The light ones are re-melted; the heavy pieces set aside. He should not allow the slur of issuing heavy pieces to rest upon him. The picking out of such heavy pieces, even if by chance a few of them should slip, does not pay; it does not pay even to pick out Australian sovereigns, which contain about 45 per mille of silver as alloy."

We are glad to perceive that nearly the whole London Press are following the lead of the *Morning Advertiser* in its opinion of Mr. Lowe's scheme, at least in so far as *Mr. J. Aytoun.*

declaring that it cannot be carried out, and must be given up. This is the opinion, strongly expressed, of the *Economist,* one of the most decided of the Ministerial organs. In its impression of Saturday last our contemporary, in a leader commenting upon the Chancellor of the Exchequer's proposal, has the following passages:—

"That the Bank Directors, or some of them, should not agree with Mr. Lowe, will not, perhaps, after what has happened, surprise many people; but what may surprise them is that all the members of the Cabinet do not agree with him. At least, last year Mr. Göschen gave elaborate evidence before the International Coinage Commissioners exactly in opposition to Mr. Lowe. He was asked:—

"'2328. Some of the witnesses who have appeared before us have thought that although the quantity of fine gold in the sovereign was reduced, and its intrinsic value therefore reduced, its value might nevertheless be maintained by levying a seigniorage of about the same per-centage value; have you ever considered at all whether that would be so?—I think it would not be so.

"'2329. Supposing that the value of the sovereign was reduced by the amount of 2$d.$, would it not be necessary, in order to discharge in the new currency any debt which had been contracted in the old, that the payment for the future should be 1$l.$ 0$s.$ 2$d.$?—It would.

"'2330. Do you think that by levying a seigniorage upon the new coin to the extent of one per cent., which is about the same value as 2$d.$ in the 1$l.$, it would be possible to avoid making that compensation with any regard to justice to the creditor?—I do not think it would remove the injustice.'"

Here we have Mr. Göschen, the member of the Cabinet the best informed upon currency matters, with the exception perhaps of Mr. Gladstone—who, we have not the shadow of a doubt, agrees with Mr. Göschen—declaring that the plan now proposed by Mr. Lowe was altogether erroneous. In the face of such opinions as these on the part of his colleague, and without even consulting the Cabinet of which he is a member, the Chancellor of the Exchequer suggests a radical change in our currency system, which, as Mr. Seyd observes in *The Times,* has excited the indignation and the ridicule of every merchant in the City conversant with the subject.

It is not worth while, however, to dwell further upon Mr. Lowe's project. We have not the slightest doubt we shall hear of it no more, at least from any member of the

Mr. J. Aytoun.

Government. Mr. Lowe must by this time be heartily ashamed of his *escapade*. But during the discussion which has arisen upon this point a question has been raised by Mr. Hubbard, a very different financier from Mr. Lowe, which it is of some importance to have decided. Mr. Hubbard, although denouncing as altogether unprincipled any plan of paying the expenses of the coinage by reducing the weight of the sovereign, is still in favour of making the possessor of bullion pay for the coinage. With this opinion of Mr. Hubbard we differ, although agreeing with him in everything else. We are of opinion with Sir Robert Peel in his definition of a pound—that it is nothing more nor less than a certain weight of gold of a certain fineness, stamped by the State, and at the expense of the State, as a certification of its weight and fineness. Such is the real nature of a pound sterling or sovereign; and if we do anything by a mintage to prevent the free conversion of sovereigns into bullion by melting them down, or of bullion being converted into sovereigns by a free coinage, we interfere with a principle of our currency upon which Sir Robert Peel laid so much stress.

Now, as a justification for changing the system of a free coinage, which has existed for two hundred years, it is necessary to point out the disadvantages arising from it. We admit that the expenses of the coinage might be thrown from the State upon the possessor of the bullion. The first point, then, to be ascertained is,—What are the expenses of the Mint? No one can ascertain this more easily than Mr. Hubbard, as he is both a Member of Parliament and a Director of the Bank of England; and we therefore consider Mr. Hubbard is bound, in order to establish his case, to inform us exactly what is the cost of the Mint. Mr. Hubbard has in his letters in *The Times* hinted vaguely about a mintage preventing a waste of sovereigns. We wish he would condescend particularly upon this point, as we cannot perceive that under the present system there can be any waste of sovereigns, or how the Mint is made to coin a single sovereign more than it would do were a mintage charged.

In supposing the contrary, people always overlook the clause in the Act of 1844 which requires the Bank to give $3l.$ $17s.$ $9d.$ in Bank notes for every ounce of gold of standard weight and fineness deposited with it. The Bank has thus always a large amount of standard bullion in bars in its cellars, and although the Bank must cash its notes in sovereigns when *sovereigns are demanded*, there is nothing to prevent it from paying its notes in bars when bars are required for exportation, as more convenient; and this is always done except when sovereigns are required for some particular purpose.

In his last letter in *The Times*, Mr. Hubbard has called in question the accuracy of Professor Jevons's calculation of the amount of sovereigns in circulation. We consider that Mr. Hubbard has succeeded in showing that Mr. Jevons's data and calculations are absurdly erroneous. There is one point in this controversy which we think is overlooked by both parties. Mr. Jevons calculates that the sovereigns in circulation are, in round numbers, 80,000,000. But he overlooks the gold which is in the Issue Department of the Bank, and upon the deposit of which an equal amount in Bank notes is in circulation. Now those Bank notes which are issued directly upon the deposit of gold, ought, we consider, to be regarded as a sovereign circulation. There are two classes of Bank of England notes—the fixed issue of $15,000,000l.$, based upon Government debt and Government securities; and there are in addition, at this moment, $20,000,000l.$ of notes based upon deposit of gold, and which have been created and issued expressly on account of that deposit.

JAMES AYTOUN.

GOLD COINAGE.

(The Times, August 24, 1869.—To the Editor.)

SIR,—Mr. Hubbard, in the *Times* of Friday last, has assailed certain calculations of mine in the hope of thereby refuting the arguments of the Chancellor of the Exchequer in favour of a modification of our Mint regulations. As you truly remark in your article of the same day, those calculations have little or no relevancy to the scheme in question. Mr. Lowe proposes to reduce very slightly the weight of the sovereign in order that our coin may be exchangeable with that of the International Monetary Convention, and that, at the same time, the cost of coining may not fall needlessly upon the nation. My calculations were directed simply to ascertaining the amount and condition of our present gold coinage, which has only a collateral bearing upon the question at issue.

To trace the precise paternity of the scheme which Mr. Lowe has so clearly put forward would be a long and needless task. That scheme is, in reality, the natural result of the establishment of an international currency in Western Europe, and it may be said to be forced upon us by a remarkable conjuncture of circumstances. After prolonged discussion, it has become at last apparent that one grain of gold in 123 grains is all that prevents us from securing some three or four great improvements in our circulating medium. This scheme, far from being due to any one person, is in reality the outcome of the efforts of several Statistical Congresses, of two International Conventions (in 1865 and 1867), and of one Royal Commission, of which Mr. Hubbard was himself a member. The eminent Continental economists who have successfully established an international money in France, Italy, Belgium, Switzerland, and elsewhere, clearly saw that the trifling reduction of the sovereign must be the concession asked from us. So far as I am aware, this view was first distinctly laid before

Englishmen by the eminent actuary Mr. Hendriks, in a most able pamphlet on decimal coinage, which was privately printed, and therefore not so readily accessible as it ought to be. The scheme was also most clearly discussed in the official report drawn up by the Master of the Mint and Mr. Rivers Wilson, of the Treasury, after their return from the International Monetary Convention of 1867, at which they officially represented the British Government. No one who has looked into the report of the International Coinage Commission can be ignorant of the able, and, to my mind, conclusive manner in which the scheme was advocated by Colonel J. T. Smith, Mr. Hendriks, and Mr. S. Brown. Moreover, that Commission published a correspondence which Sir John Herschel, then Master of the Mint, held with the Treasury and the Bank so long ago as the year 1852. It is clearly shown by Sir John that our present law of free coinage works chiefly to the advantage of the Bank and a few great bullion dealers, and that a small seigniorage is a most sound and rational measure.

I must confess that until the last few years I entirely shared the prejudice in favour of free coinage which Mr. Hubbard so strongly represents; but when independently engaged in inquiring into the amount and condition of our gold coinage, I met with facts which unmistakably showed the faulty working of our present law. Mr. Hendriks's pamphlet happened at that time to come into my hands, and seemed to me at once to point out the true remedy. It was no hastily concocted scheme, then, that Mr. Lowe set forth with so much force and completeness. The main features of the plan have been under discussion for years past, and it is only a detail or two that any single person could have added to a measure which is truly remarkable from the manifold advantages likely to flow from a very slight cause.

But even if my calculations had any important bearing on the scheme, I am not prepared to admit that Mr. Hubbard has in the least degree shaken those calculations.

Mr. W. S. Jevons.

Mr. Hubbard, as you yourself point out, has entirely missed the point and purpose of my method, and his letter is therefore full of mistakes. My purpose was to circumvent, if possible, the difficulty that we do not know how many sovereigns have in past years been exported, melted, lost, or otherwise withdrawn from circulation. It seemed obvious that these causes must have operated least upon the coinages of recent years, and that we might consequently take the proportion which those coinages appear to form of the whole circulation as a means of arriving at the total amount of that circulation. From inquiries which you have already described, it was ascertained that the coinages of 1863-4 formed rather more than one-fifth part of the circulation. I concluded, then, that the circulation could not exceed about five times the whole coinage of 1863-4. Mr. Hubbard says that I made a purely arbitrary selection of those years, and that other years, for instance 1852-3, would have given totally different results. Certainly they would, because the coinages of those years have suffered during 16 or 17 years from the destructive influences the effects of which I was trying to eliminate from the calculation. The same may be said of any other early years. My purpose was to select that part of the coinage which had suffered least as a measure of the whole, and I selected the years 1863-4 not by mere caprice, but because they were the best. The coinage of those years was very large in amount (14,578,000 *l*.), and had got thoroughly well into circulation, so as to form one-fifth of the whole circulation. Mr. Hubbard is no doubt right in saying that the years 1865-6 might have been taken, but they were less suitable, because the coins of those years formed only 1-25th part of the circulation. I took the utmost care in the paper to explain emphatically that I did not pretend to define the exact amount of the circulation, but only to ascertain a quantity (68,000,000 *l*. in sovereigns, and 12,000,000 *l*. in half-sovereigns) below which the truth certainly lay. If I have erred at all, it is on the side of caution, as a careful reader of the paper will allow, and if Mr. Hubbard could really show my estimate to be worthless and meaningless, it could only be by establishing another and lower estimate, which would only the more strengthen Mr. Lowe's assertion concerning the needless destruction of good new sovereigns.

In the latter part of his letter Mr. Hubbard shows that he does not understand the Rule of Three. He makes the extraordinary assertion that my method of calculation is fallacious, and the conclusions derived from it utterly worthless, because the first and third terms of a proportion are not of one kind. That there may be no mistake I give his words :—

"If I may presume to criticise the calculations of a Professor of Political Economy, I would say that his formula is essentially defective, inasmuch as his first and third terms are not of one kind."

I need hardly remind your readers that, so far is the Rule of Three from requiring the first and third terms to be of one kind, the rule, as given by Colenso and other eminent successors of Cocker, directs the learner to select as the third term that which is of the same kind as the answer, implying that, in the vast majority of cases, it will differ in kind from the first two. When an ordinary schoolboy has to work such a sum as this—If 100 workmen can do a piece of work in 12 days, how many men can do the work in eight days? he at once selects 100 workmen as the third term *because it is not of the same kind as the other two.*

But with a curious propensity to error, which I know not how to characterize, Mr. Hubbard has falsified at once the Rule of Three and the facts of the case. My Rule of Three happens to be one of those comparatively rare cases where the terms are all of one kind. All the terms consist of numbers of coins, as witness the "formula" stated in Mr. Hubbard's own words, "as 18,671 (examined sovereigns dated 1863 and 1864) : 100,000 (the aggregate of examined sovereigns) : : 14,000,000 (the issued coins of 1863 and 1864) : the whole circulation.

Mr. W. S. Jevons.

Nothing could have driven me to trouble your readers with such matters, had not Mr. Hubbard asserted that an important State measure rested on my figures, and that my figures were utterly fallacious. Your readers must judge to which side the charge of putting forth worthless fallacies will finally attach.

I am, Sir, yours obediently,

W. STANLEY JEVONS.

OWEN'S COLLEGE, MANCHESTER,
Aug. 21, 1869.

GOLD COINAGE.

(The Times, August 24, 1869.—To the Editor.)

SIR,—Mr. Seyd, in *The Times* of Saturday, has made statements respecting the integrity of the gold coinage which demand an answer. "The British public," your correspondent says, "are under the impression that English sovereigns stand highest as far as correctness in quality is concerned. In reality the British gold coin falls much more below its standard fineness than French, American, and Russian coin." This statement is not made by Mr. Seyd on the easily attainable evidence of an assay of the coin, but because it should be so for various reasons of more or less force which he gives. Had he taken a single sovereign of date since 1851, or, better, 100 new sovereigns, and assayed them, he would have found his mistake. The minute apparent deterioration in quality, which is observed in coin that has circulated for some time, depends upon two circumstances which have been entirely overlooked. The old coin is weighed without being cleaned. The film of oily varnish it has acquired, and which might be removed by soap and water, goes to add to the weight of the metal, but is of course burnt off and lost in the subsequent melting. The other cause is much less considerable in its action. Previous to 1851, the gold trial plate, to which the coinage

Monetarius.

is adjusted, was a shade under standard. It is unnecessary to say that all standard measures are approximative only, the best, it may be, for the time, and are liable to continued correction and improvement with the progress of science. Gold assaying has shared in this progress, and is now much in advance of what it was twenty years ago. I may be allowed to quote the following independent testimony to the accuracy in composition of our coinage. The director of the Mint of the United States, in his annual report to Congress for 1837, speaking of recent French gold coin, says,—

"We find the fineness varying from 898·5 to 899·8, and averaging 899·2. This has generally been the result for many years, and is not what should be expected. The average ought to be 000, as required by law. The British coins are kept up to the mark."

It should be added in justice to the French Mint that these slight deficiencies are known and accounted for. They appear as a small source of revenue in the French Budget. The British sovereign has fortunately had the advantage of being examined by a man of science, famous for his minute accuracy in analysis, M. Stas, Master of the Mint of Brussels. If such a disputed point were to be settled by experiment, chymists, it is believed, would unanimously refer the matter to this accomplished analyst, from his superlative qualifications. Now, M. Stas has lately stated that the British sovereign is generally rated on the Continent at 916·5 fineness, but he finds it to be 916·66. The last number is the exact description of our legal fineness. Is it necessary to go further?

Your most obedient servant,

GREAT MALVERN, MONETARIUS.
Aug. 21, 1869.

INTERNATIONAL COINAGE.

(The Morning Post, August 25, 1869.—To the Editor.)

Sir,—We all feel under obligation to the Chancellor of the Exchequer for furnishing to us a subject of discussion of greater interest than can ordinarily be found in the interval between the prorogation of Parliament and its re-meeting. That subject is the question whether or not to establish a seigniorage upon the coining of gold in this country. Mr. Lowe's own opinion inclines evidently in favour of the measure, but his mind is not made up, and he wishes, before coming to a decision, to learn what the public, and those especially who understand the subject, think of the project.

Allow me to accept this invitation, and to state briefly a few considerations which I think have material bearing on the subject.

In the first place, it is right to understand precisely what a seigniorage is, and upon whom the burthen of such an impost would fall. It is a per-centage tax levied upon the coinage of bullion. It must be paid in the first instance by the producer or importer as the condition of converting his metal into coin. If the amount levied as the condition of making this conversion equals only the difference of value given by it to the metal, it can scarcely be called a tax, for no one is a loser; and it may be, and indeed is sometimes found to be, that the value given exceeds the cost of making the conversion, in which case the State may fairly make a profit of the difference, and this seems to be the object aimed at by Mr. Lowe. But a seigniorage, when levied at the place of production, is quite a different thing. It there partakes of the character of a rent, being a portion of the profit arising from the advantage of production yielded by the locality. There is a very heavy seigniorage levied on the coinage of dollars in Mexico, and it is accompanied and enforced by a prohibition of the

P.

export of silver in any other shape. The 1 per cent. seigniorage on gold levied in the Australian colonies is of the same kind; neither of these can be said to add to the value of the precious metals in the markets of the world, because that value is fixed, like that of other commodities, by the relation of the supply to the demand, and the demand is such as to induce production in much less favourable localities, so as to yield a surplus above the cost in the nature of rent exactly similar to that which the proprietor of a rich coal mine derives from the sale of his article as compared with that of other mines.

But Europe derives its precious metals entirely from abroad. We have to deal with them, therefore, as articles of ordinary commerce. Now, a seigniorage upon imported gold can only be levied by buying that gold at one price and coining it into more pieces of the same money that expresses that price than were given for it; in other words, we give 100 sovereigns for the same weight of standard gold. Mr. Lowe's proposition is that we should purchase 123,274 sovereigns' weight in gold as now for that number of sovereigns, but should coin them into 124,274 sovereigns, each being lighter by one grain, and then pay these out as if they were equal in value with the old sovereigns. This is the manner in which the scheme will, I presume, have to be introduced if the seigniorage is levied by lightening the coin. But there is another way of establishing a seigniorage, viz., to buy gold only when you can get for 100 sovereigns a weight of standard gold equal to 101, in which case we should coin the gold into 101 sovereigns of full weight, retaining one for seigniorage, and there would be no change in the currency.

To the first method of establishing a seigniorage there is the insuperable objection that you change the measure of value in the country. The pound sterling will no longer be the pound declared by Parliament. This, however, is a part of the subject with which I will not at present deal. If you issue sovereigns only one grain less in weight and

P.

value than those in circulation (and this is what is proposed), they will not co-circulate with those already current, there will be a discount upon them. They will carry with them the stamp of inferiority, and the preference for old coin will give them an agio or batta which, once established, will lead to the necessity for money changers in every street and village, as we find them in the East, and in all countries where there is a confusion of coins in circulation.

How is the Bank of England to deal with this confusion? Will the Chancellor of the Exchequer, simultaneously with the issue of his light coin, authorize the Bank to refuse old coin of full weight in payment of notes issued with the distinct obligation of convertibility into such coin? It is argued that the seigniorage will raise the value of the coin; but this I deny. It may have the effect of lowering the value of gold bullion, because it will take away from it the great advantage it now enjoys of convertibility into coin at no charge; but its effect upon this one article is no proof of an increase of value in monetary transactions generally, as the establishment of an agio or batta in such transactions would very soon prove. It will be said that the old coin will soon disappear, because it will be used always for foreign exchanges so long as it is to be had. But this assumes that the old and new coin will be circulating at par notwithstanding the intrinsic difference of value. Now, this is contrary to the experience of all countries in which a currency has been tampered with, and if there is an agio upon the old coin giving it superior value in its own country, why should it be bought up to be used for exchanges?

The objections to issuing a lighter coin appear thus to us to be insuperable. But none of these apply to the scheme of requiring extra payment as the condition of coining. The Government having the monopoly of manufacture, may fairly say—We will not convert your gold into our coin without a payment of 1 per cent.; in other words, we will only buy gold when we can get for 100 sovereigns enough to coin 101. Let us examine the operation of such a measure. In the first place, England is now the entrepôt through which almost all the gold produced in the world finds its way to the mints and markets of Europe. Even the gold of America passes for the most part through London. This advantage—and it will not be denied to be one—we owe principally to the facility given for converting the gold into coin, and to the credit enjoyed by our gold coin, which circulates almost everywhere in Europe *pari passu* with the coin of the country. Of the 800 millions of sovereigns that have been coined since 1817, certainly not more than one-eighth are retained here, which shows that it has been profitable to convert gold into sovereigns before exporting it. But if we lay a seigniorage tax of 1 per cent. upon this operation, that profit will no longer exist. It will be said that the coined gold is increased in value by the seigniorage as well abroad as at home, but of the 700 millions exported the proportion that have been melted down will far exceed that remaining still in the condition of coin, and for that proportion a direct import from the place of production will obviously be more profitable than import through an entrepôt in which it is subjected to a duty of 1 per cent.

It may be thought that the benefit of being an entrepôt for the import of gold into Europe may be preserved to England by continuing to the Bank its privilege of paying large demands for export in bullion. But if the seigniorage be established the Bank itself would only buy bullion when it could get it at a rate to cover the seigniorage, for it is under the obligation to pay its notes in coin, and will, as now, be the channel through which the Mint would obtain its gold for coinage. It is this circumstance that will operate to lower the price of gold and to keep it out of our market. There is no doubt, therefore, that with a seigniorage the entrepôt benefit must be given up.

But it may be worth while nevertheless to establish the coinage tax, and 1 per cent. is not a higher rate than such a
P.

tax ought to bear. But let it not be imposed under the pretext of covering the expense of coinage. That expense, with a Mint in full work, ought not to be more than 2s. or 2s. 6d. for the 100 pieces, and it seems that the latitude of coinage allowed both in weight and in assay is as much as ½ per cent., or 10s. in the 100 pieces. This is not used to its full extent, yet it nevertheless gives the power, and no doubt is used to cover a coinage charge of only one-fifth that amount. But, then, the seigniorage duty is required to cover the expense of calling in and replacing the light sovereigns in circulation, which are assumed to be as many as 30 per cent. of the gold coin current in the United Kingdom. This pretext for imposing the tax assumes that the Government is under the obligation to call in and exchange for full weight sovereigns those which may have been worn or sweated down beyond a certain margin. It would be a very dangerous thing for a Government to proclaim any such intention, for it would be offering a premium to the sweaters. The Bank of England at present is, I believe, the only office or institution in which sovereigns are singly passed through the late Mr. Cotton's ingenious weighing machine for the purpose of testing their fitness for circulation under the existing law. The light coins are cut in half and returned to those who tendered them, as bullion, which the Bank is ready to purchase at a reduced rate to other standard gold. I think it a mistake not to give the full bullion value, so as to lessen as much as possible the disappointment people must feel at having their money so treated. But there would be great danger in doing more to induce the production of light coin, because of the premium any measure of that kind would offer to those who make a trade of the business of lightening gold coin.

Though I have stated objections and inconveniences that would result from the imposition of a seigniorage or coinage tax, I must not be considered to be altogether opposed to it as a measure of finance, yielding a desirable revenue. I wish it only to be clearly understood that the entire burthen of the tax must of necessity be borne by the owner or importer of the bullion presented for coinage. It cannot be divided between him and the public, under the notion that the coin will be increased in value by the tax. There is no method by which the State could realize any part of the duty from the public. Even were it to issue light coin it would receive all its dues in that coin, and they would not be increased so as to make a saving in the payment of its obligations. As for the ingenious process by which Colonel Smith proposes to prevent exchanges being influenced adversely by a reduction in the weight and value of the coin, viz., that the Bank should still be under obligation to furnish full weight of bullion to those who required it for exportation, he seems to forget that if such a regulation were established concurrently with a reduction of the coin, the Bank would be liable to be compelled upon any adverse turn of the exchanges to furnish bullion in exchange not only for the light gold, but the total amount of its notes in circulation, and this at a time when that very turn of exchange made gold dearer than usual. The exchange question, however, is one upon which I will not at present enter.

But there is another branch of the subject that must not be omitted, for it has been much dwelt upon in the discussion, and that is that by decreasing the value of our coin in the manner proposed we shall make the sovereign very nearly the exact equivalent of a gold piece of 25 francs, which the French Government intend to issue, and so England might come into the Convention for assimilating the coinages of Europe, to which many States have signed their agreement. I cannot look upon this inducement—though no doubt it is of great weight—to be sufficient to warrant a reduction of the measure of value formally established in 1819, and I doubt if the coin of France would under any circumstances co-circulate with that of England in our markets, for the French gold standard does not correspond with the English. It contains one-tenth of alloy, whereas ours has only one-

P.

twelfth, which alone would give such a different appearance to the coin as to establish for one a preference. Our coin already contains too much alloy. It would bear a much higher value as coin if it had only one-half the present proportion. Venetian ducats and Dutch sequins being nearly pure, are at a high premium in all the markets of the East because of that purity; and the Government of India, since the gold standard there was reduced under orders from this country to similarity with that of England, have ceased altogether to coin gold for individuals, whereas so long as they coined it pure there was a large receipt of a seigniorage —as high as 2 per cent. upon the conversion. I therefore cannot consent to reduce our standard to that of France, and I doubt if France would consent to raise hers. A committee of the House of Lords has been sitting upon this subject, with Lord Halifax as chairman. It has collected many discordant opinions; but has brought them to no distinct issue to assist the decision.

P.

Aug. 24, 1869.

GOLD COINAGE.

(The Times, August 26, 1869.—To the Editor.)

SIR,—Although the public are possibly tired by this time with the numerous letters and leading articles which have appeared in your paper on the subject of the gold coinage. I venture to ask you to insert one letter from myself in addition to that which you were kind enough to insert about a fortnight since.

Mr. Lowe may perhaps ere this have seen reason to doubt the expediency of recommending the consideration of this question by general discussion during the Parliamentary recess. Those who are advised by him to do so are left in entire ignorance whether the Government, as represented by the Cabinet, have formed any opinion on the subject; if

Mr. Thomson Hankey.

they have done so, many persons will seriously question the discretion of a Chancellor of the Exchequer advising its consideration until the opinions of the Government have been laid before the public in a clear and definite shape; but, without pursuing that subject further, I am induced to call attention to the safest and, indeed, in my humble opinion, the only mode by which the heavy loss from abrasion of the gold may be avoided, and that is by issuing 1 $l.$ bank-notes in addition to the present note circulation of 5 $l.$ and upwards.

Without taking into consideration the country bank-note issues, the Bank of England note is practically a Government paper; all the profit of the Bank of England note circulation, excepting about 100,000 $l.$ a year, is for the benefit of the country; if the same result—that is, the undeniable security of bank-notes—could be obtained in any other way with greater profit to the country than from the payment now made annually by the Bank of England, this might be a fair subject for consideration by a Chancellor of the Exchequer. I do not believe that by a direct issue of paper money by the Mint, secured by a gold deposit for every shilling issued above 15,000,000 $l.$, any saving to the country would ensue. On the contrary, I am satisfied that very considerable additional expense would accrue; but leaving this question, about the security of the bank-note being made perfect by the deposit of gold on its present footing, I think it can hardly be questioned that the substitution of a certain amount of 1$l.$-notes would to that extent diminish the wear and tear of our gold coinage.

The objection I have always entertained to the issue of any bank-notes under 5 $l.$, and which I still entertain to such a measure, arises from the fear that it might lead to an extension of the limit of a paper issue unrepresented by gold; the present limit of 15 millions is, in my opinion, quite enough, and I should feel very jealous of any measure which might induce any future Government to extend that limit; but if there were no risk on that score, I contend

Mr. Thomson Hankey.

with great confidence that the expense of a re-coinage of worn gold coin would be diminished by the issue of 1*l.*-notes, and this appears to me the only point worth serious consideration.

The question of a seigniorage, or of any mode of paying for the coinage of gold in this country, is really too unimportant to be pressed on public attention purely as a financial measure as long as we are not required to coin largely for other purposes than the use of the coin by British subjects, and to a very limited extent now for Brazil and Portugal. I have already, in my former letter, expressed great doubts as to the large quantity of our gold coin which is melted down for re-coinage or for use as gold in other countries. Whenever the Government may determine to recommend the assimilation of our gold coinage to the exact weight and fineness of a new French 25-franc piece, of which the present 20-franc piece will be an aliquot part, they will find that one of the main difficulties will be the far more important question—viz., How are we to remedy the inconvenience arising from wear and tear of our gold coinage?

In your leading article of yesterday I find that you do not attach much importance to the statements contained in the second or third letter from my friend and colleague Mr. Hubbard, in your paper of the same date. I believe that Mr. Hubbard understands the subject perfectly, and I am always myself inclined to doubt the correctness of my own views where they differ from any opinions deliberately expressed by him.

The Chancellor of the Exchequer's idea—if such is really his idea—of taking away the legal tender value for every sovereign of 18 years of age appears to me to be simply impracticable.

Colonel Smith's view of maintaining the full exchangeable value of a sovereign below the weight of 123·274 grains is simply by giving every holder of a sovereign of 122·274 grains the power of exchanging it at his will for one of the full standard weight. This is the only way by which a Bank of England note of 5 *l.* is now maintained at the standard value; its intrinsic value—that is, the cost of material and manufacture, is scarcely anything. By what arrangement a stock of gold could be kept and rendered always available at a moment's notice for the exchange of these small sovereigns may be a matter for serious consideration by some future Chancellor of the Exchequer, who may feel inclined to adopt Colonel Smith's views; but I must not trespass further on your indulgence; the whole question about seigniorage is well summed up in three lines, at the close of your leading article in yesterday's paper. The matter is scarcely one of sufficient moment for serious consideration at present as a means of saving the national exchequer, but the question of saving wear and tear by assimilating our paper currency to the paper currency of Scotland by the use of 1*l.*-notes is one of far greater importance, merely in a financial point of view. I do not advocate it. I am perfectly satisfied to leave all these arrangements on their present footing until we are called upon to add materially to our Mint expenditure by making a coin which will obtain much more general circulation out of this country than our present sovereigns and half-sovereigns.

I am, Sir, your most obedient servant,

THOMSON HANKEY.

CREEDY PARK, CREDITON,
August 21, 1869.

GOLD COINAGE.

(The Times, August 26, 1869.—To the Editor.)

SIR,—The high position and long experience of your correspondent Mr. Hubbard entitle any opinion expressed by him to the most attentive consideration, and as he has addressed you at considerable length in condemnation of *Col. J. T. Smith,* the proposal originally made by myself, more than a year and a half ago, and submitted to the Royal Commission, I hope you will not think me presumptuous if I request permission to offer a reply.

Mr. Hubbard's letters contain many statements and opinions in respect to which I cannot help differing from him. I shall not, however, venture to trouble you by noticing all that appears to me questionable in his writings, but only those leading facts and doctrines which are the origin and cause of the opposite conclusions we have arrived at.

One of the most important of these contained in his first letter (to which I propose chiefly to confine my remarks on this occasion) is the statement, in his 12th paragraph, that " the gold coin is not only a medium of exchange ; it is also the standard or measure of value." This statement, with the utmost respect for Mr. Hubbard, I must deny. It is impossible that a variable thing such as our sovereign, which by law may contain more or less gold, could have been established as the measure of value. The real measure is, as Mr. Hubbard himself states, the pound sterling, or 123·274 grains of gold 11-12ths fine.

It is true that it was intended that our coins should conform to the "pound sterling" as far as practicable, but exact conformity is not practicable and a variation is expressly authorized. The law now allows three-quarters of a grain to be absent from the sovereign without depriving it of its legal efficacy ; and practically the coins are at this moment far short of their nominal intrinsic value, yet the standard or measure is unchanged, being a definite and exact weight of gold; and it would make no difference, in my opinion, in the standard or measure of value if the tolerance or allowed variation in the coins were not only increased beyond the three-quarter grains, but if the whole of the gold were taken out of the coins, and paper tokens were substituted for them. To say, therefore, as in the above quotation, that the gold coin is the standard of value, and

H

that the abstraction of a portion of it must be a contraction of the measure of value, is inaccurate and unphilosophical—the confounding of two things essentially different.

Perhaps Mr. Hubbard intends merely to say that our coins are sent abroad as practically representing the pound sterling, and that if they were reduced in intrinsic value they would lower the estimate hitherto assigned to it. This might possibly be true if the coins were continually sent abroad as bullion; and I have repeatedly stated that they would in such a case lose 1 per cent. But this could not occur with the proposed new coins. Even at present our coins very seldom go abroad as bullion. Putting aside the exceptional special trade referred to by the Chancellor of the Exchequer, the selection and melting of our heaviest new coins, the use of our ordinary sovereigns as bullion is attended with a loss which makes it preferable to purchase gold for export; and, as a matter of fact, the coins are but seldom sent as mere gold. If the loss by the use of coins were greater, the certainty of their being kept at home would be obviously increased, and this is one great recommendation of the proposed seigniorage.

Hence it will be clear that Mr. Hubbard's alarm is unfounded. Our coins rarely go abroad as substitutes for the pound sterling. They exchange for gold bullion of equal market value (containing more gold than themselves), and that is sent abroad. The same will be the case *a fortiori* with the new coins, which will be of the same current value with the present sovereigns, and will buy the same amount of bullion.

The next important statement respecting which I am obliged to join issue with Mr. Hubbard is that contained in his 14th paragraph,—" That a charge for coinage can be only a charge upon the importer, and cannot enhance the value or power of the coin." This statement begs the most important question in dispute, and it is an essential one. If it be true that a Mint charge does not enhance the value (in exchange) or (purchasing) power of the coin, then I

Col. J. T. Smith.

must admit that the plan suggested by me for the accommodation of the British and foreign currencies cannot be carried out.

Let me first observe, that all the leading writers on Political Economy are of my opinion, many of them are quoted in the Report of the Royal Commissioners, and therefore ought to be known to Mr. Hubbard.

2. The authors of the celebrated Bullion Report of 1810 were of the same opinion. They say (page 12),—" They who send bullion to be coined incur a loss of interest by the detention of gold in the Mint. Their loss may hitherto have amounted to about 1*l*. per cent." This 1*l*. per cent. has formed the unit or nearly the limit to the possible rise of the value of coin above that of bullion.

3. If the charge for coining is only a charge upon the importer, are we to assume that he obtains less than the full value of his gold, or that he does obtain the full value? If the former, then we arrive at the conclusion that there is a race of men who are foolish enough to persevere in continuously supplying the Mint with gold at a less price than they could obtain in the open market. This is absurd, so we must take the other alternative, that the Mint price becomes the same as that of the open market—a fact which daily experience testifies, when proper allowance is made for delay, all expenses incident to coinage, and other circumstances.

We have now arrived at the point of disagreement; we see that when a Mint charge is made for the manufacture of coins the market price of the bullion falls. The vital question is,—does this occur because the gold is lowered or the coins raised in exchangeable value?

As it is difficult for the mind clearly to appreciate the effect of small differences, let me put the following exaggerated case. Let us suppose that the charge for coinage at the Royal Mint were 20 per cent., instead of 1 per cent.; the price of gold bullion would then be about 3*l*. 2*s*. 3½*d*., instead of 3*l*. 17*s*. 9*d*., in the open market. Now, the question is, would this be a fall in purchasing power of the gold bullion?

Mr. Hubbard says (letter ii., par. 5) that gold is estimated solely by the purity of the metal (he must have meant by the purity and weight combined), and that this purchasing power, which the world of commerce recognizes in the pure metal, constitutes the "intrinsic value of gold." He also says in the same letter (p. 3), that "subject to the slight variations attending local causes, it everywhere exhibits the same intrinsic value."

Now, at present, 1,000 ounces' weight of gold bullion exchange for a certain quantity of all kinds of commodities, the question is whether, after a Mint charge of 20 per cent. had been imposed for the conversion of any part of the general stock of gold bullion into coins, the remainder would exchange for less of commodities than before. It would exchange for fewer coins; or, in other words, it would sink in price, because every sovereign which previously was obtained by the surrender of 123·274 grains of gold would now cost nearly 147·93 grains; and therefore each sovereign which before the change would purchase about 123·274 grains would afterwards buy 147·93 grains; but would this alteration in the price of bullion affect its relations in exchange with goods? I deny that it would. I agree with Mr. Hubbard in saying that gold, as bullion, is cosmopolitan, that it is the almost universal standard or measure of value; and I infer that whatever tax may be imposed upon any special use of it, its value in general, with respect to all other purposes, will be unchanged. If there were a tax of 100 per cent. *ad valorem* on the manufacture of gold plate, then it appears to me gold plate would exchange for double the quantity of all other commodities it otherwise would; but the value of the gold would remain unchanged. If there were a tax of 100 per cent. on the manufacture of coins, then the coins would exchange for double the value of all commodities, uncoined gold included; and, in like manner, in due proportion, if the Mint

Col. J. T. Smith.

charge or tax were 50 per cent., 20 per cent., or only 1 per cent.

I refrain from troubling you with any remarks upon numerous other points of difference in Mr. Hubbard's first letter, they are most of them more or less connected with the cardinal error above explained. I must reply, however, to the challenge which Mr. Hubbard offers as a test of truth, and which is the result of a combination of various inaccuracies and misconceptions. I mean his proposal to exchange 100,000 Australian sovereigns, in Madras or Bombay, for 100,500 English. Regarding this, the first mistake is that "Australian sovereigns are coined at a charge of 1 per cent. for coinage." This is not altogether untrue; but it is untrue as it applies to the question at issue, for the charge for converting bar gold into coin, and therefore the difference in value between coins and commodities in general, is only 3 d. per oz., or about one-third per cent.

2. I have never said that a charge for coinage would enhance the value of the coins beyond the bounds of their legal circulation; hence it is not justifiable to expect that Australian coins should have their "current" value in Madras or Bombay.

3. I have never failed to draw attention to the essential condition that for any Mint charge or tax to confer value in exchange it must be unavoidable. If, therefore, sovereigns coined at a charge of 1 per cent. can be met in the same place on equal terms by others coined free, the latter would rule the market.

4. Mr. Hubbard has omitted to notice the fact, which has also been referred to by Mr. Britten, that Australian gold is of less value than English. If the price of bar gold in Melbourne or Sydney were not more than 3 l. 17 s. 6 d. per ounce standard and the charge for coinage 3 d., there would not be any margin to make the large profit Mr. Hubbard calculates.

5. Mr. Hubbard is perhaps not aware that Australian

sovereigns can be delivered in Madras and Bombay at the same cost as in England, where they are of equal value with our British sovereign. Hence, as it costs at least 3d. per sovereign to deliver the English coin in India, there would not only be no margin for profit, but a certainty of loss attending a contract to exchange the two kinds, even on equal terms.

Mr. Hubbard's alarm respecting the danger of illicit coinage will, I think, be removed by adverting to the fact he himself states, that the seigniorage on our silver coins is 10 per cent. If the inconvenience is so little felt now when the profit on capital employed in counterfeiting silver coins would be 9 per cent., how can it be thought likely to be of much consequence when the profit would be reduced to $\frac{1}{2}$ or $\frac{3}{4}$ per cent.?

I will, with your permission, reply to Mr. Hubbard's other letters hereafter.

I remain, Sir, your obedient servant,

J. T. SMITH.

FOLKESTONE,
Aug. 20, 1869.

THE COINAGE.

(The Times, August 28, 1869.—To the Editor.)

SIR,—Before proceeding to notice Mr. Hubbard's second and subsequent letters, I am anxious to insert a word respecting a paragraph in his first, commencing " Parliament is omnipotent," &c. It is there said, " a circulation of the diminished sovereign might undoubtedly be forced upon the country, and then every debtor would profit and every creditor would suffer by the difference of 1 per cent. in the value of the new currency." This warning is evidently based upon the supposition that the new currency would be less valuable in exchange than the old, but if, as I affirm, it

Col. J. T. Smith.

would have precisely the same purchasing power, then the warning, like many others based on the same foundation, falls to the ground.

The first part of Mr. Hubbard's second letter is occupied with a misconception. He takes that part of the Chancellor of the Exchequer's speech which describes what he was *not* going to propose—viz., to impose a charge for coinage without reducing the intrinsic value of the coin, and comments upon it to show the practical evils of attempting to carry it out. His question, "how long the holder of bullion will have to wait until the retention of his gold from the currency of the country raises the value of some hundred millions in coin and bank-notes now in circulation by 1 per cent.," must have been written in forgetfulness of the fact that the coins, according to Mr. Lowe's proposal, would not require to be appreciated at all. They would be of the same value as before—gold bullion would be sold to the Bank at the same price as hitherto—namely 3*l*. 17*s*. 9*d*. per ounce standard, and, as Mr. Hubbard well knows, it would be coined or not, as it might be found desirable for the convenience of that establishment and the public, without the slightest reference to, or influence upon, the interests of the importer in question.

Mr. Hubbard makes another unaccountable mistake when he says, par. 2, "The importer will send his bullion to the Mint, or sell it to the Bank, upon the new regulations, and in either case he will receive for his merchandise 1 per cent. less than he would have got last year." Had he done me the honour to read the memorandum submitted to the Royal Commission, and printed at page 148 of their Report, he would have seen that there would be not the least change in the value of gold, and that it would be sold, as I have just stated, at 3*l*. 17*s*. 9*d*. per ounce, as hitherto. As far, then, as the importer is concerned, there would be no change. He would receive the same price as formerly for his gold, and the coins in which he would be paid would have the same purchasing power as ever. Mr. Hubbard has himself remarked (letter, August 10, par. 13), that "the great mass of the people might never be aware of the transition," and I have shown in my last letter that our foreign trade would not suffer. It is unnecessary for me, therefore, to say more on this point.

In his 6th paragraph, Mr. Hubbard, alluding to some statement of mine that a Mint charge of 1 per cent. would add to the current value of the coins, says, "he is only wrong when he dreams that the same coin, worth only 25 f. at Calais, can be worth 25 f. 20 c. at Dover." This is a reiteration of the error that Mint charge cannot add to the value of coins—a fundamental question which ought to be settled at once, in order to stop the repetition of arguments founded upon it. That it is not out of the question to suppose the possibility of a coin worth only 25 f. at Calais being worth 25 f. 20 c. at Dover, may be gathered from the fact that our half-crown is worth in the former place 2s. 3d. or less, and in the latter 2s. 6d.

When Mr. Hubbard says "the pound sterling has hitherto been a truth, let it not become a sham," I agree with him; but the "pound sterling" will not be altered by reducing the weight of our sovereigns, which are only required to conform to it in value.

There appears to be nothing more in Mr. Hubbard's second letter which it is of importance for me to notice; and in the third, which, as you have pointed out, deals with the unexplained details of the proposed measure, I find, after comments upon a charge (a mintage of 1½ per cent.) which it is *not* proposed to make, a long statement of the evils to result from a supposed regulation for the withdrawal of the light coins. These denunciations are, at the least, premature. The Chancellor of the Exchequer has not yet submitted the details of his plan, and when he does, there can be little doubt that the wisdom of Parliament will decide upon a practical measure safe from the dangers to which Mr. Hubbard refers. In the meantime, I venture to suggest that if coins ceased to be legal tender after 18 years'

Col. J. T. Smith.

currency, and after 17½ were exchangeable at the Bank or Mint, provided they were not under legal weight, light coins being at all times, as now, cut and received only as bullion, the public would be relieved from an intolerable evil and practical injustice, and the currency restored and maintained much nearer to its professed standard than it has hitherto been, while the "sweaters" to whom Mr. Hubbard refers would have no greater inducement to practise their unlawful arts than at present.

In the last paragraph of this letter, Mr. Hubbard writes as follows :—

"As the Chancellor of the Exchequer has challenged public opinion (among other points) upon a scheme for a coinage sustentation fund prepared by his Mint Masters, but by them avowedly founded upon the authority of Mr. Jevons, I must distinctly declare that Mr. Jevons's method of calculation in connexion with the subject is fallacious, and the conclusions derived from it utterly worthless."

I would call your particular attention to the words "in connexion with the subject," and I would respectfully observe that when a gentleman of high position makes use of the strong language just quoted, it would be only fair that he should make sure that it is applicable to the persons he condemns. Had Mr. Hubbard attentively read the whole of the Mint Master's Report, he would have found that it contained a paragraph deducing the important result required by strict mathematical calculation from no other data than the average annual wear of the coins. The Report stated that the latest and most accurate (I have not the Report at hand to refer to) data on that point had been supplied by Professor Jevons's extensive experiments, but it was nowhere said that they were the only experiments. Because they were thought accurate, they were made use of, after comparison with former experiments made in the Royal Mint, and special experiments made under Mr. Graham's personal directions for the purpose of testing them. These facts tend to show that the data made use of were not inaccurate; nor, indeed, does Mr. Hubbard say that they are. It is only because he thinks Mr. Jevons's conclusions upon another point "in connexion with the subject" are not valid that he takes upon himself to denounce these independent calculations as "utterly worthless."

There appears to be nothing in Mr. Hubbard's fourth letter to which it is of importance for me to reply.

I am, Sir, your obedient servant,

FOLKESTONE,   J. T. SMITH.
Aug. 24, 1869.

P.S.—On re-perusing my letter of the 20th inst., I am anxious to add, regarding the Australian Mint charge, that in addition to coinage at 3$d.$ per oz., the melting is charged at from 3$d.$ to 5$d.$ per oz., making together ·86 per cent., besides delay, so that the charge has been generally considered as 1 per cent.; but it will be observed that all except 3$d.$ per oz. is for melting the bars, which are not necessarily used for coinage.

THE GOLD COINAGE.
(The Times, August 30, 1869.—To the Editor.)

SIR,—Having received many communications referring to the subject of my letter of the 20th inst., I ask you to permit me, in order to justify my assertion that the picking out of sovereigns cannot pay, to bring the matter before you in a technical shape.

In order to suit Mr. Lowe's assumption, I will agree that an operator obtains 100,000 new sovereigns (it is obvious that the sum must be large, and that new coins are required), and that 20 per cent. of this number will consist of heavy pieces—*i.e.*, pieces over-weighted by a quarter of a grain, the limit allowed by the remedy for weight. The operator would consequently be in possession of 20,000 entire ¼-grains of gold, worth 40$l.$ 11$s.$ 2$d.$

For the weighing of the 100,000 pieces, which have already been sifted by Cotton's weighing machines (at the rate of 20 per minute), delicate hand-scales are necessary;

Mr. E. Seyd.

these, with so small a difference before them, take from 6 to 12 seconds before they will "tell;" hence an hour is required, say, for 500 pieces, and 200 hours for the whole. At a charge of 6*d.* per hour the cost of the labour would be 5*l.* Now, if the operator employs ten hands at ten hours a day, it will take him two days to finish the weighing, and two days' interest at 5 per cent. per annum for 100,000*l.* costs 27*l.* 7*s.* I will assume, however, that he employs 20 hands, and thus finishes the business in one day, giving 13*l.* 14*s.* charge for interest, which, with 5*l.* for labour, deducted from 40*l.* 11*s.* 2*d.*, leaves 21*l.* 17*s.* 2*d.* as margin, or 20,021*l.* 17*s.* 2*d.* net for the 20,000*l.* retained.

How shall he realize this apparent profit? It might be suggested that he should go to the Mint and say—"I have found 20,000 pieces heavy by a quarter of a grain; what will you give me for them?" the sarcasm implied in the suggestion is obvious, but it is unnecessary to say that the Mint does not buy gold in this form. It is also unnecessary here to show why the public cannot deal with the Mint, and prefers to go to the Bank of England, where cash is paid for bar gold at 77*s.* 9*d.* per oz. standard. The 20,000 sovereigns must be melted (indeed, that is the proposal) so as to realize the extra bullion. At 123·531 grains each (instead of 123·274) they would weigh together 5,147·125oz., so that, as a matter of theory, if we value them at 77*s.* 9*d.* per oz. they will realize 20,009*l.* 9*s.*, giving, less 18*l.* 14*s.* (interest and labour), 19,990*l.* 15*s.*, or a loss of 9*l.* 5*s.* The practice, however, will give a much greater loss, as I shall show clearly by the following calculation :—

5,147·125oz. weighing, after melting into 6 bars,
Five bars, 4,300oz.; worse, 0·0¼
One bar,   845oz.; worse, 0·0¼
 Equal to standard 5,136·5oz., at 77*s.* 9*d.* per oz. ... £10,968 2 10
 To deduct,—Melting ¼*d.* per oz. £5 7 3
   Assays 1 7 0
   Interest and labour 18 14 0
               25 8 3

    Result £19,942 14 7

Therefore, if 20,000 out of 100,000 sovereigns (the proportion suitable to Cotton's scales—namely, 20 light, 60 neutral, and 20 heavy pieces, though still a disgracefully large number) are heavy by a quarter of a grain, and if 100,000 pieces can be manipulated in one day, the loss would still be 57*l*. But these are not all the "ifs." The operator must first obtain 100,000*l*. in new sovereigns. The Bank of England takes good care to issue new sovereigns only to bankers in moderate sums when convinced that they are intended for *bonâ fide* circulation. In the ordinary way, and for exporting, old sovereigns—light, say, on the average, by $\frac{3}{8}$ths of a grain, but still legal tender—are issued against notes. This judicious proceeding on the part of the Bank is a positive bar against the export of new coin, but it is especially necessary to protect the coinage against "sweating." If everybody could obtain new gold coins, would it not be likely that, rather than pick out 20 per cent. of heavy pieces at a quarter of a grain, operators would prefer to sweat off half a grain of every hundred, and thus make ten times the profit? We know, however, that little sweating is going on.

As far as I have here represented the case, the calculations apply to a supposed manufactory for melting down sovereigns in London; if such an establishment will not pay, why was it transferred to Brussels? In order to forward 100,000*l*. to Brussels the cost of shipping and insurance, amounting at the lowest possible rates to one-fifth per cent., must be incurred, or 200*l*. Three days' interest must be charged, at 41*l*. 2*s*., and then the operator there would have 20,000*l*. in heavy sovereigns, for the realization of which he must submit to deductions as heavy as those in England. He must then either return the 80,000*l*. to England at a cost of 160*l*. or sell them there at the rate of exchange, and when the exchange is in favour of England the loss might be very large. And if the 20,000 heavy pieces were picked by a London correspondent and sent over alone, the cost of forwarding and realization would still leave a loss of more than 100*l*.

Mr. E. Seyd.

Sovereigns are taken for export to Brazil and other places where the Mints are wretched, but napoleons and American eagles are quite as much used for the same purposes. In certain stages of the exchange markets, when bar gold is absent (which in England it never is), it may be necessary to use coin, or when such coin is abroad it may not pay to return it, and, rather than incur the cost of forwarding, it may be treated as bullion. Such uses are perfectly natural, and hence we in England occasionally receive foreign coins when the turn is in our favour; but it is perfectly impossible, and contrary to the theory as well as the practice of Mint regulations, that any undue advantage should be taken of coinages in the way that has been suggested; and least of all is it possible to do so with the British gold coinage.

"Monetarius" disputes the correctness of my statements respecting the quality of our coins. I herewith furnish you with the assays of a parcel of 10,000 sovereigns "cut" by the Bank. Messrs. Sillar and Co. in 1866, instead of selling these pieces by the ounce to the Bank, had them melted by a Bank melter into ten bars, and the assays, made by Dr. Miller, the Bank assayer, turned out as follows:—

Ten Bars. Nos.	English Report.	Millièmes.	Ten Bars. Nos.	English Report.	Millièmes.
74	w. 0·0$\frac{1}{8}$	915·5	79	w. 0·0$\frac{1}{8}$	915·4
75	w. 0·0$\frac{1}{8}$	915·4	80	w. 0·0$\frac{1}{4}$	915·1
76	w. 0·0$\frac{1}{4}$	915·2	81	w. 0·0$\frac{1}{4}$	914·5
77	w. 0·0$\frac{1}{8}$	915·7	82	w. 0·0$\frac{1}{4}$	914·7
78	w. 0·0$\frac{1}{4}$	914·7	83	w. 0·0$\frac{1}{8}$	915·7

These assays, inasmuch as coin when melted down loses a part of its alloy, and thereby becomes finer, are slightly above the mark—to the extent of $\frac{1}{4}$ of a millième. None of the bars, it will be seen, turned out as 916·6, or standard fine. Messrs. Sillar and Co., astounded at the result, caused No. 74 to be re-assayed by another Bank assayer, who found it 914·8 fine.

Facts like these speak for themselves, and overweigh the opinion of an American assayer in 1837, or of the Belgian assayer, who cannot have the experience of our English assayers in regard to English coin.

The average of these assays is 915·2, or from 916·6 equivalent to a loss of 1·4 per mille; while, as "Monetarius" quotes, the average of French coin is 899·2, or from 900 only 0·8 per mille. I refrain from giving you my own assays.

The British public might be furnished with the most conclusive evidence respecting the question of fineness if the Bank of England were willing to give the necessary information. That establishment, however, is very discreet in matters of this kind, and remains perfectly passive—as, indeed, it has the right to do. The Mints abroad, open as they are to the public, issue full and complete records of their proceedings and researches, and everything they do is made as clear as the sunlight. In England the public is prevented from dealing with the Mint, and forced to do business with the Bank of England, a private institution, so to speak. Hence the mystery and misunderstanding in reference to questions of coinage, and the want of information in regard to the character and quality of our own coins and that of foreign countries. I do not know whether the Chancellor of the Exchequer himself could induce the Bank of England to enlighten him on these points, but if he could obtain full and complete returns of the Bank's assays on English, Russian, French, and American coin, and give them to the public, it would be found that the statements which I have ventured to make are considerably within the actual truth.

I am, Sir, your obedient servant,

ERNEST SEYD.

1A, Princes Street, Bank,
August 28, 1869.

THE GOLD COINAGE.

(The Times, September 1, 1869.—To the Editor.)

Sir,—The differences between Colonel Smith and myself depend mainly upon two questions,—viz., What is the standard of value? and what power has legislation over that standard? The first of these questions being one of fact is capable of solution, I trust to the convictions of the contending parties. The second, depending more upon opinion and argument, is less easily disposed of; but an agreement upon the first ought to carry us a long way towards an agreement upon the second question also.

My proposition that "the gold coin is not only a medium of exchange, but is also the standard or measure of value," Colonel Smith "must deny." "It is," he says, "impossible that a variable thing such as our sovereign, which by law may contain more or less alloy, could have been established as the measure of value." I should be grieved to impugn the perfectibility which Colonel Smith desires to attribute to the standard of value, but I must attempt at least to prove that my theorem is correct, according to the law of the land, the exercise of the Royal prerogative, and every man's personal experience.

The sterling or standard pound of 240 silver pennies dates as far back as the reign of Henry II., and silver held its place as a measure of value and as a medium of exchange, with gold as an auxiliary, nominally down to the year 1816. The standard fineness of our gold coins was first fixed at 22 carats, or 11-12ths fine, by Henry VIII. The guinea of Charles II., issued in 1670 as the equivalent of 20 shillings, was soon appraised at 21 shillings, and this relation of the gold to the silver coinage was maintained with temporary variations until the suspension of cash payments by the Bank in 1797 destroyed all definiteness in the standard, and made the pound sterling a mere name. In May, 1816, a Committee of the Council, in their report upon the

Mr. J. G. Hubbard.

coinage, proposed that Parliament should forthwith enact "that the gold coin alone be the standard coin of the realm, and that silver coins be merely representative coins, and be a legal trustee for not exceeding two guineas." They further recommended that the expense of coining the gold coins be borne by the public, but that the Master of the Mint retain 4 s. out of each pound of silver as "brassage and seigniorage." In accordance with that recommendation the statute, 56 George III., cap. 68, enacted "that the gold coins made according to the indenture of the Mint be henceforth the *sole standard measure of value and legal tender for payment*, without any limitation of account." On the 1st of July, 1817, the new gold coin was made by proclamation "to be current and lawful money of the kingdom, and to be called a sovereign, or 20-shilling-piece." (*Ruding's Coinage*, vol. 2, pages 116-121.)

At the same time a coinage of silver was ordered at the rate of 66 s. to every pound troy of standard fineness, such shillings to be legal tender to the limited amount of 40 s.

The Bank of England is empowered to issue notes payable to the bearer for so many pounds. The State contracts to pay to its creditor so many pounds. In what form would Colonel Smith receive the pounds promised in the bank-note, or the pounds due in his dividend? not, surely, in a bag of dust or a lump of gold, but in *coin*. Law, prerogative, and experience combine, therefore, in substantiating the proposition which Colonel Smith denies.

When Colonel Smith describes a sovereign as "a variable thing which may contain more or less gold," he can hardly mean that the legal tolerance in weight and fineness disqualifies the coin for its office, for he adds, in the next paragraph,—" It would make no difference, in my opinion, in the standard or measure of value if the tolerance or allowed variation of the coin were not only increased beyond the three-quarters of a grain, but if the whole of the gold were taken out of the coins and paper tokens substituted for them." I can only understand this strange paragraph

Mr. J. G. Hubbard.

by supposing that Colonel Smith looks for the pound sterling, the standard of value, not in the coins where I have shown it is, but in 123 grains of standard gold embodied in a bit of a bar. This idea would explain many of Colonel Smith's expressions, but it is unfounded.

When the resumption of cash payments was under discussion after the great war, Ricardo proposed that banknotes should be issued not upon coin, but upon bullion, and that they should be redeemable down to the value of 20 oz. in bar gold. There was much to recommend the proposal. A larger circulation could have been maintained, and a great security would have been taken against the danger of a run for gold arising from panic and from popular impulses. On the other hand, convertibility would have been a delusion, as regards the holder of small notes, or of notes to a smaller amount than 80 $l.$, and, in fact, Ricardo's suggestion was not adopted, and the standard of value was vested, not in a diminutive block of gold, but in a coin.

And now, if Colonel Smith will change his point of view, we shall find very much to agree upon. I agree with him that a charge for coinage may fairly constitute the difference of value between bullion and coin, but he, taking bullion as his standard, naturally expected the "mintage" to take effect by raising the value of the coin. I, holding the coin to be the standard and invariable, forsee the mintage operate, if at all, in the diminished value of the bullion. I had stated in my first letter "that a charge for coinage can be only a charge upon the importer, and cannot enhance the value or power of the coin." Colonel Smith says,—

"This statement begs the most important question in dispute, and it is an essential one. If it be true, then, I must admit that the plan suggested by me for the accommodation of the British and foreign currencies *cannot be carried out.*"

If I have established my proposition " that our coin is our standard," I have logically established this proposition also. I might then challenge Colonel Smith to surrender

I

upon his own confession, but with all the honours of war. As, however, ours is, I trust, an amicable contest, I will pursue the controversy which he invites.

"Let me first observe," writes Colonel Smith, "that all the leading writers on Political Economy are of my opinion." This, which Colonel Smith takes as his first position, I shall ask his leave to consider last, for this reason, that opinions, however eminent, would have little weight with me if contradicted by the inexorable logic of facts, and that what I am now advancing was learnt from an experience of more than 40 years as a merchant, and of nearly 30 years in the direction of the Bank of England. I promise, however, to consult the authorities to whom he refers, and to retract any assertion which I may find untenable. Colonel Smith asks, "If the charge for coinage is only a charge upon the importer, are we to assume that he obtains less than the full value of his gold, or that he does obtain the full value?" My answer is that the importer of bullion, like the importer of any other commodity, obtains the best price he can get, and that, commercially speaking, the best price the owner of any commodity can procure is "its full value."

Colonel Smith illustrates his question in what he truly calls the exaggerated case "of a coinage charge of 20 per cent., represented by the Mint offering for gold bullion a price of $3l.\ 2s.\ 3\frac{1}{2}d.$ instead of $3l.\ 17s.\ 9d.$" "Would this," he asks, "be a fall in the purchasing power of the gold bullion?"

A Mint charge of 20 per cent. would be a tax of 20 per cent. on the importation of bullion, and would operate as prohibitory duties operate on other commodities. The producers or owners of gold bullion would not send their property for realization to this country at so serious a disadvantage. If they desired the manufactures of this country, and had no other means of paying for them, they would inquire whether from Belgium or Germany they could not obtain metal work, cotton and woollen goods, at a

Mr. J. G. Hubbard.

smaller sacrifice of gold than by buying them here subject to the tax of 20 per cent. upon the material they offer in exchange; and then, either prices of British exports would be ruinously depressed in price, or their production would cease, in proportion as their former purchasers were repelled. Australia is the chief producer both of the gold and of the wool which we import: impose a tax of 20 per cent. upon either, and the article taxed will exchange elsewhere for the products which, to the amount of millions yearly, are now supplied by British industry to our thriving dependencies.

To levy a mintage of one-sixth per cent., as I have recommended, would only be to impose a coinage charge like most other countries; it would place us at no disadvantage commercially, and its influence on prices would be quite imperceptible; but every addition to the coinage charge beyond its cost is unsound in theory and pernicious in practice, and I thank Colonel Smith for having suggested so decisive an illustration of the impolicy of levying a seigniorage upon the standard coin.

I have answered Colonel Smith's question from my stand upon the coin as standard. Had bar gold been constituted the standard of value, I could have agreed with many of his arguments, and, touching this last case, I should have said—the Legislature are competent to make the sovereign represent 25s., 50s., or 100s.; it would then become a token, a representative of value, just as the banknote is; and the supposed charge of 20 per cent. for coinage would really mean that your principal gold coin was worth a quarter of a 5 $l.$-note. The object and designation of the coin would have been altered, but the standard of value, the $123\frac{1}{4}$ grains of standard gold resident in the block, would remain the invariable measure by which the value of all contracts are determined and all obligations fulfilled. As a matter of fact, however, the standard of value is found not in a gold bar, but in a gold coin. The standard, whatever it be, cannot, and must not, be tampered with by degrading either the quantity or the quality of the gold; and, above all, we must avoid the ridiculous imposture of using old names for new things, of making a coin different from its former self, and calling it what it once had been.

Colonel Smith's communications are so rich in controversial matter that I must ask your permission to conclude my reply to him in another letter.

I remain, Sir, your obedient servant,
J. G. HUBBARD.
ADDINGTON MANOR,
August 31, 1869.

GOLD COINAGE.

(The Times, September 2, 1869.—To the Editor.)

SIR,—Finding myself referred to in more than one of the letters which have appeared in your columns on the subject of Mr. Lowe's proposal, as having so long ago as 1852 advocated in an official correspondence with the Treasury the imposition of a " Mint charge or seigniorage " on our gold coinage, I trust you will allow me, through the same medium, to offer some remarks, both on the measure so advocated, in itself, and on its bearing on the subject (not then in any way contemplated) of an international coinage.

The communication referred to, as well as the whole of a somewhat lengthy correspondence to which it led, is published *in extenso* in the Appendix to the Report of the International Coinage Committee of July 25, 1868 ; and it must, I think, be sufficiently evident on its perusal that the proposition there immediately contemplated, though spoken of indiscriminately sometimes as a Mint charge and sometimes as a seigniorage, went only to the extent of a money payment, *not more than sufficient to cover the expense of coinage*, imposed with a view to operate as a check on the

Sir J. F. W. Herschel.

rapidly increasing demand for coined gold which the then resources of the Mint were very inadequately prepared to meet, and which, it was apparent, went far beyond what was required for mere circulation, leaving it, however, open to consideration, for a reason which will subsequently appear, whether, after all, the interposition of any such check be really expedient on a consideration of general utility.

Between such a proposition as a money payment of about $1\frac{1}{2}d.$ per ounce by the " importer " (using the word in its Mint acceptation to designate the bringer of bullion to the Mint for coinage) and the abstraction of gold to the amount of an entire per cent. (or $9\frac{1}{2}d.$ per ounce) from the coin itself, there is obviously all the difference in the world. The former is a perfectly justifiable charge on the party who, for his own convenience, desires to convert his raw material into morsels transferable from hand to hand by tale : and in its practical adoption might be accomplished by an equitable transaction between the Government and the Bank (in practice the only " importer " now or likely to be), without giving any shock to the *prestige* attaching to our coin, or mooting in any way before the public the delicate and difficult discussion in which we are landed by the latter proposal. This latter, unless accompanied with a distinct provision for compensation, is liable to be regarded, and is, in fact, so regarded by the Commissioners signing the Report of 1868 (with the exception of Colonel Smith and Sir J. Lubbock)—men of eminence, and whose opinion is not to be lightly set aside—as a reduction in the intrinsic value of the pound sterling; that is to say, in plain terms, as being equivalent to a confiscation to the extent of the proposed per-centage on the total claims of the national creditor, and, practically speaking, to a perpetual income-tax (not, however, resulting in anything like a proportional revenue) of about $2\frac{1}{2}d.$ in the pound on the fundholder, as well as to the abrogation in favour of the debtor of that same per-centage on all debts contracted on the faith of the permanency of the existing system.

In opposition to this view it is contended by Colonel Smith, Mr. Jevons, and others, who advocate the diminution of the sovereign, that the new sovereign or international coin of 112 grains of fine gold would possess the same value or purchasing power as the old of 113, *at least within the area of its legal tender*, and would, in fact, *within that area* purchase 113 grains of fine gold : while Dr. Farr, putting his case of the payment of a debt from A to his creditor B contracted under the old *régime*, considers that A will have *made the same sacrifice* in paying 100 of the new coins to B (to obtain which he must have previously paid one to the State) that he would have made by the direct payment of 100*l*. sterling to him in our present sovereigns ; in reply to which, however, B might surely urge that what he bargained for was not *sacrifice* on A's part, which does him (B) no good, but the specific performance of a definite contract.

For, on the other hand, it is alleged that all our existing obligations, public and private, are based on the pound sterling, with the clear and distinct understanding that such pound is no fanciful or imaginary object—no abstract or metaphysical conception of "value" or "purchasing power," but a real and tangible thing—viz., 113 grains of fine gold in the form of a coin—a coin, that is to say, not simply *worth* in local or conventional estimation, but *bonâ fide* and in the strict grammatical sense of the words *containing* that quantity of the precious metal—a cosmopolitan, not a national coin—a coin deliberately intended and purposely calculated to be had and received (of course, when new and unworn) wherever presented—at home or abroad—among civilized or uncivilized nations, as that which it really *is*—viz., a certain definite piece of gold, no matter how highly or how lowly estimated *as such* at the time and place of its presentation in payment. All our public Acts and arrangements, from Sir R. Peel's Act of 1819 downwards, including an express provision legalizing the exportation and melting of gold coin, have been based on this definition and directed to insure its practical validity, the object having avowedly

Sir J. F. W. Herschel.

been to secure its universality of acceptance with a direct view to the maintenance of clear and intelligible commercial relations with all the world. In reference to this important and distinguishing feature of our coinage, the saving clause on the ground of general expediency to which I have above alluded is seen to have been neither unmeaning nor uncalled for.*

On this view of the subject (which is plain matter of history) any, even the smallest, diminution of the quantity of gold in the current coinage converts it into a token or representative coin, divests it of its cosmopolitan character, confines its circulation to a conventional area, and carries with it the moral as well as logical necessity for some provision for substituting the reality for the representation whenever fitting occasion shall arise; that is to say, when the representation shall cease to perform the functions of the reality. This is manifestly the case whenever the creditor in the liquidation of any claim (who is the only competent judge of his own interests) shall declare himself dissatisfied, of course on reasonable grounds, with the tender of the nominal amount in the token coinage: a case only likely to arise on the supposition of a moderate percentage such as that contemplated, when he should require the gold for exportation, or for home consumption in articles of use or ornament, or lastly in the case of a foreign holder of British securities beyond the area of the international circulation. Hence has arisen the suggestion in a recent number of the *Spectator* (August 14) to assimilate the proposed new coinage to our silver token coinage by making it legal tender only to the extent of 100*l.*, larger sums being payable, if so required, in bullion, " the State undertaking the task of verifying its weight and fineness, or not, as

* If it can be shown that we receive a *quid pro quo* in some form of national advantage in return for an exaggerated Mint outlay, the money may be well spent, and it will then only remain to provide whatever increase of power, personal or mechanical, may be required to keep the supply of coin on a level with a steady demand much exceeding its usual average.—(Report of 1868. Appendix, p. 327.)

should be found expedient." Under such an arrangement, of course, bank-notes would continue a legal tender, convertible into sovereigns of 112 grains if below, or, optionally, into bullion at 113 grains to the sovereign if above, 100*l.*, on presentation at the Bank. This, of course, would require some concerted arrangement between the Government and the Bank. This suggestion obviates the objection arising from the general rise of money prices otherwise inevitably consequent on that perpetual importation of food from abroad which our overplus of population renders necessary, and which, when not paid for in British manufactures or other produce, must be so in bullion.

Another mode of meeting the objection raised on the ground of confiscation would consist—on the principle suggested in p. 14 of the International Coinage Commissioners' Report—in writing off in the *Grand livre de la dette Publique* 101 *l.* for every 100 *l.* now standing in the names of the several creditors of the State, at the same time enacting that all debts contracted previously to the change should be nominally enhanced in the same proportion. *This would amount in effect to the formal abolition of the pound sterling* and the substitution for it of a new and inferior unit of money reckoning; it would not obviate the general rise of prices in that nominal reckoning above pointed out as necessarily consequent on our foreign commercial relations, or that less justifiable, but hardly less inevitable, rise inflicted by dealers on their customers in reimbursement for what they would persist in maintaining, any amount of scientific demonstration notwithstanding, to be a real diminution of " value " in the coin received. And, as a mode of compensatory adjustment, it is open to all those very formidable objections on the score of practicability in contracts between man and man which are urged with such force and distinctness in page 14 of the Report cited.

Placed on the avowed footing of a token coinage, and with a proviso for the mutual recognition on the part of all the contracting nations of the same principle for the

Sir J. F. W. Herschel.

exchange of coin against bullion in redemption at the rate of 113 grains of fine gold for each international coin of 112 (without which stipulation it would be most unjust to give such coins struck abroad legal currency in England), the project of an international coinage would seem to present no insuperable difficulty for so long, at least, as the contracting parties shall remain at peace with each other. The contingencies which might arise on the breaking out of hostilities and prolonged interruption of commercial relations would, however, need to be well considered, it being remembered that a declaration of war abrogates all treaties. And, moreover, all the contracting Governments should be equally bound to provide for the calling in and renewal of worn and deteriorated coin of their own striking, replacing the average loss by fair wear and tear, but not to a larger extent. This is the *quid pro quo* on which the imposition of a seigniorage, as distinct from a Mint charge, is justifiable. Where the Mint is free, no just claim can possibly be urged against a Government for such renewal; and, if undertaken on grounds of general expediency, its cost is fairly chargeable on the general revenue.

It is time to bring this long letter (my first, as I intend it to be my last, on the subject) to a close; but one word more is necessary. Gold is assumed throughout as the one and only ultimate standard of *price*. But price is not "value." Gold is pouring into the markets of the world apace. The earth is not yet, nor is likely to be for a century to come, picked clean of that metal, as it was (practically speaking) in the middle ages. In consequence, money prices must be expected for some time to come to rise, as they have done since the discovery of the Australian and other gold-fields. But this is a cause apart from and quite independent of the general rise of prices above spoken of as consequent on the proposed measure, and ought not to be mixed up with it. The effect on all fixed incomes from the one cause is already felt severely enough, and there is no reason why it should be gratuitously exaggerated by the other. *We* are wedded for better for worse to a gold standard. The question of a double standard, however, both of gold and of silver, which is one of great present interest in France, has exercised political economists since the natal day of their science, and it seems now to be pretty well agreed that one metal will be constantly tending to drive the other out of circulation, according to the variation of their relative price in the market; and such, no doubt, must be the case on the ordinary acceptation of a *double tender*, (or, as Mr. Lowe for this reason calls it, an alternate one,) under which coin in either metal may be offered, and must be accepted, in full payment of any debt. But how if our neighbours, who are in a transition state, and seem to be still hesitating on this point, should settle down to what, to distinguish it from the other, might be called a *binary tender*, under which half the value in gold and half in silver coin might be insisted on as the mode of discharge *by either party to the transaction?* Under such a convention it is self-evident that both descriptions of coin *must* be retained in circulation in such relative abundance as public convenience should require; while in determining the legal ratio, or what may be termed the monetary capacity of the two elements, such a number or fraction might be fixed upon as would make the fine gold in a 25-franc piece identical with that in the present British sovereign (according to the suggestion of Mr. Hubbard, grounded on the average price of silver from 1856 to 1865 *). Perhaps, with this modification of the meaning of a " double standard " the objections of Austria against it† might be removed, with a similar result as to the gold coinage of that nation.

I am, Sir, your obedient servant,

J. F. W. HERSCHEL.

COLLINGWOOD, HAWKHURST,
Aug. 30, 1869.

P.S.—It was not my intention to have noticed in any way the allegations of Mr. Seyd against the purity of the

* Report, p. 22.   † Report, p. 22.

British coinage, or his innuendo on the subject of the "few heavy pieces issued with the knowledge of the Master of the Mint,"—considering the letter of "Monetarius" in your paper of Aug. 20 an ample reply to the direct charge, and the report of the Pyx Jurors as to the total weight of very large masses of the coin submitted to their examination equally so to the covert sneer. Since copying the above, however, I observe in your paper of yesterday, just come to hand, that he returns to the charge fortified with assays of bars from 10,000 sovereigns "cut by the Bank" by Dr. Miller, the Bank assayer, giving results varying from 9,145 to 9,157, the standard being 9,166$\frac{1}{2}$. In Dr. Miller's accuracy I have every confidence; but has it never occurred to Mr. Seyd that among these cut sovereigns many may have *never issued from the Mint at all,* and may have owed their lightness to the fraudulent use of inferior gold? Should the Chancellor of the Exchequer act on Mr. Seyd's suggestion, and obtain returns of the Bank assays of British coin, I trust he will not omit at the same time to call for a return in full of all the assays made since 1851 by the three assayers, on whose reports the Master of the Mint depends (Dr. Miller being one of them), both of bars "passed into work," and of the coin itself previous to issue. The utter groundlessness of such a charge will thus be made strikingly apparent.

THE GOLD COINAGE.

(The Times, September 3, 1869.—To the Editor.)

Sir,—I resume my reply to Colonel Smith at his notice of my offer to give him in India 100,000 Australian for 100,500 English sovereigns—an offer which I conceived would be acceptable to him since he held that a charge of *Mr. J. G. Hubbard.*

one per cent. for coinage "raised the value of the coin one per cent."

Colonel Smith declines my offer, and pleads that my "first mistake is that Australian sovereigns are coined at a charge of 1 per cent. for coinage," and further he objects to the locality I had proposed for the transaction. Colonel Smith will pardon my mistake when he has referred to the evidence of Mr. Hendriks, who says (*Royal Commission Report on International Coinage*, question 306), " in Australia the seigniorage charged appears to average about one per cent., and the delay in delivery 20 days;" and again, question 307, "thus we have a total of very nearly one per cent., which happens to be just the rate of seigniorage on gold in Australia." "We have thus a total for seigniorage and delay of 1·33 per cent.," and to his own statement (p. 153), "at present the coinage charges in Australia, including delay, amount to fully one per cent., the consequence of which is that all gold intended for the London market comes only in bars."

As to the locality for our barter, I would ask Colonel Smith himself to name the spot anywhere within the habitable globe, but that he raises this further difficulty, "for any Mint charge to confer value in exchange it must be unavoidable. If, therefore, sovereigns coined at a charge of one per cent. can be met in the same place on equal terms by others coined free, the latter would rule the market."

I fear I must relinquish the hope of running my horse Substance against Colonel Smith's Shadow, since he makes it a condition of the match that Substance shall never appear on the same course with Shadow; but I may fairly claim forfeit if the proof of Shadow's superiority depends upon the absence of the means of comparison.

Colonel Smith rebukes me for doubting that a sovereign worth only 25f. at Calais can be worth 25f. 20c. at Dover, by the assurance that our half-crown, worth only 2s. 3d. at Calais, is worth 2s. 6d. at Dover. Here again Colonel

Mr. J. G. Hubbard.

Smith has unconsciously admitted that he proposes to treat the standard coin (at once the measure and the equivalent of value) as a *mere token*.

I now approach Colonel Smith's last impeachment. It refers to a serious charge on my part, which I will review with the care which the subject demands.

Colonel Smith takes exception to this passage of my former letter:—

" As the Chancellor of the Exchequer has challenged public opinion (among other points) upon a scheme for a coinage sustentation fund prepared by his Mint Masters, but by them avowedly founded upon the authority of Mr. Jevons, I must distinctly declare that Mr. Jevons's method of calculation in connexion with the subject is fallacious, and the conclusions derived from it utterly worthless."

Colonel Smith finishes his comment upon this passage thus:—

" It is only because Mr. Hubbard thinks Mr. Jevons's conclusions upon another point 'in connexion with the subject' are not valid that he takes upon himself to denounce these independent calculations as utterly worthless."

If Colonel Smith will refer to the very passage he has quoted from my former letter he will find that I designate as utterly worthless not his own "independent calculations," but Professor Jevons's conclusions drawn from his fallacious method of calculation. To this expression I must adhere, and I cannot exonerate Colonel Smith and his colleague, in their report to the Chancellor of the Exchequer, from blame, since every allusion in that report to Professor Jevons's researches, experiments, and observations was expressive of approval and confidence. " Because they were thought accurate so they were made use of," are Colonel Smith's own words, and this is my complaint—that he did not examine the nature of Professor Jevons's method. If he had, he must have noticed the radical defect in his most important calculation—that establishing the amount of the gold coin in circulation. If satisfied by Professor Jevons's reason for selecting the years 1863-4 as the basis of his computation—viz., the greater reduction of the sovereigns coined in more distant years by exportation, melting, and loss—he would have noticed that this reason does not touch half-sovereigns, and that although the years selected by Mr. Jevons *as the best* (for his purpose?) gave 12,000,000 *l.* as the limit of the half-sovereigns in circulation, yet that the years 1851-2 subject to the same process would give a limit of 50,203,000 *l.*, the entire coinage having been but 41,574,000 *l.* Had Colonel Smith scrutinized this "*method* of calculation," it might have struck him that, given the ages of 100,000 living coins and the numbers minted in each year, you had no means of discovering the amount of the surviving coinage. This could only be done by ascertaining the number destroyed or exported, and upon that essential inquiry the ages of the current coins throw no light whatever.

When I pointed out this to Professor Jevons, he retorted with a quibble about the Rule of Three, wholly irrelevant to the purpose, for it was to a given formula framed in the olden fashion, and not in that of Colenso, that I applied a criticism sanctioned by standard works on arithmetic, not the less accurate because they are of the last generation.

That the author of the blunder should attempt to justify it only serves to increase the distrust with which one must view any scheme propounded by those who had carelessly endorsed or credulously adopted his conclusions.

I quite admit that the independent calculations of the Mint Masters, and the scheme propounded by Mr. Lowe, might be perfectly accurate and unimpeachably wise, independently of Mr. Jevons; at present we can only judge of the intended construction by what we see of the foundation and learn of the architect.

At last I arrive at Colonel Smith's foremost and strongest position—"the agreement in his opinion of all the leading writers on Political Economy."

I have carefully read the opinions culled for the information of the International Coinage Commission, and I will notice the more important ones as briefly as I may.

Mr. J. G. Hubbard.

Sir Dudley North is quoted at some length, and I quite agree with the tenor of the citation, which is to expose the impolicy of a gratuitous coinage; but I beg Colonel Smith's attention to the following sentences not quoted to the Commissioners, but immediately succeeding in the original the paragraph last extracted:—

"That debasing the coyn is defrauding one another, and to the public there is no sort of advantage from it; for that admits no character, or value, but intrinsick.

"That the sinking by alloy or weight is all one."

Adam Smith, who is largely quoted, is clearly in favour of a "moderate seigniorage," and he holds that—

"A small duty on the coinage of both gold and silver would probably increase still more the superiority of those metals in coin above an equal quantity of either of them in bullion."

Ricardo's observations are most interesting. He lays down that—

"The limits beyond which a seigniorage cannot be advantageously extended are the actual expenses incurred by the manufacturing of bullion into coin. If a seigniorage exceeds these expenses, an advantage will accrue to false coiners by imitating the coins, although they should actually make them of their legal weight and standard."

And further on,—

"If the public could be secured from such additions to the circulating medium there could be no seigniorage so high which a Government might not advantageously exact; as the coined money would, in the same degree, exceed the value of bullion. If the seigniorage amounted to 10 per cent., bullion would necessarily be 10 per cent. under the Mint price, and if it were 50 per cent., that also would the value of coin exceed the value of bullion. . . .

"That these principles are correct may be proved from the consideration of the circumstances which give value to a *bank-note*. A bank-note is of no more intrinsic value than the piece of paper on which it is made. *It may be considered as a piece of money* on which the seigniorage is enormous, amounting to all its value; yet if the public is sufficiently protected against the too great increase of such notes, either by the indiscretion of the issuers, or by the practices of false coiners or forgers, they must, in the ordinary operations of trade, retain their value."

In this last passage, Ricardo insists upon the principle of limitation for maintaining the value either of tokens which have some intrinsic worth, or of bank-notes which have none. But no one more rigidly than Ricardo maintained the principle of intrinsic value in the standard itself, and in his own words:—

"It follows that in a country where gold is the measure of value, the price of gold bullion (where law offers no restraint against exportation) can never exceed its Mint price, and that it can never fall more below it than the expenses of coinage."

That is exactly where I hope to see it.

Thomas Tooke's evidence upon the Resumption of Cash Payments, from which extracts are given, is directed to show that " Seigniorage is synonymous with debasement unless connected with a principle of limitation." And he recommends a seigniorage of about $2\frac{1}{2}$ to 5 per cent., the coin and bank-notes of equal amounts being exchangeable for bullion as recommended by Mr. Ricardo. This, in effect, would be—as I have explained in my last letter—making bar gold the standard of value, and both coin and notes mere tokens.

M'Culloch is the next authority, and in his note on Smith's *Wealth of Nations*, there are, amid many sound and excellent statements, two short sentences which seem to concur with Colonel Smith's doctrine :—

"Coins charged with a seigniorage equal to the expense of coinage do not pass at a higher value than what naturally belongs to them, but at that precise value; whereas, if the expense of coinage be defrayed by the State, coins pass at less than their real value."

And, again :—

"Abroad, a British coin is only worth so much bullion, but if a seigniorage were charged upon it, its value here would be increased by the amount of that seigniorage."

As the learned authority himself is no longer among us to be consulted as to his real opinion upon the point in contention, I must content myself by referring to the *Essay on Money and Coins*, written in 1757 by Joseph Harris, then Master of the Mint. This treatise is described by M'Culloch, to whom we are indebted for its re-publication, " as one of the best and most valuable treatises that has ever seen the light." Nothing can be clearer than his utterances,—*e.g.*,

Mr. J. G. Hubbard.

" By debasing the standard I everywhere mean the lessening the quantity of pure silver in the pound sterling, or in the respective specie which by law makes up that sum without regarding the particular manner in or by which this may be done."—(Page 383, *Treatise on Money, &c.*, printed for the Political Economy Club, 1856.)

" To alter the value of money would be to alter uniformly and universally the prices of all commodities, a thing manifestly out of the reach of laws."—(Page 193.)

But I must not be tempted to prolong this letter even to enrich it from so tempting a mine. I commend the treatise of Joseph Harris to the attention of his successors in the office of Mint Master, satisfied that its unbiassed consideration must tend to produce unanimity in my second proposition, that " legislation has no power over the effective value of a coin which is itself the standard and measure of value in a country included in the great community of commercial nations."

I remain, Sir, your obedient servant,

J. G. HUBBARD.

September 1, 1869.

THE GOLD COINAGE.

(The Times, September 4, 1869.—To the Editor.)

SIR,—By your permission I proceed to the consideration of the light gold coin and of the mode in which it has on a former occasion been dealt with. It is rather more than 50 years since an Order of Council put the Royal Mint into action for the coinage of sovereigns and half-sovereigns. Between 1817 and 1867, 193 millions sterling were coined, and nearly 190 millions passed through the Bank of England into general circulation. How much of this vast amount now survives and fulfils its proper office within the United Kingdom is a very interesting question, but it is one of which the solution is not essential to the immediate subject of this letter. In 1842 (and perhaps

Mr. J. G. Hubbard. K

earlier) the attention of Government was drawn to the state of the coinage. Of the gold coin tendered to the Bank in 1841 the large proportion of 26 6-10ths per cent. had been rejected as light and returned into general circulation. Upon consultation with the Bank and the authorities of the Mint, Her Majesty's Government issued a proclamation, dated the 7th of June, 1842, prohibiting the circulation of the light coin, and, shortly after, they authorized the Bank to receive it by weight at the Mint price of $3l.\ 17s.\ 10\frac{1}{2}d.$ Under this authority, the Bank received between the 25th of June, 1842, and the 31st of December, 1843, a nominal amount of nearly 13 millions. The withdrawal and re-coinage of this large quantity so materially improved the average condition of the coinage that, whereas the per-centage of light gold on the amount of 6,214,000 $l.$ tendered to the Bank in the first six months of 1842 equalled $33\frac{1}{3}$ per cent., the per-centage of light gold rejected in the years 1843 to 1853 averaged only $3\frac{1}{4}$ per cent. That proportion has since materially increased, but the actual state of the coinage cannot be inferred from the aggregate operations of the Bank. The dread of the shears keeps much of the light coin away; but inquiries on a smaller scale, and more probably representing the general condition of the coinage, lead to the conclusion that it may be in nearly as bad a state as it was in 1842. It was estimated in 1842 that the loss of re-coinage would be fairly divided between the public and the Mint, the holders of the coin incurring, in virtue of the deficient weight, a loss of about $2d.$ upon each sovereign, and the Mint bearing the charges of melting, waste, and re-coinage. Coining, however, was in those days subject to serious official fees which no longer exist, and the division of the loss on a large re-coinage would now be greatly heavier on the holder of the light coin than on the Mint. Still the arrangement would be a relief to the holder of the light coin, for although he would lose $2d.$ deficient in the weight, he would save the further loss of one penny on each sovereign accruing from the

Mr. J. G. Hubbard.

reduced price of 3 *l*. 16 *s*. 6½ *d*. offered to him by the Bank. I know no reason why the Bank should not be empowered to temper the severity of its judgment upon the defective coin by greater liberality in its purchases, and by habitually receiving it on account of the Government at the price of its issue (3 *l*. 17 *s*. 10½ *d*.). This liberality, or rather this act of justice, would diminish the disposition to sort the light coin out of the parcels intended for the Bank; more light coin would be cancelled yearly, but the average condition of the coinage would be improved; it would be circulated with less hesitation, and the necessity would less frequently recur for restoring its character by a distinct proscription of pieces reduced by wear below the legal limitation.

Obviously the loss resulting from a re-coinage is aggravated by the extensive foreign circulation which the sovereign has acquired; but, whatever it be, it is better that the community bear the present burden directly at its periodical recurrence rather than that they should bear a far heavier one indirectly through the Government. A certain loss by fair wear and tear is inevitable, and if fraudulent reduction of the coin is now comparatively trifling, it is because every one in his own interest is a guardian of the integrity of the Queen's money, and the removal of this general protectorate, by the establishment of an office for the constant exchange of heavy coins for light, must in the very nature of things tend to encourage and facilitate fraud. I have sought in vain for any confirmation of the organized melting of English sovereigns either in London or in Brussels mentioned in Mr. Lowe's speech. Australian sovereigns have been largely melted with the legitimate object of utilizing the silver which they needlessly contain, but the best confutation of the fable about the Tower Hill sovereigns being systematically melted is, that it would not pay; an excess of weight in selected coins must be most discreditable to the Mint, if it can counterbalance the probable loss by the assay and the inevitable waste by melting. The only imaginable foundation for the story is the practice, natural enough, of selecting the heaviest coins for export, when an export is in itself desirable. I submit, therefore, that the best mode of reintegrating the gold coin is to return to that adopted in 1842, and, in a carefully worded proclamation, proscribe the circulation of light pieces, and authorize the Bank to buy them by weight at the Mint price of 3l. 17s. 10½d.

This last instruction I would make permanent. The policy of a coinage charge has an important bearing not only upon the habitual expenditure of the Mint, but upon the costly effort which was required in 1842, and is again required now for the maintenance of our gold coins at their legal weight. Had a "mintage" of 1½d. an ounce been adopted in 1843 the saving to this country would have been considerable. A very slight difference in the price of bar gold will ordinarily determine its export rather than that of gold coin. Cut sovereigns in bulk are readily taken by exporters at 3l. 17s. 9½d., or at 1d. only under the price of bar or coin, and an abatement of 1½d. would in almost every instance have induced the export of bar and saved the waste of coin. It is dangerous to venture even an estimate without previous computation upon reliable data, but it may be reasonably doubted whether of the 190 millions passed into circulation between 1817 and 1867, even one-half were needed for the currency of the United Kingdom. Coin exported for the use of our dependencies, or of foreign countries, must amount to many millions, and may return; but many millions have been exported and melted. In the year 1847 alone, four millions were exported in sovereigns to the United States, and there converted into American eagles. A "mintage" of 1½d. an ounce, and its practical consequence, the sale of bar gold at 3l. 17s. 9d., might have saved the wasteful destruction of those four millions. Remarking only that I am here speaking of a single country and of a single year, it seems needless to strengthen the argument in favour of a "mintage" with the attendant abatement in the selling price of bullion.

Mr. J. G. Hubbard.

Serious as the waste arising from the needless destruction of coin has actually been, it would have been still more so had not the Bank departed from its previous rule of buying American, French, and Russian gold only in the form of marketable bars, and fixed a tariff at which it would buy and sell the gold coins of the principal foreign States. French napoleons, American eagles, and Russian imperials have, under this altered system, been bought to the extent of many millions when the course of trade directed the precious metals hither, and they were re-exported whenever the country had unusually large payments to make to France, America, and Russia.

The buying price for foreign coins was fixed by the Bank with reference to their several contents in fine gold. It was so adjusted that the importer should have no inducement to melt his coin, and that the Bank, if compelled to melt, might do so without loss. Upon the same principle that the Bank fixed 3*l*. 17*s*. 7½*d*. per ounce as the price for Russian coin, which is of the same standard as our own, it fixed 3*l*. 17*s*. 6½*d*. as the price of our own light coin, which ought to be standard, but which experience has shown to be often ⅛, and sometimes ¼, carat grain worse than standard. This inaccuracy of our Mint assays was pointed out by Mr. Seyd in his intelligent and well-informed letter of the 20th ult., and I can corroborate his observations by my own experience of sovereigns sent to Russia, where the Mint, more exact than our own, ranked sovereigns at fully ⅛ carat grain worse than standard.

The extensive circulation which the sovereign has attained abroad furnishes another and a very powerful reason against the State taking upon itself the responsibility of maintaining it at its legal current weight. At present the burden of wear and tear falls on the foreign merchant or State who sends it hither. The late Brazil steamer brought some 250,000*l*. in sovereigns; if they are paid into the Bank, the loss which may arise from defective weight will be a diminution of the proceeds of the remittance, and for this loss the Brazil merchant is quite prepared. It would be a most quixotic act of generosity on the part of this country, which has already coined the Brazilian gold gratuitously, to take back, after years of wear and tear, the old, disfigured, and defective coin, and give in exchange new, bright, heavy coin piece for piece.

The Bank must in 27 years (from June, 1842, to June, 1869) have cut and bought at $3l.$ $16s.$ $6\frac{1}{2}d.$ light coin to the amount of sixteen millions, and as the value purchased in 1861 was 760,000$l.$, the purchases in late years must have reached a million.

By giving the more attractive price of $3l.$ $17s.$ $10\frac{1}{2}d.$ the Bank might so considerably extend its purchases as to maintain the coinage, when once relieved of the present accumulation of light pieces, in its improved condition, and render any subsequent intervention of the Government needless, or needful only at much wider intervals.

The proclamation of 1842, I believe, was directed only to prohibiting the currency of the light coins. It caused great alarm, and many ignorant people were frightened into parting with their sovereigns at a ridiculous abatement of their value. Any proclamation on the subject should clearly indicate that the light coins, though no longer current, were damaged only to the extent of their defect in weight, and were changeable for new ones, weight for weight, at the Bank of England and at all its branches.

The coinages of 1817 and 1818, having been struck before the bank note had regained its par value, were largely exported, and it is interesting to mark the result of the attempt then made to carry out Ricardo's suggestion of an issue of bank notes secured by bullion. Orders were given to prepare bars of 60oz. each, to the value of about half-a-million; 2,028 ingots were accordingly cast and stamped at the Mint, but not one of them was exactly the stipulated weight. The Bank sold but 13 of them; three in July, 1820, at $4l.$ $1s.$ per oz.; three in October, 1820, at $3l.$ $19s.$ $6d.$ per oz.; and seven in May, 1821, at $3l.$ $17s.$ $10\frac{1}{2}d.$

Mr. J. G. Hubbard.

One of these last was re-purchased in 1826, and is now deposited in the British Museum; the other 12 have been re-melted, and the remaining 2,015 ingots were returned to the Mint and converted into sovereigns.

The failure of this experiment furnished an additional reason for adhering to the Act of 1816, and for maintaining the sovereign of 113 grains of fine gold as the pound sterling, the sole legal tender and measure of value. It was upon no light grounds that the International Coinage Commissioners (with, at the most, two exceptions) pointed out the fitness of the sovereign, or its equivalent, as an international coin, but recommended that we should not substitute a 25-franc piece for our English sovereign.

I remain, Sir, your most obedient servant,

J. G. HUBBARD.

September 3, 1869.

GOLD COINAGE.

(The Times, September 8, 1869.—To the Editor.)

SIR,—Your correspondent, Mr. Ernest Seyd, in the two letters published in *The Times* of the 20th and 21st inst., has communicated much interesting information, most of which, although not bearing directly upon the subject under discussion, is still valuable. I observe with regret that he indulges in expressions of compassion for the ignorance of those who differ from him, which makes it not quite agreeable to notice his opinions; but, as I feel sure this is only meant to add strength to his views, I proceed to point out where I think he is mistaken.

In his first letter, dated the 13th of August, par. 3, he says that the accommodation of our currency to that of France "can" only be done in a direct and open manner, and we "must" submit to the inconveniences of the change. This assertion, as is self-evident, simply begs the question that the other plan proposed is impracticable.

Col. J. T. Smith.

In his fourth paragraph, which is not very clear, Mr. Seyd says bullion in England will be raised 1 per cent. This is a mistake. It would remain as it is, at the price of 3*l.* 17*s.* 9*d.* per oz. standard. He adds that the new pound will be worth 25f., which is now worth 25·2215f., implying that it will be lessened in value. This is also a mistake, as the value in exchange will remain unaltered, as I have shown in late letters.

In his fifth paragraph Mr. Seyd correctly states that the price of gold bullion in France will be lowered, though the effect would not be so much as he reckons. Instead of 1 per cent. the real fall would be 1 per cent. minus the present mintage, and the average cost of delay and other charges, possibly altogether amounting to $\frac{1}{3}$ to $\frac{1}{2}$ per cent. In his summary he is incorrect, in my opinion, both in saying that England will lower the value of her sovereign, and that France will lower the value of her bullion. In my letter of the 20th inst. I endeavoured to show that our sovereign will not be altered in exchangeable value; and in regard to French bullion, though altered in price, I think it is a mistake to say it is altered in value.

In his seventh paragraph Mr. Seyd asks, " Why, indeed, should we not substitute seigniorage altogether, and do without gold?" To which I reply, why not? Let those who deny the possibility show the insuperable obstacle, remembering that the doing without gold does not mean its omission from payment to obtain the currency, but only the omission of it from the circulating medium. In my opinion, if bank notes could by no possibility whatever be obtained except by the sacrifice of 123·274 grains of standard gold each, they would circulate and exchange for the same amount of goods as our sovereigns now do, and this irrespective of their being convertible into gold, so long as the currency was either receiving supplies of coin or not in the least degree redundant.

In his eighth paragraph Mr. Seyd says, " Colonel Smith maintains that the value of a thing is what it costs to

Col. J. T. Smith.

produce; other people think that the test of value depends upon what a thing will fetch." In reply to this I must observe that I have never, to my remembrance, given any opinion about what a "thing" was worth; but I have most probably said that the currency of a country will exchange for commodities of the same value as that which it necessarily costs to procure it, and, to my mind, what a thing necessarily costs is what it "fetches."

In his second letter, at the close of a good deal of valuable information, intended to prove that our coins are inferior to those of other countries, Mr. Seyd adds, "but it will be evident that our supposed free and superior coinage, together with the whole edifice of argument which Mr. Lowe has built upon it, is a huge fallacy." We are not told what the edifice is, or what the fallacy; but we have it implied shortly afterwards that the facts stated by the Chancellor of the Exchequer are untrue, and also that "the Master of the British Mint knows well that he issues very few heavy pieces," in defiance of his previous statement that "if 1,000 sovereigns new from the Mint be weighed they will be found correct or nearly correct," thus involving the certainty that the amount of overweight must be equal to that of the underweight, and if the number of heavy pieces be less than the light ones, the overweight in each must be greater, and the profit of separating them more.

In the last paragraph of his second letter Mr. Seyd denies that 1 per cent. seigniorage will prevent the export of the coins—an opinion which may be safely left to the common sense of the public. The fact is that Mr. Seyd, and many other persons whose opinions on other points are worthy of great respect, cannot perceive or in any way understand the difference between "commercial" and what they call "intrinsic" value, and Mr. Seyd evidently thinks he annihilates my claim to further hearing by stating at the close of his first letter that Colonel Smith goes so far as to say that if the "State chooses to charge 50 per cent. import duty, or seigniorage on gold, if it actually deducts this from the sovereign, the value of the 10s. remaining will nevertheless be equal to 20s." This opinion was expressed in connexion with the condition that the price of gold in the market remained steadily at $3l.$ $17s.$ $10\frac{1}{2}d.$ per oz. standard (Evidence 1,069-1,072), and it is not only true within the limits of the kingdom, but might be carried further, by saying that if the gold in the pieces were reduced to *nil*, and the coins made of paper, it would, nevertheless, be true. I am confident that this will be eventually acknowledged, but not immediately by gentlemen of Mr. Seyd's present views.

Mr. Seyd's third letter, in *The Times* of yesterday, contains much valuable information, which, as far as I can judge, seems to be fairly applied. At the same time there must be some error in his conclusions, as they are opposed to the statement of the Chancellor of the Exchequer. It may be fairly assumed that the Chancellor of the Exchequer would not have made his assertion without satisfactory assurance that the facts were as he stated them; and it may be added that a statement of a similar kind is made in Messrs. Graham and Wilson's report of the proceedings of the International Conference, published in the Appendix to the Royal Commissioners' Report, page 192. These remarks tend to show that some further inquiry is necessary.

As I have said, Mr. Seyd's statements are, in my opinion, fair and moderate, yet a different conclusion may be suggested if other information be supplied and turned to account. In the first place, he calculates the cost of weighing 100,000 pieces at $5l.$, which is not too much with the methods ordinarily in use, but I can state the fact that an easier and much simpler method may be used, with scales which could be made wholesale for $6d.$ each, at the cost of not more than $25s.$ for the whole 100,000. This method has been in practical use for more than 25 years, and many hundreds of millions of pieces separated by it. It is managed by children, and ten would do the work in one day.

Col. J. T. Smith.

Secondly, in regard to interest. If it so happened that the business was undertaken on behalf of a firm obliged to keep large balances, the charge for interest would not be necessarily incurred.

Thirdly.—Instead of picking out only the pieces heavy by ¼ gr., if the whole of the pieces heavier than standard were taken, the work would be easier, and the result somewhat more favourable.

Fourthly.—Especially if the coins were sold to a foreign mint contractor, by which the charge for melting and assay would be avoided.

Fifthly.—And if the practice were only adopted at a time when the exchanges were adverse and gold must be sent abroad, the charges for freight and assurance would be saved, being covered by the rate of exchange.

These suggestions are merely thrown out by way of reconciling apparently contradictory statements, which I doubt not are equally true.

I remain, Sir, your obedient servant,

J. T. SMITH.

8, QUEEN STREET PLACE, E.C.,
August 31, 1809.

THE COINAGE.

(The Times, September 9, 1809.—To the Editor.)

SIR,—Mr. Hubbard has endeavoured in two long letters published in *The Times* of the 1st and 3rd inst. to meet my arguments upon two questions, viz., as he states them—1st, " What is the standard of value ? " and 2nd, " What power has legislation over that standard ? "

2. In regard to the second, I beg to say I have never expressed any opinion about legislation, that I am aware of, and I decline to add to the number of issues, till those first put forward are disposed of. What I have stated in my

Col. J. T. Smith.

letter as a vital point in the discussion of the Chancellor of the Exchequer's proposal is, whether a Mint charge adds to the exchangeable value of the coins or not, and I must ask Mr. Hubbard to confine himself to his denial that it does, or say that he admits it.

3. Now, in regard to the first point, I have denied the statement that "the gold coin is the standard or measure of value," and I have given my reasons. Mr. Hubbard, in reply to this, after giving a good deal of valuable historical information, quotes the statute 56 George III., cap. 68, which, he says, " enacted that the gold coins made according to the indenture of the Mint be henceforth the sole standard measure of value and legal tender for payment without any limitation whatever." Hence, he concludes that "law, prerogative, and experience combine, therefore, in substantiating the proposition which Colonel Smith denies."

4. What Mr. Hubbard means by prerogative and experience substantiating the fact he does not explain, but it appears certain that if his proposition be not better substantiated than as it is by law it has not much to support it; for if he will be so good as to refer to the Act of Parliament itself, sec. 11, he will find that the enactment is very different from the words he has given, and, especially, it is not enacted that the coin should be the standard measure of value.

5. It is stated in the preamble to this section that whereas great inconvenience had arisen from the double standard measure of gold and silver having prevailed, it was expedient that gold coin should thenceforth be the sole standard measure of value and legal tender for payment, without any limit of amount, yet the enactment which follows is confined to making gold coin according to the Mint indenture the only "legal tender for payments." And the exclusion of all enactment as to its being the standard measure of value is all the more marked from the fact of its having been previously noticed.

6. Now, to resume the second question. I have denied Mr. Hubbard's statement "that a charge for coinage can

Col. J. T. Smith.

be only a charge upon the importer, and cannot enhance the value or power of the coin." I have stated it to be a vital question, and I have given reasons at length for my opinion. One of these reasons was that " all the leading writers on Political Economy are of my opinion," this statement obviously referring distinctly to the one question of the effect of a Mint charge. Mr. Hubbard meets this argument by making extracts from some of the writers, and another of his own, on the subject of Mint charge, the impolicy of gratuitous coinage, debasing coin, seigniorage, and altering the value of money, thus making confusion in the minds of those who are not fully conversant with the subject.

7. The fair answer to my argument on this head, could it have been made, would have been that the seven authors quoted, or some of them, do not agree that a Mint charge adds to the market value of coin; but the simple truth is, as I affirm, that every one of them agrees with my statement, and Mr. Hubbard might have frankly admitted this instead of introducing other questions.

8. It is not necessary to pursue this subject much further, although, as I have said, it is a most important and vital one; because Mr. Hubbard has himself settled it in my favour, as will be shown presently. I have first to remark that in the 12th paragraph of his letter in *The Times* of the 1st inst. he begins, " A Mint charge of 20 per cent. would be a tax of 20 per cent. on the importation of bullion." This is a mistake. A Mint charge and an import duty on gold bullion are not identical,—a Mint charge might be called a tax on the manufacture of coin, but it would not affect bullion otherwise than by reducing its price, in common with all other commodities. An import duty on gold would not reduce its price, if there were no separate Mint charge, but would increase its value compared with commodities, which latter would be reduced in price. Thus the difference in effect between a Mint charge and an import duty on bullion is, that with the former the Mint price of bullion would be reduced, but with the latter not.

9. The solution of the question as to the effect of a Mint charge on the exchangeable value of coins is contained in the same paragraph of the letter just quoted. Mr. Hubbard says, speaking of the effects of a Mint charge of 20 per cent., " The producers and owners of gold bullion would not send their property to this country;" and further on, " and then either prices of British exports would be ruinously depressed in price, or their productions would cease to the same extent that their former purchasers were excluded."

10. What is the meaning, in other words, of exports being ruinously depressed in price? Simply, that the currency has increased in exchangeable value. If this be the effect, as Mr. Hubbard declares, and as I doubt not it would be, of a Mint charge, as supposed, it proves that the operation of such a charge is to increase the exchangeable value of the coins.

11. But the latter part of the sentence above quoted contains a mistake which it is somewhat important to rectify. It is not the fact that the former purchasers would be excluded; and it is remarkable that it did not occur to Mr. Hubbard that, although there would seem to be a great disadvantage to the importer of gold, there would appear to be a vast advantage to the purchaser of exports. But the truth is there would be neither one nor the other. Affairs would go on just as at present, the new state of things being reconciled to the present by an alteration of the course of exchange; the commercial par of exchange with France, for instance, which is now 25·20¾, or thereabout, would become thereafter 31½ (31·46). A merchant sending gold from Paris, who would now receive 3*l*. 17*s*. 9*d*. for it, capable of purchasing a bill for nearly 98f., would, after the change, receive only 3*l*. 2*s*. 3½*d*., which would either purchase the same amount of goods, owing to the reduction of prices, as 3*l*. 17*s*. 9*d*. would have done previously, or would procure a bill on Paris for nearly 98f., at the exchange of 31·46f., as before.

Col. J. T. Smith.

12. These facts Mr. Hubbard's experience of more than 40 years as a merchant, and of nearly 30 years in the direction of the Bank of England, will no doubt lead him instantly to recognize and confirm.

13. We have at last arrived at a demonstration, out of Mr. Hubbard's writings, that a Mint charge does add to the commercial or exchangeable value of coin. I will now turn to a third question which Mr. Hubbard has superadded to the discussion—viz., his paragraph on the subject of the Mint Masters' scheme for a sustentation fund. I give it below, as follows:—

"Mr. Jevons's treatise contains much interesting matter, and facts industriously collected, the accuracy of which I am at present unprepared either to corroborate or deny. But as the Chancellor of the Exchequer has challenged public opinion (among other points) upon a scheme for a coinage sustentation fund, prepared by his Mint Masters, but by them avowedly founded upon the authority of Mr. Jevons, I must distinctly declare that Mr. Jevons's method of calculation in connexion with the subject is fallacious, and the conclusions derived from it utterly worthless."

14. This paragraph appears to me, and will, I think, to all who read it, to be calculated to convey the impression that a certain scheme was based upon Mr. Jevons's authority, that the conclusions of Mr. Jevons are worthless, consequently that the scheme is worthless also. I explained to Mr. Hubbard that the Mint Masters' Report was separately founded on *data*—that is, facts—collected by Mr. Jevons, and adopted after comparison with other facts, and special experiments made to test them, and the result deduced by strict mathematical calculation; the effect of this explanation being to show that, unless an objector is prepared either to dispute the facts, or the mathematical reasoning on them, it is vain and useless to dispute the result.

15. Mr. Hubbard, in the paragraph above quoted, stated that he was not prepared to deny the facts, and he has never, as yet, said that he disputed the mathematical reasoning. Unless he can show it to be wrong, it is clear that he never had the least ground for impeaching the accuracy of the Mint Masters' Report. If he had, I challenge him to say what it was, and let its value be tested; if not,

to state frankly that he never had the least ground for the implied imputation.

16. Mr. Hubbard now says that he did not designate our independent calculations as worthless, but Professor Jevons's conclusions, drawn from his fallacious method of calculation. This explanation I willingly accept; but it must be remembered that the Mint Masters' Report had a foundation not only based upon facts Mr. Hubbard was not prepared to deny, but also not in the smallest degree connected with the conclusions he holds to be worthless. Under these circumstances it is surely most unfortunate that Mr. Hubbard should have spoken of the Mint Masters' Report and Mr. Jevons's conclusions in such close connexion, declaring that the former was " avowedly founded on Mr. Jevons's authority," and adding that "his conclusions are utterly worthless."

17. It will, perhaps, occur to the readers of this letter as also remarkable, that when this was pointed out to Mr. Hubbard he did not hasten to acknowledge and rectify the mistake he had inadvertently made.

18. I will only add that, in my opinion, Mr. Jevons has earned the thanks of the country for his valuable contribution to our knowledge on a most important subject. I have refrained from noticing Mr. Hubbard's attack upon his calculations, because I am desirous to confine our attention to the specific points at issue between ourselves, and Mr. Jevons has himself defended them.

19. I presume Mr. Hubbard will not again repeat his denial of my assertion that a Mint charge adds to the exchangeable value of coin, and I shall, therefore, for the future take it as admitted that it is so.

20. With your permission I am exceedingly anxious to make a few remarks on Sir John Herschel's letter in *The Times* of the 2nd inst., as there are some points contained in it which evidently need further investigation.

I remain, Sir, your most obedient servant,

8, QUEEN STREET PLACE, E.C.,   J. T. SMITH.
Sept. 7, 1869.

THE GOLD COINAGE.

(The Times, September 10, 1869.—To the Editor.)

SIR,—The *Economist* of last Saturday remarks that no complete answer has been given to the letter of Mr. Ernest Seyd in *The Times* of August 30, impugning the goodness of our gold coin, and showing apparently that loss must follow from its melting or exportation. You will, perhaps, allow me, therefore, to point out that, though Mr. Seyd's facts and figures may be accurate in themselves, they will not in the least bear the construction which he puts upon them.

To show the quality of the gold coinage, Mr. Seyd quotes the assays of ten bars of gold composed of 10,000 sovereigns " cut " by the Bank and melted by Messrs. Sillar & Co., in 1866. The average fineness of the gold was 915·2, instead of 916·6 as it should have been. These numbers I am perfectly prepared to accept; but if he implies that they reflect upon the conduct of the Mint, I may point out that at p. 390 of his own recent work on bullion Mr. Seyd himself calculates the value of new British sovereigns at a very different figure,—namely, 916. Mr. Seyd ought to be aware, after reading the letter of " Monetarius," if not before, that there is a difference in fineness between sovereigns coined before, and those coined since, 1851. In that year a reform of the Mint was made, and the management of the coining, as well as of the assaying, was placed in the hands of the most eminent scientific men. The change effected is thus referred to in the letter of the Director of the United States' Mint to the Secretary of the Treasury, dated the 28th of January, 1854, and published in the proceedings of the 33rd Congress (1st Sess. Ex. Doc., No. 68):—

"The law provides that 'gold coins of Great Britain, not less than 915½ thousandths fine, shall be received at 94 6-10ths cents per pennyweight.' In a long series of years, and operating at times upon large quantities of such coin, we have not been able to find a higher average result than 915½, and it was upon this basis that the enactment was framed. But under the present management of the British Mint, and of its assay department, beginning fairly with the year 1852, there is an upward tendency more strictly conforming with the legal standard of 916 2-3rds. The assay of a few pieces of 1852 and 1853 (the course of trade preventing the receipt of large quantities here) gives an average of 916¼, and the consequent rate would be 94 7-10ths cents per pennyweight. But it will evidently require a large emission at this rate to make a perceptible improvement in any promiscuous parcel."

As the sovereigns melted by Messrs. Sillar were all cut for lightness by the Bank, they would for the most part be old ones coined before 1851, and Mr. Seyd's facts therefore have not the least reference to the conduct of the Mint since that year. Nor do they at all affect the good faith of the previous management. The art of assaying is a very ancient one, and the assayers of the old Mint Company performed it faithfully in the traditional manner. But the progress of chymical science showed that what had previously been esteemed pure gold was not perfectly pure. The analysis of the gold and its alloy had been imperfectly accomplished, and about the year 1851, Mr. Graham and Dr. Allen Miller brought the coinage up to its true fineness by the employment of more scientific methods. With these facts I happen to be familiar, owing to my former connexion with the Sydney branch of the Royal Mint.

The more recent reports of the Director of the United States' Mint contain an official table of the weight and fineness of foreign coins, prepared according to the law of the United States of the year 1857. On looking over these we find that up to the year 1863 the sovereign is quoted as follows:—

"England.—Pound or sovereign, new .. 916·5
Pound or sovereign, average .. 915·5"

But, beginning with the year 1864, we find:—

"England.—Pound or sovereign, new .. 916·5
Pound or sovereign, average .. 916·0"

The exact theoretical standard fineness of our coin is 916·66, and the American assayers certify that it comes within from one to two parts in 10,000 of the truth. I may

Mr. W. S. Jevons.

add, however, that when the question comes to these very small fractions it becomes purely a matter of opinion. The gold assay process even now does not admit of certain accuracy to one or two parts in 10,000. Under these circumstances we can surely rest satisfied with the fact that three of the most eminent English chymists are concerned in the production of the English sovereign, and that M. Stas, who is, I believe, esteemed above all other living chymists for the extreme accuracy of his analytical determinations, has certified the fineness of the British sovereign to be 916·66.

The French gold coin is quoted by the American assayers at 899 in their recent report in 1868, or just ten parts in 10,000 below the true standard. The Russian coin is quoted at 916, or about six parts in 10,000 too low. So much for the accuracy of Mr. Seyd's statement that "in reality the British gold coin falls much more below its standard fineness than French, American, and Russian coin."

Mr. Seyd, again, adduces figures to show that sovereigns cannot be profitably picked and melted in the way asserted by Mr. Lowe. Such arguments are not calculated to meet the fact that they are or have been so picked and melted; but I think it is not difficult to show how Mr. Seyd puts a completely wrong construction on his figures. If Mr. Seyd proves anything he proves that sovereigns cannot be profitably exported at all, and that, owing to the supposed want of fineness, and the costs of the operation, exportation must leave a loss. How is this to be reconciled with the fact that from 1858 to 1866 the acknowledged and registered exports of British gold coin averaged 4,300,000*l.* a year (*Report of Royal Commission on International Coinage,* p. 341), not including what is sent unregistered at the Custom-house, or what is first melted in London and then exported as bullion? In order that such large quantities of coin may be sent it must pay to send them, and it is of course the state of the foreign exchanges which enables the exporter to bear all the expenses and yet make a profit.

Now, the question which Mr. Seyd has not really touched is this :—When sovereigns are actually going to be exported is it profitable or not to pick out the heaviest? It is a secondary and unimportant question whether the expense of melting be incurred in this country or not, for it is universally allowed that at present, when our sovereigns are not current on the Continent, they there become mere bullion, and are bought and sold by weight. The real point, disentangled from irrelevant considerations, is this—Can the operation of weighing and picking out the heaviest sovereigns be profitably performed?

According to Mr. Seyd's own figures there will clearly be a profit. He supposes 20,000 sovereigns of an average weight of 123·531 grains each to be picked by weighing out of a mass of 100,000*l.*, the cost being as follows :— Weighing 100,000 sovereigns at 6*d.* per 500, 5*l.* ; interest at 5 per cent., 13*l.* 14*s.*—total 18*l.* 14*s.* Now, the excess of weight of the sovereigns above the standard weight (123·274 grains) is ·257 grain per sovereign, or in all 5,140 grains of standard gold, worth at 77*s.* 9*d.* per oz. 41*l.* 12*s.* 6*d.*

Subtracting the expenses, there remains a net profit on the operation of 22*l.* 18*s.* 6*d.*

It is by no means clear, however, that we ought to debit the operation with interest at 5 per cent., for money can often be borrowed for a few days at a very low rate of interest, and it is possible that the operation might sometimes be carried out upon sovereigns which are temporarily detained for some other cause. If we throw out of account this very doubtful item of interest, there remains a profit of 36*l.* 12*s.* 6*d.*

The reader will clearly understand that this is not the whole profit which may arise from remitting sovereigns abroad. It is merely the accessory and incidental profit which that bullion-broker will make who can carry out this picking operation. Mr. Seyd confuses the whole matter when he implies that the excess of weight of some sove-

Mr. W. S. Jevons.

reigns is not only to pay all the expenses, but is to be the motive for melting and exporting the coin. That sovereigns are exported to countries where they are bought and sold by weight cannot be doubted, and Mr. Seyd's own data, I repeat, show that when sovereigns are about to be exported it will pay to pick out the heaviest.

This practice of picking might, no doubt, be prevented by issuing none but sovereigns close to the standard weight, but this would increase the cost of coining. A larger proportion of blanks and coined sovereigns would have to be turned back and re-melted. The true remedy is so to fit the sovereign for currency abroad that it would be valued there as here, by tale, and not by weight. All motive for melting or picking would thus be done away with, because the gold would, abroad, as well as at home, be more valuable as coin than as bullion.

I wish to add to my last letter that though the reduction of the sovereign and the imposition of a Mint charge have been discussed in various quarters during several years past, the scheme stated by Mr. Lowe was first put forth with all its main features in Colonel Smith's work, entitled *Remarks on a Gold Currency for India*. This book was published early in 1868, and at the end is given "A Suggestion regarding International Coinage," in which the peculiar feature of the scheme—namely, the exact equivalence of the Mint charge and the gold subtracted from the sovereign—is clearly explained. This equivalence is the turning point of the whole matter, since it enables us to avoid altogether any disturbance of the standard of value.

I should be trifling with your readers' patience if I noticed again at any length the difference of opinion on an arithmetical point which still exists between Mr. Hubbard and myself. He demolished all my calculations by pointing out the fact (which, by the way, happened not to be the fact), that the first and third terms of a proportion were not of the same kind. In his latest utterance Mr. Hubbard says of me :—

"He retorted with a quibble about the Rule of Three, wholly irrelevant to the purpose, for it was to a given formula framed in the olden fashion, and not in that of Colenso, that I applied a criticism sanctioned by standard works on arithmetic, not the less accurate because they are of the last generation."

If I can extract any meaning from this almost unintelligible sentence, it is that Colenso's heresies are not confined to the numbers of the Old Testament, but that he has corrupted the principles of arithmetic accepted by a past generation, of which Mr. Hubbard is the living representative.

I am, Sir, yours obediently,

W. STANLEY JEVONS.

OWEN'S COLLEGE,
Sept. 7, 1869.

THE GOLD COINAGE.

(The Times, September 11, 1869.—To the Editor.)

SIR,—I have read Colonel Smith's letter of to-day most attentively, but I cannot, as he desires, revoke or qualify any expression I have used. I do distinctly deny that a Mint charge can add to the exchangeable value of a standard coin like the sovereign. I have endeavoured to substantiate my denial by argument, and I have challenged Colonel Smith to the test of a practical experiment. I regret that my argument has failed to convince him, and that my challenge has been declined; but I trust Colonel Smith will not think me uncourteous if I decline to follow him a second time over the whole field of controversy—"to fight the battle o'er again, again to slay the slain."

I am, Sir, your obedient servant,

J. G. HUBBARD.

ADDINGTON MANOR,
Sept. 9, 1869.

THE OBSERVER.

(September 12, 1869.)

A VERY ardent discussion has been carried on during some time in the columns of *The Times* with respect to our gold coinage. Mr. Hubbard, one of the Directors of the Bank of England, and Colonel Smith, late Master of the Mint at Calcutta, are the two principal disputants, although several other correspondents have entered into the field of controversy. Mr. Hubbard and Colonel Smith are agreed upon one point, viz., that the system of free coinage at present in operation should be done away with, and that a mintage charge or seigniory should be established, differing, however, as to what this should be. Before, however, entering into a discussion as to this difference, we have to request attention to the question as to whether a free coinage is not an advantage to the community fully compensating for the expense of a free mint.

Those in favour of a seigniory being imposed are always urging as a reason that this would prevent sovereigns being sent abroad instead of bullion during an adverse exchange. But, supposing that sovereigns are exported and reduced to bullion, their place is immediately supplied by more sovereigns coined by the Mint out of that bullion which would otherwise have been sent abroad. The whole disadvantage, then, of a free coinage reduces itself into the expenses of a Mint maintained by the State. Those expenses do not, we believe, amount to 20,000*l.* a year, and for such a *bagatelle* as this it is proposed to alter a system which has been in force for more than 200 years.

Sir Robert Peel used to define a pound sterling, or sovereign, to be a certain amount of gold bullion of a certain fineness, stamped by the State to certify its weight and quality. This is our standard coin and our measure of value. It is not a token having an artificial value given to it by an act of the Government. It is a piece of money having nothing more or less than the intrinsic value of the gold of which it is composed. It can be melted down and reduced to the original bullion out of which it was formed, and all bullion of the requisite fineness can be converted by the possessor into sovereigns without expense by a free mint. The sovereign is thus the mere identification of 113 grains of fine gold, and is a universal coin with which we can as easily buy claret in Bordeaux as whisky in Islay. We have no occasion for international coinage, our sovereign—held over the whole world in the highest estimation —being nothing more than a piece of bullion, can at once be compared with, and adjusted to, the coins of all nations.

One of the principal causes assigned, as we have already stated, for the imposition of a seigniorage is, that this would prevent exporting sovereigns instead of bullion. Professor Jevons, in a letter in *The Times* of last Friday, maintains this most elaborately. Now there is not the slightest occasion to send sovereigns out of the country when bullion is required; for the Bank has always in its cellars large amounts of bar or standard gold, which the exporter can have in place of sovereigns when bullion is required. But, says Mr. Jevons, the sovereigns are sent abroad to make profit of them. Those above the average weight are picked out and then melted down into a larger amount of fine gold than the standard weight. To this we have simply to reply, that, if a profit could be made by such a process—which we do not believe—why, in the name of common sense, should it not be carried on in London, without incurring the expense of the exportation, now that the law against melting the coin has been repealed? We perceive that Mr. Hubbard, Mr. Seyd, and all the other well-informed correspondents of *The Times*, characterize as utterly ridiculous and absurd the idea of sovereigns being sent abroad for the purpose of being melted into a larger amount of bullion than what they nominally contain. Still, Mr. Jevons, in his letter of last Friday, sticks to his point, and refers to the *Report of the Royal Commission on International*
  The Observer.

Coinage, p. 341, by which it is shown that a large amount of sovereigns are exported every year. Professor Jevons asserts that no sovereign is sent out except for the purpose of being melted down. Upon this assumption is based the whole argument about the practice of melting our gold coin. Had Mr. Jevons examined the tables he quotes with a little more care, he would have found that, while sovereigns are exported, large amounts are at the very same time re-imported. For instance, in the last year referred to—1866—4,007,089 *l.* were exported, while 4,053,723 *l.*, a larger amount of sovereigns, were re-imported. Does not this fact upset the whole theory of Mr. Jevons? Does it not prove that sovereigns are not exported for the purpose of being melted down? That when sent abroad in place of bullion, it is for circulation or other special objects; and that they are also carefully preserved as a coin in the highest estimation which will be readily received in every country.

Such is one great advantage of our free coinage. We shall now mention another. It is a notorious fact, that almost the whole bullion obtained from the gold fields comes first to England—not only from Australia, but from California and other regions. This arises from our free coinage, which makes it more advantageous to the importer to take his gold to England than to France, or other countries where a seigniorage is charged. Now gold is never brought to a country without a certain amount of goods being taken in exchange. We do not mean to say that all the gold brought to this country is exchanged for our manufactures, but a very considerable part is, and by this our trade and commerce is increased, and all owing to our free coinage.

We shall return to the subject next week, when we shall explain and comment upon the controversy now being carried on betwixt Mr. Hubbard and Colonel Smith.

THE GOLD COINAGE.

(The Times, September 13, 1869.—To the Editor.)

SIR,—The controversy respecting the proposed new gold coinage has not elicited much information to the general public. Assertions without proof have been met by denials with very little argument, and even the terms " standard " and " value " appear to be used with different meanings by the two opposite parties. Many details having little or no connexion with the real question at issue have also been introduced, and tend much to embarrass the inquiry. The ostensible purport of the plan is to give an additional source of revenue to the Exchequer, and also to prevent this country being called upon to coin gratis the gold which it is not intended should be used for our own wants. Its real object, however, seems to be the introduction of the international coinage scheme.

It is time, therefore, that we should dismiss collateral points, and direct our attention exclusively to the system itself. Whenever a new plan is proposed, which is supported by a long chain of reasoning, based on principles which are not universally accepted, and expressed in terms which are not received in the same sense by the opposite parties, it would appear that the easiest mode to come to a decision on its merits would be to try it: that is, to take some acknowledged facts and figures, and work them out by both plans; and then compare the results.

The main arguments in favour of obtaining by this plan an admission into the International Coinage League may be briefly comprised in the following four points:—

1. The Mint par between England and France is 1l. sterling = 25f. 22½c., meaning that when coined strictly according to the Mint regulations these two amounts of English and French money contain exactly the same quantities of pure gold.

Most of your correspondents assume that practically the *Par.*

pound sterling is worth 25f. 20c., which is sufficiently near the truth.

2. If one grain of gold is abstracted from each sovereign, this coin becomes exactly equal in value to 25f., and therefore abroad it would be placed on a par with the coinages of France, Belgium, Switzerland, and Italy.

3. The new and depreciated coin can be made by the Legislature to pass at home for the full value of the old sovereign. This, when expressed in the terms of the currency school, means that a seigniorage imposed by law becomes up to its amount an integral part of the value of the coin.

4. Our entry by this means into the League would be attended with great advantages to commerce and convenience to travellers.

The first two terms may be accepted as being mere matters of fact. The third is denied *in toto*, and the fourth is at present very doubtful, and is still open to discussion.

There is, however, some ground of complaint against the manner in which this controversy has been hitherto carried on. Many of the gentlemen who have engaged in the discussion (some illustrious for their talents and position) have addressed the public as if every reader was as well acquainted with foreign weights and exchanges as themselves; whereas most of the persons who have to run the chance of the venture, should the plan ever be adopted, cannot follow their reasoning from inability to comprehend the terms in which it is expressed.

So far as regards the general reader, this obscurity has existed from the very commencement. What per-centage of our fundholders has a definite idea of the results of the proposal that one grain of gold is in future to be abstracted from our sovereign? And how many of them know that it means an extra income-tax of 2d. in the pound imposed on them, should the third proposition, given above, turn out to be false?

The old mode of defining the coinage of gold in this

country appears to be more easily comprehended than the one now adopted of stating the weight of the sovereign in grains. By law, 40 lbs. troy weight of gold of the standard of 11-12ths fine and 1-12th alloy, was ordered to be coined into 1,869 sovereigns. The reason of this peculiarly odd number of pieces being coined out of a definite number of ounces has more of an antiquarian than practical interest, and need not be referred to here. But it may perhaps be incidentally remarked that this number has been found very difficult to remember by persons not accustomed to bullion calculations. Hereafter this trouble will be saved to them, as they have in future only to recollect that the figures 1,869 not only represent the number of sovereigns which are by law to be coined out of 40 lbs. of gold, but they also indicate the exact year when an English Chancellor of the Exchequer proposed to depreciate the British standard of value.

Hence, if the 40 lbs. or 480 ounces of bullion are reduced into grains, and divided by 1,869, we obtain 123·274 grains, being the true weight each sovereign should have when issued, and which explains why this odd amount of grains is used.

We also derive from this the meaning of our terms " legal standard of value," which is that one sovereign of the proper weight is the 1-1869th part of 480 troy ounces of gold of English standard fineness.

If, on the contrary, we divide 1,869 sovereigns by 480 ounces, from which they are made, we obtain 3·89375 $l.$ (3$l.$ 17$s.$ 10½$d.$) as the value of one ounce, and which is commonly called the Mint price per ounce.

There appears to be a difference of opinion respecting the actual mode by which the deduction from the sovereign is proposed to be made; some supposing that one grain standard gold is to be taken away; others assuming that one grain pure is to be abstracted. The value of the first would be a small fraction below 2$d.$, and the other a trifle above that sum. From the explanation of the plan in your
Par.

paper of the 9th of August, it would seem that the proposal is to coin sovereigns of the present standard of fineness, but weighing only 122¼ grains each, instead of 123·274 grains, as at present. This would leave the Chancellor a gain of 1·024 grain of standard gold, the value of which is as nearly as possible 2d. Therefore, this is also the loss in intrinsic value on each sovereign, and which is rather more than 8-10ths per cent.

The mode of operation would therefore be that every 480 ounces of standard gold would hereafter be coined into pieces weighing each 122¼ grains, of which there would consequently be produced 1,884·662, or about 1,884⅔. Of these the Mint would return to the owner of the bullion the former number of pieces—that is, 1,869—and retain 15⅔ pieces for gross profit to pay for coinage, &c. The contemptible 2d. in the pound thus assumes the form of 8l. abstracted from every 1,000l.

But is this a loss to the public? And the answer depends on the solution of the question implied in the third proposition. Does the imposition of a seigniorage of the description proposed by the new plan add the value of itself to the intrinsic worth of the 122 grains left in the coin, so as to bring this new one up to the same value at home as the old one of 123 grains?

Before entering on the discussion of the above proposition, which is, in fact, the main point at issue, it is necessary to quote a paragraph from the letter of Mr. J. G. Hubbard, inserted in your paper of the 1st of September :—

"The standard, whatever it be, cannot and must not be tampered with by degrading either the quantity or the quality of the gold; and, above all, we must avoid the ridiculous imposture of using old names for new things; of making a coin different from its former self, and calling it what it once had been."

Please observe that the strong language in the latter part of this extract comes from a man of deservedly high authority in these matters. Although cordially agreeing with him in the purport of the whole of the above paragraph, it would not have been becoming in an unknown individual like myself to have put the sentiment forward in so plain a manner. I can only, therefore, thank Mr. Hubbard for having endorsed his respected name to this explicit declaration of the truth. The words "new" and "old" have been so constantly alternating throughout this discussion, that it has become troublesome to read articles on the subject. The promoters of the plan having as yet abstained from christening their prodigy, which it was their duty to have done before this time, the writer would respectfully suggest that, as the intrinsic value of our coin is proposed to be lowered by 1 grain of gold, the new coin which is to take its place should be called a "Lowe." The word, of course, would be used by the proposer to express the inferiority of the coin when compared with the sovereign; but it might also be employed with great propriety by the opposite party, as a graceful tribute to their illustrious convert. By adopting this plan the parties on both sides of this controversy will be at least able to understand each other, which it is sometimes very difficult to do at present.

It is necessary before further investigating the subject to repeat a few facts on a point which has already been more fully explained by one of your correspondents. The French Mint coins from one kilogramme of gold of their standard fineness (9-10ths pure) an amount of coins of 20f., 10f., or 5f. each, as the case may be, which, collectively, are of the value of 3,100f.; but they retain 6·70f. for mintage, and return only 3,093·30f. to the owner of the bullion. Hence, if a man has one kilogramme of gold of the French standard of purity and wishes to dispose of it, he obtains from the purchaser only 3,093·30f., the amount that he would have received had he taken it to the Mint to be coined. This is, therefore, called the tariff rate for gold of the French standard.

There is a separate tariff rate in the French bullion market for each different fineness of gold.

Par.

In the French Mint the charge for coinage is, therefore, rather more than 2-10ths per cent., and the additional loss for interest when a delay occurs in the delivery need not here be taken into account. This delay is short and does not frequently occur, while here it is certain and of longer duration, so that on this point the advantage is in favour of dealing with the French Mint.

It appears singular that while the French system of mintage is so constantly held up as an object for our imitation, the principal admirers of it should propose a plan which is completely opposed to it on two main points. They recommend a seigniorage of 8-10ths per cent. instead of a brassage of 2-10ths per cent., thus making the English Mint levy four times the amount the French one does. And they deduct this enhanced charge from the weight of the coin, instead of making the owner of the bullion pay it. A moment's consideration will, however, give the explanation of this apparent paradox. The pretended advantage to the Treasury is the bait thrown out; the hook they want the Chancellor to swallow is the reduction of one grain from each sovereign, and thus bring down its value to 25 f., and complete their *beau ideal* of an international coinage.

With the *data* we now have, let us fix our attention on some particular parcel of exactly 480 ounces troy of foreign gold and investigate the possibility of our coinage being kept up under the new system.

In order to simplify our future calculations, we will assume that these 480 ounces are exactly of the English standard of purity. And for the same reason we will concede that during the time of our experiments with this gold the international coinage is a complete success, and the exchange between London and Paris is at par. Therefore, one "Lowe" here will purchase a sight bill on Paris for 25 francs; and conversely, 25 francs there will purchase a sight bill on London for one "Lowe." If it is desired, we will also concede that the English and French coins pass at the same value indifferently in the two countries.

As a starting-point to be used in our future comparisons we must, therefore, remember that under the present arrangements of the English and French Mints,—

1. 480 oz. of English standard gold would produce 1,869 sovereigns if coined here;

2. The same gold coined in Paris would yield about 47,040 f.

It is useless to give the details of the calculation by which this last result is obtained. To practical men like your correspondent, Mr. E. Seyd, the writer has no fact to communicate respecting the ratio of ounces to kilogrammes, or the tariff rate of gold of the British standard, which they do not already know, and to your other readers the calculations would be but an unmeaning mass of figures. Any one may, however, easily convince himself that the above amount of francs is not grossly untrue, by considering that these 480 ounces are here coined into 1,869 sovereigns, and that at the very moderate estimate of 25 f. 17 c. per pound sterling they will produce 47,042 f. 73 c., which he can prove for himself by merely multiplying the figures.

We are now in a position to examine how the matter would stand under the proposed new regulations in this country, and we will first take the case when the proceeds of the gold sent to Europe are intended to be used in France.

If the 480 ounces are sent direct to Paris, the proceeds will be, as before stated, about 47,040 f., because the French Mint will not have altered their regulations. But if it is first sent to London and sold to our Mint the delivery of 480 ounces will result in the receipt by the importers of 1,869 Lowes, which amount remitted to Paris at sight at the current rate of 25 f. per Lowe, or drawn against from Paris at the same rate, would give only 46,725 f., so that there is a loss to the shipper of about 315 f. or above 6-10ths per cent., which is the difference between 8-10ths and 2-10ths, the two Mint charges. The Chancellor of the Exchequer may, therefore, be congratulated that he will be

Par.

no longer obliged to coin the gold free of charge which is intended for exportation to the Continent. But we must at the same time offer him our condolence for the loss of the profit which he fondly imagined would under the new plan result from this employment of his services.

Next let it be assumed that the gold is sent to Europe for the purpose of the proceeds being employed in England. If the 480 oz. are sent direct here and coined they produce, as before, 1,869 Lowes. But, if first sent to Paris, these 480 ounces yield, as above mentioned, 47,040 f., which when transferred here, either by draught from London or remittance from Paris at the par exchange of 25 f. per Lowe, will give in London rather more than 1,881 Lowes. The difference of upwards of 12 Lowes is therefore a saving of more than 6-10ths per cent. in favour of the plan of sending the gold to France for coinage.

The alternative of forwarding the actual coined gold either way is here purposely left out of the question, because the international coinage system is founded mainly on the idea that we shall by its means get rid of the frequent alterations in the exchanges; and even if this expectation should prove false the gain of 6-10ths per cent. on the coinage is amply sufficient to pay the cost of transport and leave a profit.

Whenever, therefore, it was requisite to coin fresh money for home use, the Bank (acting in this case for the Government) must go into the market and purchase gold at the lowest rate at which it was obtainable. The Chancellor, in his anxiety to obtain the 8-10ths per cent. which were promised to him by the promoters of the plan, appears to have forgotten that his neighbour across the Channel offers to perform the work at one-fourth of the charge, and may, therefore, be reasonably expected to carry off all the business. Must the success of this wonderful scheme depend upon the chance of the French also altering their mode of coinage by changing their present brassage of about 2-10ths per cent. into a seigniorage of about 8-10ths per cent.?

Pray observe that this hitch in the arrangement cannot be corrected by clipping the French coin of part of its present contents, as the 25 f. in gold would not then be equal in value to the Lowe; and thus if we by these means get into the League the French would go out of it.

Three-fourths of the Chancellor's golden dreams of a gross profit of 8-10ths per cent. obtainable by a seigniorage have thus suddenly vanished, and the very utmost that he can hope to obtain is a brassage of 2-10ths per cent., like the French, to pay for the cost of coinage.

The difficulties which the Government will have to contend with, even in converting the present into the new currency, are based upon the same principles, and will be referred to in the next letter, which will follow up the depreciation of the "Lowe" as compared with the sovereign, even in the home market.

Your obedient servant,

EXCHANGE BUILDINGS,   PAR.
Sept. 9, 1869.

P.S.—The writer having thus coined a name for the new currency (and without any charge for seigniorage) trusts that a sense of justice will induce the promoters of the new plan to do the same for the proposed 25-franc piece. The name of any foreigner who has distinguished himself on their side of the argument would probably be the best; but this is, of course, left entirely to themselves.

GOLD COINAGE.
(The Times, September 14, 1869.—To the Editor.)

SIR,—In the last letter it was shown that it was impossible under the proposed new plan that our Mint could obtain foreign gold to keep up the currency, and yet retain at the same time the full 8-10ths per cent. profit which was *Par.*

expected, as the bullion would go in preference to France, where it could be coined at an expense to the owner of only 2-10ths per cent. A similar difficulty, and arising from the same cause, would be experienced in converting our present stock of sovereigns into Lowes. Those romantic retreats for "sifting" sovereigns which have been alluded to by the Chancellor or his advisers, might then be employed in dividing the coins into those which would pay the cost of sending over to be coined at 2-10ths per cent., and those, if any, which would not bear the charges of transport.

This impossibility of keeping up our gold currency has been shown by employing the actual state of our present Mint regulations as our standard, and this plan is attended with peculiar advantages in making the required comparisons between the old and new systems. The 40 lbs. of bullion is the smallest weight which can be coined, under present regulations, into a definite number of sovereigns, without employing fractional parts either in the quantity of bullion used or the number of pieces produced. This forms, therefore, the most convenient integer of weight which can be used in showing the relative results of the two methods.

On the most general principles, however, the thing can be proved to be impracticable, if attempted to be carried out on the terms proposed. By the projected plan it is necessary, if we are to participate in the supposed benefits of the International Coinage League, that the French and English coins should be of exactly the same intrinsic value, in order that they circulate on a par with each other in the commerce of the world. The only difference between a Lowe and a French 25-franc piece should be in their external ornaments and inscriptions. But neither England nor France are producers of gold, and both must depend for their necessary supplies for their materials to coin from on the bullion sent to them from abroad. The two countries are such near neighbours, that the cost of sending gold from distant sources of production may be considered as almost, if not quite, the same. Therefore, if England charges 8-10ths per cent. for manufacturing a Lowe, and France will make their 25-franc piece (which is of exactly the same value) for the small charge of 2-10ths per cent., it scarcely requires an appeal to the wisdom of Solomon to decide which of the two will monopolize the whole trade.

The reasoning, therefore, of the promoters of the scheme is of the most extraordinary description. They start with the assertion that, from the circumstance of this country coining *gratis*, while other continental nations make a charge, a very large quantity of bullion is sent here for coinage which is not wanted, nor is intended for our home use. Suppose this granted. It would be a very good argument to support the expediency of imposing a brassage of about 2-10ths per cent., to be levied in the French mode, and thus taking away the inducement for gold not wanted here being sent for coinage. But this would not suit the plans of the International Coinage Committee: for their purpose 8-10ths per cent. must be abstracted from our coin to make it equal to the 25-franc piece, and thus, in their eager pursuit of the end they have in view, they have entirely lost sight of the fact that their mode would prevent gold coming here at all.

Let us now consider what bearing these facts have on the dogma laid down by the promoters of the new plan, that the seigniorage may be considered as so much added to the value of a coin, at least so far as regards its circulation at home. We have taken gold, the foreign material from which our coins are made, and find that its present price in the market is 3*l*. 17*s*. 9*d*. per ounce when paid for in sovereigns, but that this price would require to be increased by upwards of 6-10ths per cent. if paid for in Lowes; and without this additional charge not an ounce could be procured for coinage. Let us next take the case of the purchase of a cargo of corn in France for importation into England, the price for which in France is exactly 50,000 f. The debtor in England would now be able to cancel the obligation by
Par.

buying and remitting a bill for 50,000 f., which, at the average exchange of 25 f. 20 c. per pound sterling, would cost him about 1,984 *l*. Under the new *régime*, the debt expressed in foreign money would be the same as before; but when the Lowe is exactly worth 25 f., the importer would have to expend 2,000 Lowes to obtain a bill for 50,000 f. The difference of 16 between 1,984 and 2,000, or about 8-10ths per cent., is the exact measure of the depreciation of the new coin in this case. The Lowe "does not go so far" in purchasing power as the sovereign, and hence 16 more coins are required to liquidate the same debt.

It may be here objected that the 50,000 f. due for the corn is a foreign debt in payment of which the Lowe only exerts its intrinsic or weight value; but the grain is intended for use here, and how does the consumer pay for it? Supposing, for the sake of avoiding unnecessary calculations, that the importer was willing in both cases to sell to the miller at cost price. The corn he imported this year he must sell for 1,984 sovereigns, the exact amount he paid for it. Next year, if the new plan were in operation, he would acquit the same debt of 50,000 f. by the payment of 2,000 Lowes; and must, consequently, in order to sell without loss, receive from the miller 2,000 Lowes. The consumer would then find to his cost that, though all the external conditions of the market remain the same, he has to expend 16 more Lowes than he did in sovereigns to obtain the same quantity of goods. Is not the coinage affected in value even in the home market?

The above case is selected because it refers only to the two coinages at present under discussion—the French and English; but the same inevitable result must ensue whatever foreign produce we select which is required for our home manufactures. Take the instance of the cotton-spinners and weavers. Under the circumstances now existing, the Mint par between England and America, deduced as in other cases from the pure gold in the two coinages, is about $109\frac{1}{2}$ per cent. when expressed according to the usual mode of quoting the exchanges between the two countries. The commercial exchange varies above and below this according to supply and demand for bills, but not to any considerable degree, because if much above, gold is sent here, and if much below, gold is sent from here. With the new coinage now proposed for this country the par would be about 108⅝ per cent., and this diminished par would be the regulator of the course of exchange. Here, again, we have the irrepressible 8-10ths per cent. loss starting up against us. The manufacturer, in his turn, will find that his Lowes do not go so far as the old sovereigns. With the same number of cents per lb. as the price in New Orleans, and, consequently, the same debt to extinguish, the English-man will be drawn upon from America for more Lowes than is now the case with sovereigns. He must, therefore, raise the price expressed in Lowes of the goods he produces, and thus again consumers will awake to the conviction that abstracting one grain of gold from our coinage really makes a Lowe 8-10ths per cent. less in purchasing power as compared with a sovereign even in the home market.

It thus appears evident that for all articles which we do not produce (gold, cotton, tobacco, &c.), and also for those things of which we do not always produce a sufficient quantity for our consumption (wheat, &c.), the Lowe will not have, even when the goods are dealt in here, the same purchasing power as is possessed by the present coin called a sovereign. Or, in other words, we must expend more Lowes than we did sovereigns to obtain possession of the same quantity of any commodity we want. This is what has hitherto been called a depreciation of the coinage, and if even a more pleasing name should be invented, the unpleasant fact will remain.

Nor will the effect stop here. Suppose a man whose business it is to sell or make up a strictly English production. Should he in his innocence implicitly believe the Chancellor, and, therefore, charge for his goods the same number of Lowes as he now does of sovereigns, he, also,
Par.

will find when he wants to employ the money he has received in the purchase of cotton goods, tobacco, or almost anything that can be mentioned, that his Lowes have lost 8-10ths per cent. of their buying power. Annuitants and every one with a fixed income will then discover that they have paid very dearly for the facilities supposed to be in store for tourists, and those whose business it is to make exchange calculations.

And this brings us to the consideration of the fourth proposition—viz., whether there is any real or considerable advantage to the trader or the traveller in adopting the international coinage. This has been purposely left to the last, as being by far of less importance than the question of whether lowering our standard does or does not impair its purchasing powers even when used at home.

Your obedient servant,
PAR.

EXCHANGE BUILDINGS,
Sept. 13, 1869.

GOLD COINAGE.
(The Times, September 14, 1869.—To the Editor.)

SIR,—Sir John Herschel, in the postscript to his letter of the 30th of August, says that in the parcels of sovereigns assayed by Dr. Miller there "may have been many never issued by the Mint at all, and may have owed their lightness to the fraudulent use of inferior gold." It is not at all likely that such base coin should escape detection at the Bank of England or elsewhere. The first test is that of weight; the coin must weigh near to 122 grains, and the specific gravity of standard gold taken at 18·4, it follows that if any greater quantity than two carats of alloy—say copper of the specific gravity of 9—be used, the weight must either be reduced, or the thickness of the coin must be increased.

Half-gold and half-copper would thus either weigh 91 grains, or the piece must be more than one-third thicker; three parts gold and one part of copper would give a specific gravity of 16·7, equal to 111 grains, or 1-10th thicker. In *Mr. E. Seyd.*

order to cause a worseness of 2 per mille in any parcel of coin, it is necessary that 12 pieces of 750 fine should be present in the 1,000; of 850 fine, 30 such base coins are necessary. Is it at all likely that either of these descriptions of base pieces should have escaped the attention of the examiners at the Bank who returned the parcel to Messrs. Sillar and Co. as light coin? I presume Sir John Herschel only means that this particular parcel of sovereigns was mixed with bad coins, for if he means that a private mint is actually at work systematically manufacturing inferior pounds, it would appear that at 750 fine there must be about one million, and at 850 fine there must be three millions of such undetected pieces in circulation in order to account for the habitual worseness of bars melted from light coin.

Attempts are now and then made to pass inferior coins, but they are instantly detected by the laws of specific weight, independently of the forged impression and other indications. Coins have been made of platina gilt, this metal being heavier than gold. They are easily found out by their size; and as platina does not melt, it cannot possibly influence the fineness of a bar made from coin.

Turning now to Mr. Jevons's letter of the 7th inst., I find that he states—"Mr. Seyd himself calculates the value of the new British sovereign at 916." On page 390 of the book alluded to I give this as the tariff rate in France, not as the result of my calculation; in other parts of the book I show that British coin is actually below this rate. Mr. Jevons's quotation from the American assays, showing an average of $915\frac{1}{2}$ up to 1852, furnishes evidence that the tariff rates of other nations are no reliable guide, and altogether there is a curious contrast between the quotation made by "Monetarius," who, in his letter of the 30th of August, says that in 1837 the British coin was found up to the mark, and that furnished from the same authority by Mr. Jevons saying that up to 1852 the average was $915\frac{1}{4}$. It is clear that such contradictory evidence is not reliable.

Mr. E. Seyd.

I cannot understand why Mr. Jevons should seek for evidence of this kind abroad, when here, in England, where the sovereign is born, lives, and dies, there must be at hand far more abundant and reliable testimony than can be obtained elsewhere, and in so serious a question as this our home evidence must outweigh everything else. I have indicated in a previous letter how this can be done. I am further prepared to point out a complete plan of investigation, with the details of which *The Times* need not be troubled. And if this plan be followed out, I am also quite prepared to concede beforehand that since the abolition of the Mint Company and under the management of the late and the present Master of the Mint the coinage has much improved. The issues made since then cannot, however, compensate for the general want of fineness in the bulk of our coinage; in the parcels, for instance, usually melted down there are always a great many pieces of issues since 1851, and yet the fineness remains much inferior.

The tone of Sir John Herschel's and Mr. Jevons's letters seems to imply that I meant to convey insinuations unfavourable to the Mint Master. I have no such intention; my object is merely that of bringing before the public the real state of the case, and in so doing I have faithfully adhered to figures, while my opponents have recourse to speculations, without giving figures. Mr. Jevons says:—

"The reader will clearly understand that this is not the whole profit which may arise from remitting sovereigns abroad. It is merely the accessory and incidental profit which that bullion broker will make who can carry out this picking operation. Mr. Seyd confuses the whole matter when he implies that the excess of weight of some sovereigns is not only to pay all the expenses, but is to be the motive for melting and exporting the coin," &c.

I do not think that any political economist, however high his standing may be, has the right to call upon his readers "clearly to understand" such a proposition, without at the same time making it clear by figures and by facts. What are these other profits? With the exception of the refining of a few Australian sovereigns holding silver, and the natural course of exchange matters, as dictated by the balance of trade, what are the extra profits alluded to? Can Mr. Jevons answer this question? The fact is that no commodity is less liable to speculation and to mysterious dealings than gold. Its value can be ascertained with mathematical precision, and persons only unable to fully comprehend the pure logic and the unfailing arithmetic of exchange matters can have the hardihood to bring forth such statements without figures.

I recommend to Mr. Jevons the following experiment:— Let him take 100,000 sovereigns of the late issues; let him pick out the heavy pieces, without making any charge for time or for interest; let them be melted here and disposed of as he thinks best. Or let them be sent to Brussels to be realized there; the moment is favourable, because the exchange is in favour of Belgium. Mr. Jevons's evidence respecting the melting establishment in Brussels is, no doubt, complete enough to enable him to find out how the coins are there realized; and if he should find it impracticable actually to make an experiment of this kind, then let him, for the information of the British public, calculate the transaction out in such a form as to show the complete result. I have set him the example, and it is only fair that he should accept my challenge. If he is unable to do this in a proper form, subject to true criticism, he is clearly not justified in maintaining his statements.

The question might well be asked, why does not Mr. Lowe or Mr. Jevons furnish the public with the whole evidence respecting the Brussels melting establishment? Do they hesitate to do so because it will give offence to the operators engaged in the practice? Surely, about such a matter as this, the groundwork for an important State measure, it is desirable that no mystery should be maintained.

I have only just returned from abroad, and beg your permission to answer other matters in a subsequent letter.

I am, Sir, your obedient servant,

1A, PRINCES STREET, BANK,   ERNEST SEYD.
Sept. 13, 1869.

GOLD COINAGE.

(The Times, September 14, 1869.—To the Editor.)

Sir,—After the voluminous correspondence on this subject, I will only venture upon a few observations which my experience in the bullion business of over 20 years may warrant.

Mr. Jevons states that "the export of British gold coin averaged 4,300,000*l.* a year from 1858 to 1866." This statement is likely to mislead your readers into the belief that these sovereigns have all been melted, when the fact is that large amounts of sovereigns are retained in foreign mints and national banks, and returned to this country when the exchange alters sufficiently to render the operation profitable. Large quantities of sovereigns have been received from America and paid into the Liverpool branch of the Bank of England; also English sovereigns have often been returned from Australia and Brazils, while the Banks of Holland and Belgium do not melt the sovereigns they buy, but re-sell them when the exchange proves favourable.

It is also necessary to consider that sovereigns are required for circulation in our Colonies, and that the exports to Ceylon are in dragon sovereigns, which are too light for home circulation, and even in India it is doubtful if any large proportion of the sovereigns we export is melted. It is true that the bulk of the arrivals of Australian sovereigns is melted down for refining purposes, but that concerns the Australian Mints, and is occasioned by the silver being left in the coins, owing to the absence of sufficient refining facilities in Australia. If you make all these deductions, the statement made by the Chancellor of the Exchequer that sovereigns are largely exported will be found to be erroneous. With the exception of exports to countries such as Turkey, Brazils, and occasionally to Russia, where the Mints may find it more convenient to

Bullionist.

coin from our sovereigns (their standard being the same as our own) than to alloy bar gold, I maintain that for bullion purposes it is always more profitable to export bar gold. I do not dispute that Mr. Jevons's statement may be correct in theory, that it might pay to pick out very heavy sovereigns; but in practice it is not done, as when sovereigns are exported they are simply drawn from the Bank of England, and, the notice being generally short, the delay necessary for the selection of very heavy sovereigns would not be obtainable, or would risk the operation being forestalled by other shippers.

There can be little doubt that a seigniorage would be preferable to a reduction in the weight of the coin; the former would simply be a question of revenue, and would only affect the price of imported gold. The Bank of England would no doubt lose business by being unable to buy bar gold at the present price—3l. 17s. 9d.; while importers would hold over for the chance of selling to exporters. If the weight of the sovereign should be reduced and the Bank continue to sell bar gold at 3l. 17s. 10$\frac{1}{2}d$., of course gold bars would be used to pay the balances due to foreign countries, and they would be one standard of value. If bar gold could not be obtainable at the Bank at the present price, violent fluctuations in the exchanges would result. For example, the French exchange cannot approach 25f. per pound without its being checked by gold exports, and cannot exceed 25f. 35c. without the reverse operation—viz., imports of gold from France—being resorted to. With sovereigns of diminished weight, say to the extent of 1 per cent., the range would be from 24f. 80c. to 25f. 35c. (over 2 per cent. variation between London and Paris), while sudden changes would be caused by arrivals of gold suitable for export. There is another argument against the proposed reduction in weight. Our standard being 916·6, the gold is softer than the usual quality of gold used abroad, and wears sooner. At present there are large quantities of sovereigns in circulation which would be cut at the Bank.

Bullionist.

The loss of 3*d*. to 4*d*. each entailed by that process keeps large sums from the Bank. What, then, would be the result of an increased loss on cut sovereigns—say, of 6*d*. each? It is quite impossible to distinguish by sight a sovereign which will not turn the scale from one that will; yet the penalty of presenting such light sovereigns at the Bank would be considerable. It has been stated that if a thousand sovereigns be taken from one department of the Bank and paid into another, there is a possibility of a few being cut, no doubt through some fault in the weighing machines. In no other country is such a loss imposed upon the public as in this, and in consequence a large amount in sovereigns is held by banks, even when the stock of gold at the Bank of England is reduced to a dangerous point. It would be a useful alteration to assimilate our standard to that of France, America, and many other countries—viz., nine-tenths fine. The weight of the sovereign could be increased so as to contain the same quantity of pure gold. The only argument advanced in favour of reducing the weight of our gold coin is the possibility of making our sovereign pass for 25 francs. This is a very questionable advantage. The traveller would find a small advantage if he carried English gold with him, but bank-notes and circular-notes would often be at a discount, as at present Belgian notes or bills lose in Paris from $\frac{1}{4}$ to $\frac{1}{2}$ per cent., although their gold is current in France.

I am, &c.,

Sept. 11, 1869.   BULLIONIST.

THE SOVEREIGN.
(The Times, September 16, 1869.—To the Editor.)

SIR,—As one of the Royal Commissioners, I have naturally given much attention to the correspondence which has appeared in your columns on the above subject, and though I do not wish to discuss the advisability of
Sir J. Lubbock.

charging a mintage, still, as I do not quite agree with any of your correspondents, I should be glad to say a few words on the effect of such a charge if made.

At present each ounce of bullion is coined into $3l.\ 17s.\ 10\frac{1}{2}d$. No charge is made for doing so, and any one taking bullion to the Mint will receive back the same amount of gold in the form of coin; but practically, as he would have to wait some time before receiving the coin, the holder of the bullion prefers to sell his commodity to the Bank at the slightly lower rate of $3l.\ 17s.\ 9d.$, because he calculates that the loss of interest would amount to more than the $1\frac{1}{2}d$.

Under ordinary circumstances the value of a manufactured article is that of the raw material *plus* the expense of manufacture; but in the case of the pound sterling (if we leave out of consideration the trifling difference of $1\frac{1}{2}d$.) we have the anomaly of a manufactured article which is worth no more than the raw material of which it is composed; this is due to the fact that Government bears the expense of the manufacture, and hence I should not say, with some of your correspondents, that a mintage raises the value of the sovereign, but rather that the absence of any charge for mintage depresses the value of the coin, and prevents it from being worth more than the same weight of bullion.

To assert that a coin cannot be worth more than the bullion contained in it is practically to deny the advantage of a coinage, to assert that a manufactured article cannot be worth more than the raw material of which it is composed, and to ignore the fact that there is actually a difference in value of $1\frac{1}{2}d$. an ounce, which, though small, is sufficient to establish the principle.

Suppose the Government undertook to make shoes gratis. Shoes would be worth no more than shoe leather, and if subsequently the Government imposed a charge of 1 per cent. for manufacture, shoes would become worth 1 per cent. more than before.

Sir J. Lubbock.

So it is with coin: as long as Government coins gratis, coin and bullion will be of equal value; if Government charge 1 per cent. for coining, coin will become one per cent. more valuable than bullion.

It is surely incredible that the charge of a mintage should produce no effect on the value of the coin.

By the conditions of the case, if a mintage of 1 per cent. be imposed, new sovereigns will only be obtainable at a cost of 1 per cent. higher than before; and certainly no one will pay the Mint 1 per cent. for coining bullion, unless the coins thus obtained are worth as much as the bullion given for them; hence a mintage must either raise the value of the coin or put a stop to coinage altogether.

On the other hand, if a mintage of 1 per cent. is charged, and 1 per cent. of gold is deducted from the sovereign, these two charges will counterbalance one another, and the value of the sovereign will, in my opinion, be the same as it is now.

I thoroughly concur in all that has been said as to the importance of maintaining public faith and the integrity of the pound sterling, but, while we must be careful not to cheat creditors by lowering the value of the pound, we must, on the other hand, be equally careful not to cheat debtors by raising it, and it seems to me clear that if a mintage of 1 per cent. be imposed, and all other circumstances left as at present, we shall raise the value of the sovereign to that extent, compel every debtor to pay one per cent. more than he contracted for, and add 8,000,000*l*. to the National Debt.

It is surely a curious circumstance that on one of the simplest possible questions of Political Economy we should have on one side such high practical authorities as Sir J. Herschel, Mr. Hubbard, and Mr. Hankey, and on the other Adam Smith, Ricardo, John Stuart Mill, Colonel Smith, Dr. Farr, and Mr. Lowe.

I am, Sir, your obedient servant,

15, LOMBARD STREET.   JOHN LUBBOCK.

THE SOVEREIGN.

(The Times, September 16, 1869.—To the Editor.)

SIR,—In the previous letters it was proved that the third proposition put forward by the promoters of the new system was not true—that is, it was shown that a seigniorage of the description proposed by the new plan did not add its own amount to the intrinsic worth of the coin, even when employed in purchases at home. It was further argued that if even the benefits arising from entering into the League were a sufficient inducement to us to undergo the mere temporary inconveniences always attending a change, some other method must be adopted which should insure our obtaining a proper supply of gold when we required it.

The question, therefore, remaining for discussion is the expediency of making the change, if an honourable mode of doing it were hereafter to be pointed out. One inevitable inconvenience would be the future rise of nearly one per cent. in all commodities, and this is certainly a great one.

Now the benefits and conveniences promised by the new system may be divided into three classes:—

1. The cessation of foreign exchange quotations, and the calculations consequent on them, by the abolition of which great benefits are expected to be derived by the trading community.

2. The convenience and diminution of expense to travellers.

3. The total, or nearly total, cessation of exports of gold to restore the balance of trade.

The actual calculations themselves—that is, the reduction of a certain amount of pounds sterling into their equivalent in francs and cents at a given exchange, or its opposite, francs into pounds—appear to the writer to offer no greater difficulties than in finding out the value of so
Par.

many tons, hundredweights, quarters, and pounds, at a specified price per ton, being both performed by the same well-known rules of common arithmetic. Neither is it supposed, even if the extra difficulty really existed, that it would be thought of much account by the so-called friends of the manufacturer and trader; first, because this labour is performed in most cases by the regular dealers in bills, and not by the makers of them; and, secondly, because these dealers are looked upon with suspicion by the trader in goods, it being supposed that, by the mysterious nature of the exchange quotations, an unfair profit is made out of the sale of foreign bills. The extreme competition now existing among these dealers is an effectual answer to this absurd supposition.

The variations constantly occurring here in foreign exchange quotations arise mainly from three causes:—

1. The different degrees of mercantile credit accorded by the purchasers to the names already on the bills as drawers or endorsers.

2. The different dates at which the bills become due.

3. The variations in supply and demand of bills on any particular place which occur from day to day.

The first case may be dismissed in very few words. It is based on precisely the same principles as prevail in the money market when sterling inland bills are required to be discounted. Bills bearing the acceptances of some few first-rate houses are discounted generally rather under the Bank rate. Others of not such good credit can only be parted with at or above this rate. There must be a similar mode of expressing this discrimination with foreign bills, and the only method possible is by an alteration in the rate of exchange at which they are purchased.

The second case also finds its analogy in the home market for bills payable here. A good bill payable immediately is taken as cash for the sum represented on its face. One due three months hence is taken less the discount. The same deduction must be made in negotiating foreign bills. If the exchange on Paris is supposed to be to-day 25 f. 20 c. for a bill at sight, and the rate of interest in France is 3 per cent., then a bill that has three months to run before maturity can only be sold at about 20 c. above that rate—that is, 25 f. 40 c. The alteration in the exchange is the only mode by which the buyer can be recompensed for the loss of three months' interest. He is willing to take 25 f. 40 c. *after* three months, instead of 25 f. 20 c. immediately.

And, lastly, supply and demand in the foreign bill market is the same as in the home discount market. When few bills are offered, the money-lender is content with $2\frac{3}{4}$ to 3 per cent. interest, because he can get no more. When there is a rush for discount, he gradually raises his rate until it may perchance be 8 per cent., or upwards. The purchaser of bills on abroad merely does the same thing, but his alteration of rate, according to whether a scarcity of bills or their abundance prevails, can only be expressed by the exchange he is willing or able to give.

These elementary truths are not published for the information of either Mr. Hubbard or Mr. Seyd, both of whom had probably arrived far beyond them during the first year of their entry into commercial business. The purpose of the writer is to point out to general readers some facts which have a great influence in the solution of the present question, and which they would probably find omitted in the writings or lectures of political economists. The reason of this omission it is not here necessary to investigate.

It will be perceived that the variations in the exchanges above enumerated depend on the nature of things bought and sold, and not on the particular manner in which the quotations are made. Consequently, variations from day to day must exist even under the new system of an international coinage. Good and inferior bills—sight and three months' date bills—cannot all be quoted at the same rate under any system. What, therefore, is the form in which this variation would in future be expressed? Perhaps a *Par.*

reference to the dealings between countries which have already joined the League will give us some hints upon this point.

From a recent Paris exchange list we may extract the following information:—Bills on Belgium are current at from $\frac{1}{2}$ to $\frac{1}{4}$ per cent. discount, if at sight. Therefore on the day the list was published a bill at sight for 100 f. on Belgium would have produced 99 f. 50 c. to 99 f. 75 c. The list further informs us that if the bill is not at sight, but has a certain term to run before it becomes due, a further discount at the rate of $2\frac{1}{2}$ per cent. per annum will be deducted, according to the days to elapse before it is payable. Thus, if the bill has three months to run, a further sum of about 15 cents has to be deducted, leaving 99 f. 35 c. to 99 f. 60 c. as the price in Paris to be paid for the bill.

We have, therefore, two alternatives before us respecting the manner in which the exchange on Paris will be quoted under the new system:—

1. If 25-franc pieces are coined (a sort of French Lowes of equal value to the English Lowes), then the exchange on France may be expressed here by a per-centage quotation similar to the mode adopted between France and Belgium, and varying by eighths and quarters per cent., according to the quality of the bills, the term they are drawn at, and the state of the market, whether well or short supplied with bills.

2. If the French refuse to coin pieces of 25 f. each, then the exchange must continue to be quoted as at present, but with a reduced number of cents in the quotation. Our Lowe would be intrinsically worth 25 f. exactly, instead of the sovereign being worth about 25 f. 20 c., as at present. But supposing that to-day a bill, having a certain number of days to run, could be sold at 25 f. $27\frac{1}{2}$ c. to 25 f. 30 c. per pound sterling, then a bill of the same term, and under similar circumstances of the market, would under the new system be quoted 25 f. $07\frac{1}{2}$ c. to 25 f. 10 c. per Lowe.

Some method of quoting the variations in the exchange,

arising from either of the three causes given above, must therefore always exist. If the last method just mentioned —that is, 25 f. 07½ c. per Lowe—should be the one we are compelled to adopt, it is identically the same with our present mode. If we obtain the French Lowe, then the per-centage system, the same as now prevails between France and Belgium, would also be our lot; and it is needless to hint to those who are accustomed to the trade, that calculations performed according to per-centage variations are certainly not easier than those which are required when the exchange alters by centimes.

The labour expended by mere bill dealers is, however, of no moment in the eyes of our modern reformers; it is the saving of trouble to the manufacturers who draw the trade bills which is the real point with them. Let us, therefore, examine and compare their position under the old and new systems. From the many thousands of these bills which have passed under the hands of the present writer, he thinks himself competent to give an opinion, at least regarding their present general form.

The only real market in England for the sale of bills on the Continent is London, for it is there only that the exchange can be fixed. Suppose a manufacturer in the country sells parcels of goods of equal value to two Frenchmen, the *cash* value of each being 1,000*l*. The first foreigner, having money lying to his credit in Paris, requests he may be drawn upon at sight. The other, for his own convenience, stipulates for the bill on himself being made out at three months' date. Now, the drawer cannot in a provincial town in England fix a rate of exchange at which to draw the bills in foreign money, and he therefore employs a form of bill expressly suited to meet his case. His bill would then read:—" Pay 1,000*l*. sterling at the exchange as per first endorsement in London."

These bills come into the hands of a London banker, who sells them through a broker in the usual manner. Now, if on the arrival of the bills the quotation for a bill

Par.

on Paris at sight was 25 f. 20 c. per 1 l. sterling, the banker would mention that exchange in his endorsement of the first, or sight bill, which would immediately become a draft for 25,200 f., and must be paid for that sum.

The other bill, however, is at three months' date. No one will on the same day give as much for a long-termed bill as he would be willing to pay for a sight one; but the difficulty is got over by putting a *different* rate in the endorsement, say 25 f. 40 c. more or less according to the rate of interest then prevailing in France. The next day the manufacturer gets his sterling cash price (less the very small charge for negotiating the bills), and need not trouble himself with the rate at which they were sold; which, in point of fact, he seldom knows. Neither are the men who are drawn upon injured by the process. The first disburses only 25,200 f., because he pays at once. The other is called upon for 25,400 f., but only after three months' time, and thus has had the use of the money (in the shape of the goods) for the three months before he pays for them.

What, however, would be the position of the manufacturer, supposing the new scheme entirely carried out? That is, how would he stand if the proposed 25 f. pieces are actually coined, and we conduct our exchange business with France as that country now manages it with Belgium? It would be totally impossible for him to fix in the country the exact discount at which a bill might be negotiated a few days afterwards in London, so the drawer must remain in doubt until the actual proceeds are advised to him of what his bills will really net him. Then, indeed, the maker of trade bills will find out what exchange calculations mean. His sight bill may have been sold at one-eighth per cent. discount, and the three months' date one at the same price, with a further reduction of 3 per cent. per annum for the days it has to run. The magic charm of "exchange per endorsement," which in former times saved him all trouble, will serve him no longer. The bills must be drawn in the International Lowe of the value of 25 f., and paid in the same. It would, indeed, be a rare chance to find any one willing to give him in cash 1,000 Lowes for a bill of the same amount, but payable only after three months.

The manufacturer certainly can and would avoid the loss of the interest by insisting on adding it to his invoice whenever payment is offered in a three months' date bill, which is the usual term. But he will have to keep himself acquainted with the rates of interest prevailing abroad as well as at home; and as to the constant rises and falls in the exchanges, resulting from short or redundant supplies of bills in the market, he can have no protection against this source of error in his calculations. Surely, he will have some cause for regret when his talisman, with the cabalistic signs " Exc. pr. Endt." engraved on it, is thus snatched from his hands.

The attempt to do away with exchange quotations and calculations, or even to render them easier to the makers of trade bills, is therefore hopeless, unless some of the professors in the new system can devise the means of destroying the variation in the value of bills arising from all the three causes already enumerated—that is, different degrees of credit in the drawers, different terms at which bills are drawn, variations in the supply of and demand for bills offered in the market.

Before they can expect to make even this part of their scheme work well, they must devote their energies to further investigations on this point.

EXCHANGE BUILDINGS,   PAR.
    Sept. 14, 1869.

MR. LOWE AND THE COINAGE.

(The Economist, Sept. 18, 1869.—To the Editor.)

SIR,—Mr. Lowe, the Chancellor of the Exchequer, has invited the public to consider the three following propositions, and they have attracted a good deal of attention:—

Mr. T. N. Hunt.

The first proposition is, that when any person applies to the Mint to have bar gold coined into sovereigns, the Mint ought to be paid not only mintage, which is the expense of converting the bar into coin, but also seigniorage, which is the profit which a Government is enabled to take by means of its monopoly of coining,—the two charges together to amount to about one per cent.

The second is, that the most just and proper manner of obtaining this payment is by the Mint making 101 sovereigns in future out of the same bar of gold out of which it now makes 100,—returning 100 of the new sovereigns to the person applying for the work to be done, and keeping the remaining one for itself.

The third is, that each of the 101 new sovereigns will be of the same value as each of the present 100.

It is true that the cost in bar gold to the person applying to have the sovereigns made will be just the same as it is now, except about the one-sixth of a grain which he now pays in the Mint charge of $1\frac{1}{2}d$. per ounce to the Bank; but it does not follow that the cost of any article is at all times and under all circumstances the measure of its value, unless its value is intrinsic, as is the case with our present sovereign to the extent of 113 grains of gold, but will not be to the same extent with the proposed new one.

Mr. Lowe evidently depends on the charge for coining creating such a scarcity of sovereigns as will at all times keep their current value above their intrinsic value by the whole amount of the charge made by the Mint. But that will not be the case any more than it is with the present sovereign now, which, although there is practically a Mint charge of $1\frac{1}{2}d$. per ounce for converting bar gold into coin, passes for no more than its intrinsic value whenever the Bank sells bar gold; because it never sells an ounce under $3l.$ $17s.$ $10\frac{1}{2}d.$, which reduces the sovereign to the intrinsic value of the gold contained in it, without any addition whatever for the Mint charge of conversion. This present charge of three halfpence per ounce will be extended by

Mr. Lowe's proposal to whatever the amount of the new Mint charge may be, and we now arrive at the cause and explanation of the error in Mr. Lowe's proposal.

The value of a sovereign in comparison with bar gold is always fluctuating between its two extremes, the minimum, being its intrinsic value, which is the actual quantity of gold contained in it, and the maximum, its artificial value, consisting of the gold contained in it, plus the charge for coining. It may fall as low as the intrinsic value, but cannot be lower. It may rise as high as the intrinsic value, plus the charge for coining, but cannot be higher. Consequently the present sovereign, perfect from the Mint, can never be worth less than 113 grains of bar gold, because it can be melted into a bar of that weight. And it may be worth more, as actually happens whenever bar gold is sold to the Bank at 3*l*. 17*s*. 9*d*. per ounce, being an increase in the value of the sovereign at the rate of three halfpence per ounce, which is now practically the whole charge of converting the bar into sovereigns.

By the same rule, the value of the proposed sovereign may fall as low as 112 grains, the quantity of gold it will contain, but it can never rise above 113, being the price for which the new sovereign may be demanded from the Mint.

Thus the maximum value of the proposed sovereign cannot be greater than the minimum value of the present sovereign; but its minimum value may, and will be at times, below the minimum value of the present, by the whole amount charged for coining, whatever that may be.

By the present regulations, the fluctuations in the value of the sovereign are confined to the narrowest possible limits, that is, between 113 grains and 113 grains plus $1\frac{1}{2}d$. per ounce, or about $113\frac{1}{6}$ grains of bar gold. By the proposed plan, the value of the sovereign will fluctuate between 112 and 113 grains of bar gold.

These observations apply equally to any charge made by the Mint, whether for mintage or seigniorage.

The danger of seigniorage, as distinguished from mint-

Mr. T. N. Hunt.

age, is that it immediately makes it the interest of the State to buy bar gold of intrinsic value, and coin it into sovereigns of the artificial value caused by the seigniorage, and to continue the operation until the sovereigns have become so abundant that all difference between their artificial and intrinsic values has ceased, which is nothing more or less than the ordinary course of debasing the coin.

On the 20th October, 1696, the following resolution was passed by the House of Commons:—"That this House will not alter the standard of the gold and silver coins of this kingdom in fineness, weight, or denomination."

And on the 12th June, 1822, the same resolution was passed again in the same words.

If the question is raised again next year, I trust the same resolution will be passed again for the third time.

Yours, &c.,
THOS. N. HUNT.

THE SOVEREIGN.
(The Times, September 20, 1869.—To the Editor.)

SIR,—In my last letter it was pointed out that it was very doubtful if any advantage would be gained either to the maker of foreign commercial bills or the dealer in them by a change in the mode of quoting the exchanges. The question which next requires our attention is whether any great convenience or benefit would be derived by the traveller were the International Coinage League to be really joined by England.

With regard to those who run over to Paris for a few days' recreation, they may be classed with others who select Margate for the same purpose, with respect to convenience, should the first-named "traveller" omit to provide himself in London with French coin before his departure, or the second take his cash in 20*l.* bank-notes,

Par.

any annoyance either may experience in getting change is of their own seeking. With respect to any losses incurred by the first one in the exchanges, the promoters of the plan who look with complacency at the 8-10ths per cent. loss on each sovereign entailed by their scheme on all the inhabitants of England who remain at home must surely possess in their countenances a considerable portion of their favourite word " brassage," to enable them to bring forward as an argument the losses of travellers by foreign exchanges, which amount on an average to not half that sum.

Leaving these two—the one to drink his *vin ordinaire* and the other to enjoy his donkey-ride on the sands—let us turn our attention to the *bonâ fide* traveller, the man who takes his family for some months' tour on the Continent. As long as the amount of Lowes he takes with him will last, he has nothing to trouble him in the way of exchange calculations. Perhaps hotel-keepers abroad may get into the habit of distributing over the items of their bills the profit they formerly made by exchanging sovereigns into francs at rates fixed by themselves; but this point is left for their future consideration should the occasion arise. The question then comes—can a man take with him a sufficiency of coined money to defray the expenses of a long journey without either inconvenience or risk? Would not tourists of this description prefer the old modes of providing themselves with letters of credit or circular notes? They would then be in the position they now hold. The tourist wants money from the Paris banker to whom his letter is addressed, and, perhaps, at a time when a sight bill on London is at a slight discount. Discussions about the exchange commence as usual, only varied from former times by the controversy being about eighths per cent. instead of the same depreciation being, as now, expressed in centimes.

Then comes the question of commission. Can a traveller expect that no charge under this denomination is in future to be made for the trouble of furnishing him with money and negotiating his draught on London merely because his *Par.*

bill is now expressed in Lowes instead of sovereigns as in former times?

The expected advantage to travellers does not appear to increase by a nearer inspection.

Before alluding to the last inquiry which remains to be made it is necessary to quote a passage from the proceedings of the British Association for the Advancement of Science, as given in your paper of the 26th of August. A scientific baronet was proclaiming his adhesion to the theory of seigniorage, and added :—

"The sovereign among ourselves would be of the present value, and in exchange with other countries the difficulty suggested by Mr. Fellowes would not arise, for we do not pay for imports with coins, but with bills, and the value of bills would remain unaltered."

The name of the speaker need not be mentioned, from the conviction that some important part of the paragraph could not have been heard, as it is impossible to imagine that any one likely to have obtained a hearing at that meeting could have maintained that the balance of trade arising from our imports exceeding exports could be adjusted by bills alone.

There is no doctrine which more amuses men of business than the very common one that a fall in the French exchange *causes* the exportation of gold. That it is generally a good indication of a tendency in that direction they know, and act accordingly. But the fall in the rate is itself a result and not a cause. Whenever any serious and unexpected addition is made to the amount of our ordinary imports there are not enough bills in the market, representing drawings against our usual exports, to satisfy this new demand added to our ordinary requirements; and, therefore, the exchange must fall, owing to competition among buyers of bills. A bad harvest here, and consequent large importations of wheat, is perhaps the best instance to be given, on a great scale, of a derangement caused by circumstances which we could not prevent. A more unpretending and limited instance may, perhaps, set the matter clearly before some persons to whom the other is too great to be grasped.

Suppose a man who in ordinary times manages to maintain his family by his weekly wages finds that by the long-continued illness of one of his children he has become indebted to the doctors for more than he can pay, and is consequently compelled to part with some of the few silver spoons possessed by his household. This poor man, if he laid his unfortunate case before the British Association, would not probably have used the language of political economists by explaining,—

"That his imports and exports to his own home (wages and expenses of living) were on an average at par, or in equilibrium with each other, but that an unforeseen event had destroyed the balance between them, in consequence of which he had been compelled to export some of his bullion, which had always been looked upon by him as intended for home use only. He was, however, glad that when he commenced housekeeping he did not listen to the advice of some who recommended him to provide himself with articles formed of base Britannia metal, as they would not have helped him now, being of themselves of no intrinsic value."

But let him put his case in whatever words he chose, it is evident that his view of the matter is much nearer the truth than that of many professors of the science of Political Economy.

Now, making our coinage on a par of value with that of the French would not alter this balance against us when other circumstances should have created it. We should owe for the corn the same amount in francs, and this must be equivalent to a certain number of Lowes instead of a rather smaller number of sovereigns, as at present; but the debt must be paid, and, therefore, bullion go out in extreme cases. Neither would an alteration in the mode of quoting the exchange alter in the slightest degree the main fact. It would only change the mode of expressing it. At present we bid against each other, offering 1*l.* sterling successively for less and less francs and cents, as the exchange goes down. Then under the new system we should bid up from day to day, first one Lowe, one Lowe and $\frac{1}{8}$
Par.

per cent. premium, one Lowe and ¼ per cent. premium, for the piece of 25 francs, until the point is at last arrived at when the cost of sending the Lowe itself is found to be less than the premium asked for the bill, and then the Lowe must depart on its continental tour.

And now let us sum up the whole of the argument. The consequences usually predicted when a man starts in pursuit of two hares appear to have befallen the proposers of the scheme. They had three objects in view which cannot all be accomplished together by the same process.

1. Saving the cost of coining *gratis* for other nations.
2. Obtaining a profit out of the charge for coining by demanding more than the mere cost of the operation.
3. Enabling us to enter the International Coinage League by means of reducing our standard.

The first object could, of course, be attained by charging a brassage of 2-10ths per cent., collected as in France, if upon principle, and taking other circumstances into consideration, this course should prove to be desirable. But this plan would destroy their chance of obtaining advantage No. 3.

The second is impracticable, because it has been already shown that if we demand 8-10ths per cent. for a service the French consent to perform for 2-10ths per cent., we cannot even obtain gold for our own use except by sacrificing three-fourths of this charge, which forms the whole of the profit anticipated by the Chancellor.

The third object would certainly be accomplished, but at the expense of our honesty and fair dealing. The fallacy of expecting that a seigniorage adds its own amount to the value of the reduced coin has already been shown. It is strange that the advocates of this doctrine did not perceive that the difference between the rise in the price of *one* article in this or any other country, and a general rise in all commodities, depends on whether the occasion of the rise is from circumstances beyond our control, or caused by our own internal changes. Thus, with a bad harvest here, the price of wheat and bread is enhanced without any corresponding rise in commodities which are not main articles of food. Again, the American war, by diminishing the supplies of cotton, enhanced the price of that article in England to an enormous extent. Did our iron or other staple commodities of home produce increase in value at the same rate, or did they even rise at all? In these examples the causes of the rise in price were external, and not of our making. But when we depreciate the standard with which all things are bought and sold, the loss of purchasing power in our money is general. It first shows itself in the enhanced price of all foreign articles imported either for use in their natural state, or to be employed in manufactures. These articles are neither few nor unimportant, and a tolerably correct list would employ some time in compiling. After this first step, the rise must inevitably show itself in all things, even those of strictly home production.

This doctrine is again brought forward by Sir John Lubbock, but he has failed to perceive that, even granting the truth of his dogma, the mere act of coining adds to the value of the bullion employed; his reasoning is not applicable in the present case, although likely to be employed by others in that way. With so highly scientific a man I must, however, depart from my former homely mode of reasoning, and express my argument in algebraic form.

By his reasoning, and under present circumstances, 123 grains of standard gold *plus* the Queen's head are equal to x, the real value of our sovereign.

Under the new system we shall have 122 grains of standard gold *plus* the Queen's head, equal to y, the real value of a Lowe.

Now, if any little boy who has begun Algebra should bring out any other result than $y = x - 1$ grain of gold, it is to be hoped the teacher will advance him to a conspicuous situation in the schoolroom, with the addition of the usual appendage on his head.

The first question at the commencement of the inquiry
Par.

must therefore be answered in the affirmative. The fundholder really has an additional income-tax of 2d. in the pound imposed on him—a sort of perpetual Abyssinian war without a particle of glory to compensate for its pecuniary inconveniences.

If, therefore, we enter the League by reducing our standard (which must be by some amended plan, the present one being impossible from other circumstances), let us at least try to act with common honesty. Let us secure the parties interested in former contracts from being made victims to our modern ideas of convenience in exchange transactions. We have the example of France when she changed the old livres into francs; and the proceedings of all the countries which had joined the League. They all provided a par between the former and the new currencies, by which old contracts were to be liquidated when payments of them were made in the recently established coins.

The idea that the new system would prevent gold coin from being exported when circumstances required it, has been proved to be erroneous.

Traders and tourists do not derive such great advantages as would compensate for the certain troubles and annoyances of the change.

The chief faults of the proposed plan may therefore be summed up thus:—

1. It is dishonest, inasmuch as it does not provide for the faithful fulfilment of previous contracts.

2. It is impracticable, because under its arrangements we should get no gold for our own currency.

3. It is useless, because the great advantages promised to traders and tourists vanish upon closer inspection.

EXCHANGE BUILDINGS,   PAR.
Sept. 16, 1869.

P.S.—The case given above of the solicitude of France to provide for the due performance of previous contracts is an instructive example. The difference between the old and the new coins was not very great—81 livres being equal to 80 francs in intrinsic value; and which was, consequently, the par at which it was arranged that all previous debts were to be fulfilled. This, therefore, amounts to $1\frac{1}{4}$ per cent. in favour of the franc. The French, in the midst of their revolution at the beginning of this century, recoiled from the idea of defrauding any one to the extent of $1\frac{1}{4}$ per cent. The International Coinage men think it is quite allowable to abstract 8-10ths per cent. from all payments under previous contracts. Hence we most unexpectedly arrive at a real arithmetical expression for the difference between honesty and its opposite. This difference, according to modern theories, is rather less than $\frac{1}{2}$ per cent., or, in other words, it is perfectly justifiable to abstract twopence in your payment of a debt of one pound, but beware of retaining threepence, for that is most certainly improper. Can the fact that the establishment of this tariff of payments under old contracts acted in the case of France in favour of the Government, and that the enactment of this regulation would in the present instance be unfavourable to our Treasury, be the cause of its omission in the present scheme?

BULLION *VERSUS* COIN.

(The Times, September 20, 1869.—To the Editor.)

SIR,—In his letter which appeared in your journal of Thursday, Sir John Lubbock has brought to the solution of this knotty question the illustration of raw leather and manufactured shoes, and it has been very happily chosen for the purpose.

Shoes will be worth the value of the raw leather *plus* the cost of manufacturing them; and, similarly, coin will be worth the bullion *plus* the expense of coining (mintage), subject to the provision in each case that too many shoes or

Lord Overstone.

too many coins are not manufactured. And if the expense of manufacturing the shoes or coining the bullion be charged in each case upon the owner of the raw material, we shall have good security against undue depreciation of the manufactured article through excess of supply. But this security is, of course, lost if the cost of making shoes or coins is defrayed by some other party, while the owner of the raw material is still entitled to the manufactured article free of cost.

Thus far it is difficult to believe that there can be any difference of opinion. The next step, however, in the discussion brings us to that which is the really important question. What is the true standard of value in this country? By what means can the debtor legally discharge his debt? Is it sufficient if he tenders raw leather (bullion), or is he bound to pay in shoes (coin)?

By the letter of the law and by usage the debtor has hitherto been held bound to discharge his debt in coin. Is it, then, consistent with justice and good faith to turn round upon the creditor and declare that his claim shall be sufficiently discharged by the tender to him of the raw material (bullion), instead of the manufactured article (coin), which has hitherto been recognized as his right and been treated as the only medium in which debts can be faithfully discharged? Is not this a change in the standard of value and a debasement of it? " In fact, 113 grains of fine gold *in bar* are substituted for a *coin* containing that quantity of fine gold as the standard pound and measure of value in this country."—(*Report of the Royal Commissioners.*)

This proposition, then, being established—viz., that the debtor can discharge his obligation only in coined gold,— let us now take another step, and assume that the State ceases to coin *gratis*, and that any person possessing bullion and wishing to have it converted into coin must pay the expense of the process. What will be the result of this? The cost of mintage, hitherto defrayed by the State, will hereafter be necessarily paid by those who bring bullion to be manufactured into coin; in other words, the cost of mintage will fall upon the importer of bullion.

It has been proposed that the cost of mintage, and far more than the cost of mintage,—that a charge of even one per cent., under the name of seigniorage,—shall be deducted from the coin itself—that 112 grains shall be substituted for 113 grains in the sovereign; and to give to this the appearance of justice it is contended that the sovereign, reduced as regards its quantity of fine gold, will, nevertheless, remain undiminished as to its purchasing power. It is wholly unnecessary to enter into this question, upon which so much specious reasoning and so many doubtful theories have been hazarded.

The established standard of value in this country is not any imaginary or theoretic amount of purchasing power which is necessarily unsusceptible of accurate measurement; it is something of a far more simple, practical, and definite nature.

Gold of fixed weight and fineness, certified by the stamp of the State (*i. e.*, coined), is the medium in which all money obligations are to be adjusted; the debtor and creditor classes are equally bound to give and to accept the specified amount of gold, without reference to any supposed fluctuations in its purchasing power. The gold findings may have reduced, other causes may enhance, the purchasing power of gold; but these considerations afford no justification whatever for an increase or diminution in the *quantity* of gold which is to represent a pound sterling.

It appears, therefore, that the elaborate and ingenious discussions respecting the effect of a seigniorage upon the purchasing power of the sovereign are altogether wide of the question to which the public attention ought to be directed.

Can any portion of the gold now contained in a sovereign be taken out of it without debasing our present established standard of value—without depriving the credi-

Lord Overstone.

tor of a portion of that amount of gold which he is entitled to receive in discharge of his claim?

These questions, it would seem, admit but of one answer.

The amount of gold, then, contained in a sovereign cannot be diminished without tampering with the standard, and a violation of good faith.

The cost of coining, therefore, cannot be charged in the form of a deduction from the weight of the sovereign. It must, therefore, be defrayed either by the State as heretofore, or by a direct charge upon the owner of bullion who may bring it to be coined.

In all controversies it is a great point to obtain a clear and precise view of the question which is really at issue, and if these remarks tend in any degree to promote that result, the object of the writer will have been fully accomplished, his wish being, not to dictate his own opinions as infallible, but simply to assist in the making of truth.

The sovereign is now a legal tender for the discharge of debts to an unlimited amount, because it contains the exact quantity of gold which the creditor is entitled to receive for his pound sterling.

If the amount of gold in the sovereign be diminished, no matter on what plea, the sovereign must cease to be a legal tender (except to some very limited amount), because it will no longer contain the exact quantity of gold to which the creditor is entitled. It must descend from its present high and universally recognized character, " a cosmopolitan coin, really containing what it purports to contain, a fixed quantity of gold " (see Sir John Herschel's letter, Sept. 2), and must take rank with the inferior token coins of our monetary system. It will cease to be the thing signified; it will become merely a sign or symbol, the value of which can be maintained only by convertibility into the thing signified.

It is unfortunate that discussions should have been raised which may tend to produce a perilous disturbance of public confidence as to the very foundation of our monetary system—the integrity of our standard of value. But the question having been mooted under high authority, it is essential that it be sifted to the very bottom.

The well-known boast of Elizabeth's reign was "*Moneta in justum valorem reducta.*" That great Queen, under the advice of Burleigh, "had the manliness to reform the coin of her kingdom" by restoring to it the just number of ounces of silver. Surely, the good sense and good faith of the present age, with or without the advice and encouragement of a Burleigh, will "have the manliness to maintain the just value of its money" by a steady rejection of every plan, however specious the disguise, by which it is proposed to withdraw one single grain of gold from the legal, well-known, and universally recognized weight of the sovereign.

Let me conclude these remarks in the memorable words of Sir Robert Peel, in his speech on the resumption of cash payments, in 1819:—

"That great man, Sir Isaac Newton, came back at last to the old, the vulgar doctrine, as it was called by some, that the true standard of value consisted in a definite quantity of gold bullion. Every sound writer on the subject came to the same conclusion, that a certain weight of gold bullion, with an impression on it, denoting it to be of that certain weight, and of a certain fineness, constituted the only true, intelligible, and adequate standard of value."

Your obedient servant,
LOCKINGE,   OVERSTONE.
Sept. 17, 1869.

THE GOLD COINAGE.
(The Daily Telegraph, September 20, 1869.—To the Editor.)

SIR,—A suggestion was thrown out by the Chancellor of the Exchequer, towards the end of last session, that by the imposition of a small coinage charge and the diminution of a single grain of gold, we may, without disturbing the

Mr. L. Levi.

measure of value, render the sovereign equal to 25 francs, and thereby bring about a complete system of international coinage. Let us understand what are the real points at issue, and see whether the adoption of the proposal will involve, as is alleged, any departure from the practice of the country in matters of coinage, or alter in any way the monetary standard which is universally acknowledged as the test of national good faith and the anchor of good credit and safety. We must do justice to the Chancellor of the Exchequer by stating that the question is not of his own seeking. It originated with the movement for obtaining an international and decimal coinage, which is gaining ground all the world over, and is the immediate result of the International Monetary Conference, held in Paris in 1867, in which this country was officially represented. And it is well to realize the fact that the question of assimilating the weights, measures, and coins of all countries is no longer either the theory of philosophers or the dream of enthusiasts. Nation after nation made it the subject of practical legislation, and we are fast advancing towards the realization of the desideratum. Even as it is, the metric system of weights and measures has become a common language among a large number of States, and the coinage of some of the most influential nations of Europe is now identical. But the question is progressing still more, and as we have felt the necessity of moving in the same direction as regards weights and measures, by rendering the use of the metric system permissive in England, so we will find that we cannot long remain strangers to the negotiations for the adoption of an international coinage.

The first change involved in the proposition of the Chancellor of the Exchequer is the imposition of a charge for the manufacture of the coin and the maintenance of the Mint. In former days the Sovereign considered himself entitled to a seigniorage in return for his affixing to pieces of the precious metals his Royal stamp, as a voucher for their containing specific weights of a specific fineness, and as a warrant for their currency at specific values. Such demands were, of course, objectionable, and were liable to much abuse. What is now suggested by charging a seigniorage, or rather mintage, is simply that the amount expended in the production of the coinage shall no longer be inserted in the estimates and paid by the nation in the shape of taxes, but defrayed by a charge on the commodity produced. Any one visiting the Mint will see that it is a large manufacturing establishment, converting gold, silver, and bronze as raw materials into coins of different values, and that that work is undertaken, not for the State, but for money-dealers and bankers. It is a mistake to suppose that the Queen issues the money. Though the coining of money is here, as in all States, the act of the Sovereign power, and the stamping is the unquestionable prerogative of the Crown, still, practically, the Mint performs these offices on behalf of any one bringing gold, silver, or bronze to the Mint for the purpose. In practice, the Bank of England is the great provider of gold, the Bank receiving the bullion from the importers at $3l.$ $17s.$ $9d.$ per oz., and paying for it in bank-notes at the rate of $3l.$ $17s.$ $10\frac{1}{2}d.$ per oz. The other metals are purchased. For example, in 1868 the Mint received from the Bank of England 940,505 ozs. of gold bullion, and purchased 318,410 ozs. of silver bullion at $60\frac{3}{4}d.$ per oz., 388,878 ozs. of silver worn coin at $77\frac{1}{8}d.$ per oz., and nearly 21 tons of old copper coins at $242l.$ per ton, and converted them into so many sovereigns and half-sovereigns, and silver and copper coins. But to perform this conversion a considerable expenditure is annually incurred. The cost of the Mint, in salaries, machinery, alloy metal, loss on coinage, and loss on worn silver coin withdrawn from circulation, being put down at $45,820l.$ Calculated on each sovereign, it appears that the cost varies considerably with the number turned out from the Mint. With an average production of 5 million sovereigns the cost of each is stated to be $0·72$ of a penny, or nearly three-farthings; for an annual production approach-

Mr. L. Levi.

ing ten millions, the cost may be taken at a halfpenny for each sovereign. But this is not all. To the cost of production we must add the cost of maintaining the currency at its full legal weight. So that, when all is calculated, one to one-and-a-half per cent. would have to be charged to defray all the expenses. Yet under the present regulation a person bringing to the Mint 123·274 grains of gold 11-12ths fine, receives back a sovereign of precisely the same weight. But why not charge the cost of manufacture to the parties who bring the gold for coinage ? In almost all other countries a mintage charge is levied. In France the mintage is 6 f. 70 c. per kilogramme of standard gold, or between one-fourth and one-fifth per cent. Such expense is kept back from the sum to be returned. A kilogramme of gold is divided in France into 3,100 f., but the bearer of the raw material receives back 3,093 f. 30 c., because the State takes 6 f. 70 c. to pay the Mint for the expense of coinage. The entire quantity of gold brought in is coined, but the Mint is paid with part of the coin produced by it. And the exaction is perfectly fair. In the United States the mintage charge is a half per cent. In Prussia it is the same. And what is the consequence of the different practice? It is that a large quantity of sovereigns is annually exported from this country. And no wonder. In the words of the Royal Commissioners, if coins having currency in several countries are struck in different mints, in some of which a heavy charge is made for coinage, and in others the coins are struck either at a less charge or free of expense, surely bullion will be brought in greater quantities for coinage to those mints where there is the least charge (unless the cost of transmission to those mints should exceed the difference of charge), and a large and unnecessary expense will be thrown upon the countries where such is the case. But there is no reason why we should undertake the expense of coining for the circulation of other countries. Therefore, even if there were no other reasons, as a measure of self-defence, we should charge what shall at least defray the average cost of coining. And this is what the Chancellor of the Exchequer proposed.

Admitting, then, that the imposition of a mintage charge is expedient, or, we may say, has become a necessity, and that, to cover the expense, such charge must be at least one per cent., or twopence on each sovereign, what is the best manner of introducing such a change? We may either charge twopence extra for every sovereign of the present weight of gold, or take off one grain of gold without changing the weight of the sovereign. The former plan would be clearly inconvenient, and cannot be thought of. The latter is easier, and accomplishes, besides, the ulterior object of an international coinage. But it is objected that, if we reduce the weight of the sovereign by one single grain of gold, we necessarily alter its exchangeable value. Doubtless the absolute relation of weight to value is the best guarantee against abuses in the coinage; yet we must remember that the legitimate value of any article is that of the raw material, plus the cost of manufacture, that the State has perfect right to consider how best it can reimburse itself of the cost of coinage, and that the creditor has no right to demand a sovereign of higher value than what is represented in twenty shillings' worth of gold, including the cost of coinage. It is very true that, if we take off one grain from the present weight of the sovereign, its intrinsic value will be so much less; but, by the uniform testimony of political economists, the current value of a coin is enhanced by the amount of seigniorage imposed upon it. A sovereign of 112 grains of fine gold, plus the one per cent. of mintage, would in effect exchange for exactly the same amount as a sovereign of 113 grains without such a charge. Some may question the expediency of imposing such a mintage, and reasons might be adduced why, instead of diminishing the weight of pure gold in the sovereign, we should, if necessary, add the twopence to its value. But it is an undoubted fact, that, if we do take off such grain of

Mr. L. Levi.

gold and add one per cent. of mintage, the exchangeable value of the sovereign will be precisely the same.

But what will be the effect of such a charge in our financial relations with foreign countries? A distinction must be made here between those countries to which payments are made in bullion, and those to which we must send sovereigns. As regards the former, no change whatever will take place. As regards the latter, we must remember, it is always intended that the conditions of coinage shall be precisely the same in all countries entering into the monetary convention. Even at present the sovereign of 113·001 grains of fine gold is worth in France only a trifle above 25 francs, and ordinarily passes for that amount only. Let us enter into the convention, and the sovereign of 112 grains will exchange precisely for a 25-franc piece in gold of equal fineness. To bring about an international coinage, we must bridge over this difference between the coinage of the countries of the convention and our own; and it is a matter for congratulation, that by remedying a decided defect in our system of coinage we are enabled to avoid all the complications of a tariff. The idea itself is perfectly simple. It is acted upon in every country where a mintage is charged, and is advocated in this by men of practical knowledge. Mr. Lowe adopted it, and in a masterly speech brought the whole subject before the House of Commons, and through them before the nation at large. The suggestion being novel, necessarily created surprise among many, while many more, naturally adverse to the change, seem disposed to turn a deaf ear to reasoning. Nevertheless, I do not hesitate to declare my entire adhesion to the proposal, and my expectation that public opinion will fully sanction the contemplated reform.

I am, yours obediently,

LEONE LEVI.

Sept. 18, 1869.

THE DAILY TELEGRAPH.

(September 21, 1869.)

"THE whole foundation of the proposal I am about to make rests upon the assumption that, according to practice, according to law, according to the ancient monetary policy of this country, that which is implied by the word 'pound' is a certain definite quantity of gold, with a mark upon it to determine its weight and fineness; and that the engagement to pay a pound means nothing, and can mean nothing, else than the promise to pay to the holder, when he demands it, that definite quantity of gold." In presence of the coinage controversy still raging, it may not seem out of place to recall these words of Sir Robert Peel when he proposed the Bank Charter Act of 1844. All the advocates, on either side, we presume, will concede the fundamental position, that contracts between buyer and seller must be discharged in a circulating medium accepted by both; and the great statesman whom we have quoted did no more than provide an effective means of facilitating the completion of such engagements. Sir Robert never professed to have discovered a standard of value absolutely free from fluctuations. On the contrary, he asserted, in the broadest manner, that nobody pretended to have discovered an absolutely fixed and invariable standard. But he chose one particular metal as enjoying certain conspicuous advantages over all other substances—such as certainty of supply, universality of demand, and ready currency—not only in all civilized, but in many savage countries; and he declared that the same qualities which, since the Middle Ages, had fitted it to be a representative of value, still existed, and were likely to continue. Promises to pay, therefore, he said, shall be expressed in words which mean a particular quantity and fineness of this metal—gold—in a coined state, stamped by the Sovereign, a legal tender, and consequently sure to pass from hand to hand in discharging old obligations or contracting fresh liabilities. Of course Sir Robert was in no sense compelled to recommend that the pound should be represented by 113 grains of fine gold, or 123¼ grains of 11-12ths fineness; he might have said 112 and 122¼ grains, and all contracts would have been arranged accordingly. But, whatever the representative chosen, the settlement of the transactions between the debtor and creditor at home would have been regulated by that standard; while foreign countries, not recognizing our coinage for the purposes of their own internal currency, would simply take our " pound " for the weight and fineness of bullion which it was known to contain. Peel's pound, then, became the basis of our home circulation, and was accepted by foreigners as the equivalent of so much bullion. Mr. Lowe proposes that the gold coin representing the unit of value shall contain a smaller quantity of the precious metal, and shall nevertheless pass current for the value measured by its predecessor. What foreign nations would think of the change is, of course, understood. They would treat Lowe's sovereign on the same principle as that which they apply to Peel's: the coin would be worth the quantity of gold that was in it, neither more nor less. It is the effects on our home transactions, resulting from such a change, that concern us most closely; and we should endeavour to estimate those consequences before committing ourselves to a hasty judgment upon the new plan.

There can be no doubt whatever, that an universal disturbance of values would be an almost immediate consequence of any change which altered, either by increasing or by diminishing, the quantity of gold contained in the sovereign. The value of the metal may fluctuate slightly; but it always has a value, and a grain less or more would be distinctly appreciable. Diminish the amount of metal in the coin, and you so far reduce its intrinsic value—we use the phrase in its popular and intelligible meaning; you necessarily, therefore, lessen its purchasing power. Augment the amount of gold, and you produce exactly the converse effect. We are aware, indeed, that many authorities of deserved eminence question the conclusion that a general disturbance of values would follow the official announcement of a deduction from the intrinsic value of the sovereign. Professor Leone Levi, echoing the opinion of Mr. Lowe and of other political economists, has asserted with characteristic ability, in our own columns, that "the current value of a coin is enhanced by the amount of seigniorage imposed upon it." "A sovereign of 112 grains of fine gold, *plus* the one per cent. of mintage, would in effect exchange for exactly the same amount as a sovereign of 113 grains without such a charge." No doubt, if we were now for the first time determining what should be our internal currency, we might enact that the sovereign should be exchangeable for twenty shillings, whether it contained 112 grains or any smaller number. There is no imaginable extent of depreciation which a State might not sanction if it pleased. But our present gold coin is a measure of value—that is, its known intrinsic worth is taken as a gauge by which to determine the value of any other commodities at home or abroad. It is something more than a token or symbol; it is a thing which has in itself an ascertained worth. If we take away any part of that which is its characteristic and essential substance—namely, the metal—what must necessarily follow? It is futile to suppose that, irrespectively of the Mint stamp, confidence in its worth will remain the same, whatever be the quantity of gold in it. Every man's judgment will tell him that, since in the markets of the whole world 112 grains of gold are worth less than 113 grains, they cannot be of equal value in a single market—England. Again, we cannot imagine by what process it would be possible to convince the public that Mint labour is the equivalent of the gold abstracted. Hitherto, they will agree, 113 grains of fine gold *plus* labour have not been worth, when coined, 114 grains; how is it that the natural law has been suspended in the past, and is only now coming into operation at the bidding of a select band of political

The Daily Telegraph.

economists? But, further, the Professor has made no allowance for an influence which, as men in business would tell him, must prove fatal to his theory, no matter how much disposed public opinion would be to take on trust the reduced sovereign. We need not remind so learned and able an observer, that all the European nations are becoming every year more intimately connected in trade and other relations. The sentiment of one is instantly reflected upon its neighbour, deepened rather than lightened in the passage. As a matter of course, our reduced sovereign would be taken at its bullion value in France, and what we chose to declare worth twenty shillings would there represent only nineteen shillings and tenpence, or its equivalent in French money. Is it conceivable that our confidence in our artificially upheld sovereign would remain unshaken when we saw it universally depreciated elsewhere? The process of disturbance might not be so speedy in commencing; but, once started, its operations would probably be all the more marked, from the fact that discredit abroad was the initial impulse. We do not believe that any amount of reasoning would then persuade an Englishman that a coin which had fallen in value across the Channel maintained its exchangeable value at home. In the struggle between fact and theory, argument and practice, there can be no doubt which would go to the wall. The British Philistine has an intense perception of the obvious, and he would promptly appraise the Lowe sovereign by the same rules as those used by his neighbour across the Channel—that is, he would treat it as worth twopence less than its Peel predecessor. All future bargains would be adjusted accordingly, and all past contracts would be settled in a sense highly favourable to the debtor who liquidated the claims against him in a depreciated currency—and proportionately unfavourable to the just and recorded claims of the creditor.

Before we go any further, then, in discussing the new proposal, let us quite understand what it implies. The substitution of Lowe's pound for Peel's pound—two things essentially different—would involve a change in existing contracts. The change might be arithmetically small; but it would be sufficiently tangible, and in its operation universal. Hence it must create a general unsettlement in the highest degree prejudicial, not merely to our industry, but to our social comfort. To the Englishman bent on completing his bargain honestly according to the original contract, the new coin would be a Lowe, or a Jevons, or a Farr; but it would not have the familiar ring of unexceptionable sterling gold with which the careful Peel gave life to our monetary system, while he put the currency doctors of Birmingham to shame. The citizen would have more to pay or less to receive, and nothing would convince him that a coin whose essence was changed continued essentially the same. On the alternative plan of a seigniorage to be paid by the sender of bullion to the Mint, it is unnecessary to say much, as Mr. Lowe himself discouraged the idea. If high enough to yield a sufficient profit to the Mint, the charge would deter importers from sending their gold to be coined; if low enough not to discourage them, it would hardly be worth anything to the Mint; and a middle term would not be easy to find. The present arrangement has the advantage of offering an inducement to bullion holders to turn their metal into coin; a practice which, of itself, is good for the nation, since it replenishes our stock, and is a natural counteractive of that constant wear and tear which Mr. Lowe laments. But assuredly the expense of minting gold is a miserably insufficient ground on which to base such a revolution as the Chancellor of the Exchequer contemplates. What is 40,000*l*. or 50,000*l*. a year, or even 400,000*l*.—the amount at which Mr. Lowe estimates the cost of renewing our gold coinage—distributed over the whole community? The cost of our Mint is simply the tax which the nation contributes for supplying itself with one of the best coinages in the world—with an unquestionable medium of exchange; and

The Daily Telegraph.

whether it pays that tax directly in the support of the Mint, or indirectly by an abstraction of gold to that extent, the charge equally falls on the taxpayer, with this difference, that the direct form involves the least amount of hindrance, and therefore the least ratio of loss on the whole transaction. An impost more universal in its application, more fair in its incidence, it is difficult to imagine; and it is one which is as inevitable as the use of money itself. There is no doubt that much of our coinage needs renewal; the nation desires it, and, we are firmly convinced, is quite willing to pay for an improvement the cost of which would be returned to the consumer twice over in the saving of risk, loss, and trouble. But that is a point which has no necessary connection with altering the basis of our currency; and it is only right that the consequences which must follow a derangement of our monetary standard, with the confusion of contracts, the covert depreciation of existing values, the shock to confidence, and the countless social inconveniences, should be deliberately examined and thoroughly understood by every class of the public, before the Government or the Parliament should be committed to any irretrievable step.

THE SOVEREIGN.

(The Times, September 22, 1869.—To the Editor.)

SIR,—Having always felt the most sincere respect for Lord Overstone's opinions on the currency, I have read his letter in this morning's *Times* with no little surprise. Lord Overstone says that " security against undue depreciation of the manufactured article (money) is, of course, lost if the cost of making it (*i. e.*, coining) is defrayed by the other party (*i. e.*, the manufacturer), while the owner of the raw material is still entitled to the manufactured article free of cost." It follows that our present system of coining,
Aliquis.

which is exactly described in the above sentence, and of which Lord Overstone approves, offers, in his opinion, no security against undue depreciation of money.

Next, Lord Overstone tells us that "by the letter of the law and by usage a debtor has hitherto been held bound to discharge his debt in coin," and he proceeds to argue that it would be unjust to declare that a debt shall be discharged by bullion instead of coin. As no one has made this proposal, I need not stop to discuss it, but I should like to ask Lord Overstone how, on these principles, he accounts for the fact that a debt can by law and usage be legally discharged by that which is neither coin nor bullion—a bank-note. Let him not say that a bank-note has this efficacy because it is convertible into gold. When it was not so convertible, between 1817-1819, it had this power derived from that law, the existence of which Lord Overstone denies. It is, therefore, untrue, as Lord Overstone asserts, "that the debtor can discharge his obligation only in coined gold."

After having argued for the right of the debtor to be paid in coin, and protested against the substitution of 113 grains of fine gold for a sovereign, Lord Overstone now turns round and insists on the right of the creditor to receive 113 grains for his debt, a right so absolute that he will not even discuss the question whether it be not possible to give him the full value of his debt in a way as convenient to him and more beneficial to the public.

Passing by this inconsistency, I come to the statements "that the amount of gold in a sovereign cannot be diminished without tampering with the standard," and that "the sovereign contains the exact quantity of gold which the creditor is entitled to receive for his pound sterling, and that if the amount of gold in the sovereign be diminished, the sovereign must cease to be a legal tender (except to some very limited amount), because it will no longer contain *the exact quantity* of gold to which the creditor is entitled. How does Lord Overstone reconcile these assertions with
Aliquis.

the fact of which he is, of course, well aware, that the gold in a sovereign may be diminished by about three-halfpence without the sovereign ceasing to be a legal tender for a debt? Is not this a sensible diminution of "the amount of gold in the sovereign?" Does such a sovereign contain the exact amount of gold which the creditor is entitled to receive for his pound sterling? Why does not the sovereign cease to be a legal tender, as Lord Overstone says it must, and as the law says it must not? Simply because, taking his stand upon the law, Lord Overstone has misstated the law, has assumed a state of things which does not exist, and founded on it imaginary rights which every day's experience negatives.

I am, Sir, your obedient servant,

Sept. 20, 1869. ALIQUIS.

THE SOVEREIGN.
(The Times, September 22, 1869.—To the Editor.)

SIR,—The letter which you did me the honour of inserting in *The Times* on Thursday last has brought me several answers and various objections, which, however, generally resolve themselves into one or other of the two following, viz.:—

1. That the sovereign cannot be worth more than the gold which is in it; that the mintage adds nothing to the purity or quantity of gold, and cannot, therefore, affect the value.

2. That, as your correspondent "Par" observes, if the mere act of coining adds to the value of the gold, coin would even now be worth more than bullion.

The first objection was met, and as it seems to me conclusively, by the fourth paragraph of my previous letter, but as an additional illustration I will call attention to the effect of Customs duties.

Let us suppose that a duty of 10s. per cent. is imposed on any given article. Ninety ounces (duty paid) will then be as valuable as a hundred were before; and, practically, every one knows that the duties on wine and tobacco raise

Sir J. Lubbock. P

the price of sherry and cigars, though nothing is thereby added to their quantity or flavour.

As regards the second objection, it is obvious that the act of coining will not add to the value of the gold as long as the expense is defrayed by Government, just as the duty on tobacco would not raise the price of cigars if it were paid by the Government.

This was clearly pointed out by Lord Overstone, with whose letter, so far as Political Economy is concerned, I agree in the main, while, on the other hand, I venture to differ from him as to the requirements of justice. Lord Overstone admits, if I understand him correctly, that the imposition of a mintage would raise the value of a sovereign, and yet maintains that all pending contracts should be fulfilled in the then more valuable coin. Surely, however, this is adhering to the letter rather than the spirit of the law.

I fully admit that the increased supplies of gold "may have reduced, other causes may enhance, the purchasing power of gold," and that " these considerations afford no justification whatever for an increase or diminution in the quantity of gold which is to represent a pound sterling;" but it seems to me that if Parliament deliberately takes a course which, as Lord Overstone admits, raises the value of the pound sterling to the extent of 1 per cent., justice requires that contracts should be re-adjusted.

Permit me to repeat that I am not advocating the imposition of a mintage; the expediency of such a step must be discussed on other grounds, and certainly no change ought to be made excepting after the gravest consideration. My object has merely been to point out the effect which such a change would certainly produce; and although I feel much hesitation in differing from so great an authority as Lord Overstone, still it seems to me that it would be quite as unjust to raise as to lower the value of the pound sterling.

I am, Sir, your obedient servant,

15, LOMBARD STREET, E.C.,   JOHN LUBBOCK.
Sept. 21, 1869.

THE SOVEREIGN.

(The Times, September 22, 1869.—To the Editor.)

Sir,—I cannot understand why practical men go on repeating the statement that our gold coinage is gratuitous, when they well know that private persons do not send gold to the Mint, and that the Bank of England levies an import duty of 2,320*l.* on every million's worth of gold bullion which it buys with its bank-notes. This is equal to 4*s.* 7½*d.* per cent., and it is in every sense of the word a mintage, with the difference that it is paid to the Bank, and not to the Mint, as it ought to be. The 1½*d.*, or difference between the Bank and Mint price, which Sir John Lubbock makes so little of, enables the Bank to give 934*l.* 10*s.* in its bank-notes for 935*l.* 10*s.* in gold bullion; the assay fraction and the turn of the scale make up the rest.

M. Chevalier first pointed this out (*La Monnaie,* last edition, page 328). He says that the actual charge paid by the importer of each kilogramme of French standard gold for coinage purposes in England is 8 f. 52 c., while in France it is 6 f. 70 c., "de sorte que le système, qui s'appelle gratuit, serait sensiblement le plus cher."

So far, then, from our coining sovereigns gratis for all the world, we are now making importers of gold for coinage purposes pay more in England than they do in France. The fact that the Bank receives the import duty instead of the Mint does not alter the nature of the tax at all; the importer must pay it in order to get sovereigns; it remains a mintage still.

Mr. Hubbard and Mr. Seyd both agree in recommending a mintage charge which is not to exceed the actual cost of manufacturing the gold coin, and which is to be paid by the bearer of the metal to the Mint, but without deduction from the present weight of the sovereign.

Mr. Hubbard considers that one-sixth per cent. would be a sufficient charge; he suggests that the Mint should charge 1½*d.* per oz. for coinage, or buy gold at 3*l.* 17*s.* 9*d.*,

Mr. N. A. Nicholson.

but he makes no provision for delay in returning the coin at the Mint, and, as he would lower the Bank price to 3*l*. 17*s*. 7½*d*., importers would prefer bank-notes at the latter price when they wanted cash for their gold, and send it, as they do now, to the Bank, instead of sending it to the Mint and having to wait, perhaps, a considerable time for the coin. This would raise Mr. Hubbard's mintage charge in practice to one-third per cent., or 2*s*. 0½*d*. above the actual charge at present levied by the Bank. As your correspondent "Par" has done his country such good service by preventing the embryo "Lowes" from becoming actual debased sovereigns, permit me to turn the attention of your able correspondents to the best means of transferring the existing mintage charge from the Bank to the State, as represented by the Mint. There are but two ways of dealing with our existing arrangements, if the future mintage is not to exceed the actual cost of manufacturing our gold coin. Every hundred sovereigns coined in England cost at present 10*s*. 10½*d*., made up of 4*s*. 7½*d*. import duty levied by the Bank, and 6*s*. 3*d*. actual cost of manufacture at the Mint.

1. We may separate the Mint from the Bank altogether, allowing no gold for coinage purposes to go to the Bank at all. This would necessitate an increase in the number of our Mints, the introduction of State bank-notes, and the abolition in England of any bank-notes not issued by the State.

2. We may unite the Mint more closely to the Bank, which would then deduct the mintage when it bought gold bullion with its bank-notes, and pay it over to the State. The Mint would not then be obliged to re-melt and re-assay the Bank bars, as it does now. Of one thing we may be certain, that we cannot continue our present system and yet reduce our mintage charge to the mere actual cost of manufacturing our gold coin. There are too many cooks just now for this; although I do not believe they spoil the broth, they add to its cost.

I remain, Sir, your obedient servant,

TRINITY COLLEGE, OXFORD,   N. A. NICHOLSON.
Sept. 20, 1869.

THE SOVEREIGN.

(The Times, September 25, 1869.—To the Editor.)

Sir,—I have neither time nor the inclination to enter into all the sinuosities of the question of "the sovereign," as it has been discussed by the various correspondents in your journal. *Abesse a controversiis* is a maxim the wisdom of which I recognize more and more as. I advance in years.

The purpose of these few lines, and they are the last the insertion of which I shall venture to request, is simply to prevent misapprehension of the true meaning of my former letter.

First,—As regards the remarks of "Aliquis":—

"Our present system of coinage, according to Lord Overstone's view, offers no security against undue depreciation of money."

My statement was that, so long as the State defrays the expenses of coinage, more bullion may probably be converted into coin than would be the case if the expense of coinage were charged upon the owner of the bullion, and that some excess in the supply of coin might thus arise. But the moment this excess of coin became appreciable, the corrective would be found in re-melting the coin, and thus bringing it back to the state of bullion. This is the security against undue depreciation of coined money through excess of supply, and this security is derived from the fact that the coin contains the full amount of bullion which was brought to be coined, without any deduction upon the plea of mintage, seigniorage, &c.

Next, "Aliquis" says:—

"I should like to ask Lord Overstone how, on his principle, he accounts for the fact that a debt can by law and usage be legally discharged by that which is neither coin nor bullion—a bank-note."

My answer is,—The bank-note discharges a debt equally with the coin or bullion, because it is an engagement or promise to give the coin in exchange for the bank-note, whenever it is called for.

Lord Overstone.

"But this was not the case previous to 1819," says "Aliquis." No doubt the suspension of cash payments was the suspension of all sound law and sound principle. It was an anomalous state of the monetary system, to which sound reasoning is inapplicable. It can be explained and defended only on the tyrant's plea of necessity.

Again:—

"Lord Overstone is, of course, aware that the gold in a sovereign may be diminished by about three-halfpence without the sovereign ceasing to be a legal tender for a debt. Is not this a sensible diminution of the amount of gold in the sovereign?"

Here is a vital misconception of the fact of the case. In the case there put there is no diminution of the gold in the sovereign. The party who brings bullion to be coined receives in return an amount in sovereigns less than the amount of bullion which he paid in, in the proportion of $1\frac{1}{2}d.$ on every ounce of gold. He receives fewer sovereigns in that proportion; but the sovereigns which he does receive contain the full legal amount of gold; and on that account, and on that account only, they pass into circulation, containing the exact amount of gold which the creditor is entitled to receive for his pound sterling.

Between myself and Sir John Lubbock, so clear-headed and intelligent on all occasions, there can, I think, be no final difference of opinion when we once come to understand each other correctly :—

"Lord Overstone admits that the imposition of a mintage would raise the value of a sovereign."

This is an ambiguous statement. I admit that bar gold may by the process of coinage be increased in value; that the sovereign may be more valuable than the same amount of gold in the state of bullion. But it must be remembered that it is the gold with this additional value—it is not bar gold, but coined gold—it is bullion, *plus* mintage, which constitutes the standard of value in this country. The *Lord Overstone.*

coin supposed to be more valuable than the bullion is the medium in which all pending contracts must be fulfilled. To depart from this would be to violate the spirit quite as much as the letter of the law, and would be in opposition to established usage.

These remarks it will, of course, be understood are directed against any proposal for deducting the cost of mintage from the present weight of gold in the sovereign. It is the integrity of the sovereign as essential to the good faith of the country for which I contend. I leave untouched the question whether the necessary cost of coining ought to be defrayed, as is now the case, by the State, or by the importer of bullion.

Again, Sir John Lubbock says:—

"It seems to me that it would be quite as unjust to raise as to lower the value of the pound sterling."

I cordially concur in condemning any measure which may be resorted to for the express purpose of raising or lowering the value of the pound sterling. It is for the interest of justice and for the well-being of the community that the value of the pound sterling should continue as nearly as possible invariable. With this end in view our duty is to leave it alone. Natural and uncontrollable causes will produce some variations in the value of gold. This, when it occurs, is unfortunate, but it is not unjust. Let us not aggravate this evil by endeavouring to produce artificial variations of its value. This will be both unfortunate and unjust.

What, then, are we to think of a measure by which it is proposed to effect a double variation in the value of the pound sterling or sovereign. First, to reduce its value by the distinct act of diminishing the quantity of gold, and then to increase its value by the mysterious process of seigniorage—first to cut the throat, and then to sew it up again. Remove a certain quantity of gold from the sovereign, and cover the wound with a seigniorage plaster.

This leads me to one concluding remark. Mintage we

can understand; it is a distinct charge, the cost of a well-known process, which may be confined within narrow, well-defined limits.

But what is seigniorage? Upon what principle does it depend? Within what limits can its operation be restricted? At present its mysterious influence is invoked to the extent of one per cent., because that meets the convenience of the present difficulty. But is there any principle which will prevent the same influence being hereafter called into action to the extent of 10 per cent., should that at some future day be deemed convenient for the further improvement of our standard of value; ten grains of gold abstracted, ten per cent. of value added by this *undefinable something*, seigniorage.

There were wisdom and good faith in the resolution more than once solemnly pronounced by the Legislature, " that it will not alter the standard of the gold and silver coins of this kingdom in fineness, *weight*, or denomination." Shall we now roll back the current of intelligence and declare that the standard of gold coin in this kingdom shall be altered in weight? A fraudulent practice which has been considered the disgrace of barbarous ages, from which modern civilization had emancipated itself.

Let the public keep its attention steadily fixed upon the plain consideration that gold of fixed weight and fineness, and in the form of coin, is the medium in which every creditor is entitled to receive, and every debtor is bound to discharge, a debt. This is a plain, distinct right on one side, and obligation on the other side, which cannot be affected or disturbed by any supposed variation in the value or purchasing power of that fixed quantity of gold. To introduce any other rule is to introduce endless confusion, conflict, and injustice, and to afford facility and encouragement to that most dangerous tendency from which a community is never altogether free to seek immediate ease, and a state of hollow factitious prosperity, by the

Lord Overstone.

gradual debasement of the standard of value. *Facilis descensus Averno ; sed revocare gradum !*

Your obedient servant,

LOCKINGE, OVERSTONE.
Sept. 23, 1869.

Let me again draw attention to the almost prophetic words of Sir Robert Peel, spoken in debate, June 12, 1822 :—

" The causes of variation in the value of money no man could determine ; but if this House once established the fatal precedent of disturbing existing contracts to meet such variations in value the idea of a fixed standard for the country was at an end for ever. Fluctuation in the value of money had always occurred, and must continue to occur ; but far better would it be to take to the paper system again than to set the example of reviewing the contracts of the country on account of an alteration in the value of its currency."

THE SOVEREIGN.
(The Times, September 25, 1869.—To the Editor.)

SIR,—In Sir John Lubbock's letter in *The Times* of to-day he adopts a plan which has already been too frequently employed in this controversy—that is, giving only part of an argument; the benefit of which proceeding to himself is more apparent than its justice to those he quotes. In my letter inserted in *The Times* of September 20, which he does me the honour to refer to, it was stated that—

" Granting the truth of his dogma, that the mere act of coining adds to the value of the bullion employed, his reasoning is not applicable in the present case, although likely to be employed by others in that way."

This evidently points out that the advocates of the new plan would naturally avail themselves of the advantage of " standing in Sir John's shoes," in order to prove the truth of their general doctrine, which is, that any seigniorage adds its own amount to the intrinsic value of the coin. Sir John Lubbock is undoubtedly not a man who would go

Par.

this length; and he must by this time have found out that during the greater part of the discussion two very different questions have been frequently confounded together, although having in reality no connexion with each other.

1. Can we impose a tax on the importer of gold, so as to make him pay the mintage charges, in exchange for the benefits he derives from having his bullion converted into coin?

2. Can we levy a tax of about 8-10ths per cent. by abstracting one grain of gold from each sovereign?

Now, experience (a much better guide in these cases than abstract theory) points out that the first question must be answered in the affirmative. We find that under ordinary circumstances importers are willing to sacrifice $1\frac{1}{2}d.$ per ounce in order to get their bullion converted into our coins. This is shown by their readiness to sell to the Bank at 77s. 9d. per ounce, thus avoiding the loss of interest and trouble by sending to the Mint. As explained already by some of your correspondents, this loss, with other petty charges added, amounts on an average to about 2-10ths per cent. We also find that the French Mint gets supplied with gold for coinage at about the same rate. From undeniable facts we thus arrive at the conclusion that up to 2-10ths per cent. for charges of coinage the tax can be, and actually is, levied both here and in France.

Before the year 1835 the French Mint charged 9f. per kilogramme (say 3-10ths per cent.), but reduced it at that time to about its present amount of 2-10ths per cent. This is a very strong indication that the latter is nearly the extreme limit of the charge. It also shows that the French mode of collecting the tax is by far the best, as in the case of a mistake in its amount, the error can be corrected without interfering with the coin already in circulation.

The arguments into which some of your correspondents have entered, as to whether the tax on the importation of gold into this country should be devoted to defray the expenses of coining, or permitted to be retained by the Bank of England, have nothing whatever to do with the present question. Let
Par.

us first ascertain how much we can obtain by these means. We can afterwards discuss its legitimate appropriation.

The second question must be answered in the negative. It has been proved from facts that it cannot be carried into operation under the present circumstances of other countries and by the means proposed. Its dishonesty has been shown in the same manner.

It is difficult to imagine how two such different questions could be so mixed up and confounded. With a standard of value already established (the sovereign here and the franc in France), the amount of tax which the importer of bullion will pay could have been easily ascertained. If reasoning would not solve the question, then trial will, as is seen in the example of the French Mint. But the attempt to obtain the benefit of this tax by abstracting one grain from our already existing standard, has been shown to be so unreasonable, that it could only have been put forward by men who had a totally different object in view, and were unable to calculate the collateral effects of their own scheme.

There is another circumstance having an important bearing on the present question, and which the advocates of the new system have hitherto omitted to explain. If a man sent his gold and agreed to the retaining of 8-10ths per cent. for seigniorage, as proposed by the Chancellor, would the Mint deliver to him at once the quantity of sovereigns he is entitled to receive according to the terms of the contract, or would they still keep up the usual delays and trouble? If the owner of the bullion is paid *at once*, then he loses about 6-10ths per cent. more than he does at present—that is, 8-10ths per cent. in all. If, however, the usual delay is still to occur, the owner pays the present 2-10ths per cent. occasioned by the delay, and an additional 8-10ths per cent. retained by the Chancellor, thus making in all about 1 per cent. Surely this is a point of sufficient importance to require elucidation.

Your obedient servant,

EXCHANGE BUILDINGS,
Sept. 22, 1860.

PAR.

THE GOLD COINAGE.

(The Daily Telegraph, September 25, 1869.—To the Editor.)

Sir,—I have read with much interest the letter of Professor Leone Levi in your columns of this day; but I am sorry to say I cannot concur in the strong approval the Professor expresses of the suggestion thrown out by the Chancellor of the Exchequer towards the close of the last session of Parliament, for the imposition of a seigniorage of 1 per cent. (nearly), or, in other words, the depreciation of the present sovereign to that extent.

In the first place, it appears to me that not even the ingenuity of the present Chancellor of the Exchequer, nor all the enthusiasm of Professor Levi in behalf of a uniform international coinage, can make the exchangeable value of 112 grains of fine gold equal to that of 113 grains of fine gold. But I do not presume to set up my humble opinion against that of such high authorities, and therefore I will, with your permission, Sir, ask the Professor to reconcile this difficulty; and I think it would be desirable that he should also enlighten the public on a few other points—for example:

When the new English 25-franc piece, containing 122·274 grains, is issued in lieu of the present sovereign, containing 123·274 grains, are all the sovereigns at present in circulation to be called in, or are both to be in circulation at the same time, and be declared of the same value?

If the former, is it not clear that the holders of the estimated 80 millions to 100 millions of sovereigns now in circulation must lose the 1 per cent.—say, from 800,000 *l.* to 1,000,000 *l.* ?

If the latter, shall we not have two coins in circulation of the same nominal value, but the one (I must not say intrinsically, as the Chancellor of the Exchequer denies that anything has an intrinsic value) relatively of less value than the other, or at a discount? And will not such a state

Mr. Leonard Bruton.

of things involve serious evils? Putting these alternatives aside, does not another arise, namely, as the coins are to be internationally legal tenders, how long will the French or other money-dealers be in discovering that their 122·274 grain—25-franc—piece is exchangeable for the English 123·274 grain sovereign, and in superseding the Queen's head by that of the Emperor, and in thus driving the former altogether out of circulation for the sake of the 1 per cent. profit.

A word as to the proposal for an international coinage, or rather for an international coin, which appears to be the ultimate object in the present proposal. It should not be forgotten that at present there is no such coin as a 25-franc piece in any country, and it does not appear that even France proposes to issue such a coin for general use, but only as a kind of sample—unless, indeed, England could be induced first to issue it, and then no doubt the French Mint would be busy enough in making them for the purpose of being exchanged for our sovereign, for the reason just mentioned, viz., the profit of 1 per cent. Further, it should be observed that the advantage to be gained by carrying out this proposal would be exceedingly limited. It would not affect the mode of keeping accounts or make them more internationally uniform; although it would in some cases get rid of some decimal fractions, inasmuch as the 1*l.* English would be expressed by 25 francs instead of 25·20—except to express different rates of exchange. The English would still keep their accounts in pounds, shillings, and pence, and the French theirs in francs; and it is a question whether or not the English is not the most comprehensive, after all, to those who understand both.

Professor Levi has referred to the Report of the Royal Commissioners on International Coinage (dated 25th July, 1868), in a manner to almost lead to the inference that that official document bears out the views of himself and the Chancellor of the Exchequer; but it is quite the contrary.

Out of fourteen Commissioners who signed that Report, only one (Mr. J. B. Smith) concurs in those views; and the Report distinctly states, that, "upon full consideration of all these circumstances, we do not recommend that this country should merely adopt a gold coin of the value of 25 francs to be substituted for the sovereign" (*Report*, p. 18). And in another part of their Report the Commissioners say :—

"The recommendation which we have hitherto considered—*i. e.*, that of reducing the value of the English pound to that of 25 francs—naturally proceeded from a conference in which four of the nations represented have already a currency founded on the basis of the franc. But the question as naturally suggests itself to persons in this country, whether the English pound might not more advantageously be adopted as the general monetary unit, and the value of the piece of 25 francs raised to that of the pound. Many reasons of considerable weight may be urged in favour of this course, by which the object proposed by the French Government, of establishing a convenient relation between the British coinage and that of the countries which have joined the convention, and of securing a common basis for a general international currency, would equally be attained."—(*Report*, p. 15.)

And then the Commissioners proceed to cite a number of the "weighty reasons" referred to, but it would occupy too much of your space to quote them.

In conclusion, I would strongly recommend every one who takes an interest in this very important question to read this valuable Report before coming to a hasty decision upon so difficult a question. For my own part, I must add that I have come to the same conclusion (at present) as the Commissioners—that, inasmuch as the object can be as well or better accomplished by the appreciation of a new foreign coin to the extent of twopence on 25 francs, that would be preferable as an alternative to the depreciation of the so long established English sovereign by the same amount. For whether under the name of seigniorage, mintage, or otherwise, or whether by the State or individuals, that depreciation to the extent already mentioned, of from 800,000*l*. to 1,000,000*l*., must be borne by this country—at least, so it appears to me—without any corresponding advantage accruing to it; whereas the same object may be accomplished, according to the Report of the Royal Com-

Mr. Leonard Bruton.

missioners, without any sacrifice whatever on the part of foreign States, except the trouble of creating a new 25-franc piece equal in value to the English sovereign.

If, however, Professor Levi desires that the question should be publicly discussed, an excellent opportunity will be afforded him for reading a paper, or otherwise raising it, at the approaching meeting of the National Association for the Promotion of Social Science at Bristol; and the Professor would, moreover, be thus promoting the object of the Chancellor of the Exchequer when he made his startling speech on the subject, at the close of the last session of Parliament, which was, he said, "to give the public an opportunity of ventilating the matter during the recess."

I am, Sir, your obedient servant,

LEONARD BRUTON,
BRISTOL, *Secretary to the Bristol Chamber of Commerce.*
Sept. 20, 1869.

THE BULLIONIST.
(September 25, 1869.)

LORD OVERSTONE, ON THE STANDARD OF VALUE.

To all earnest-minded persons the discussion of the proposed debasement of the gold coin of the realm must now seem to be closed. It has been summed up in a commendably brief and characteristically pregnant letter of Lord Overstone, which we publish, and which really leaves nothing more to be said on the ostensible purport of Mr. Lowe's proposal. On one of the latest days of the session the Chancellor of the Exchequer, it will be remembered, replying to Alderman Lawrence, declared that his object would not be attained in any other mode than by diminishing the quantity of standard gold in the sovereign, by about one per cent.—from 113 grains to 112 grains. On this basis the question has been argued, and column after column has been written to prove that the smaller quantity would still retain equal purchasing power with the larger, while the Mint would be—as it is not now—paid for the cost of coining. We observed early in the controversy that this consideration was altogether beside the real question which the public had soberly to consider, which was the maintenance intact or the degradation of the legal standard of money. As was to be expected, Lord Overstone simply declines to discuss topics as to purchasing power. The venerable member for Oxfordshire, a short time since, humorously described the various attempts made at bankruptcy reform as repeated efforts to get something out of nothing. What Mr. Lowe and the gentlemen who have made him their mouthpiece propose to accomplish is really nothing less than this act of creative power. By their plan the smaller sovereign is to remain of the same value as before, the Mint is to be paid for coining the bar gold and something more, and nobody is to defray the cost. The proposal is one which deserves to be dismissed simply with a laugh.

With Lord Overstone and Mr. Hubbard we say that a pound of legal account does not mean this or that amount of purchasing power, which is a constantly fluctuating quantity, and unsusceptible of measurement; as defined by law, a pound is 5 dwts. $3\frac{1}{6}\frac{7}{2}\frac{1}{3}$ grs. of standard gold. This is "the medium in which all money obligations are to be adjusted; the debtor and creditor classes are equally bound to give and to accept the specified amount of gold without reference to any amount of supposed purchasing power." These are the words of Lord Overstone, but the truth they convey does not really gain anything, except its clear enunciation from the recognized high authority of his lordship. A fact which is not denied, and which is declared in the plainest language by the Legislature, claims no support from authority. The service he has done is to have brought the weight of his great name in these matters to a statement of the true question before the public, and to have swept aside a mass of controversies wholly irrelevant and

The Bullionist.

likely to obscure in many minds the only practical point at issue. Is or is not our gold coin to be reduced in weight, on no matter what pretext? This is the question. Nor can we doubt that the answer of the country when it comes to be given in the House of Commons, if Mr. Lowe should persist in challenging an answer there, will be more or less in the language of the letters we refer to: "the amount of gold contained in a sovereign cannot be diminished without tampering with the standard, and a violation of good faith."

Lord Overstone's reasoning could not of course escape a certain amount of carping criticism. It is perfectly true that a large quantity of gold coin added to the circulation will depreciate the currency; but how can that fact possibly affect the conclusion above enunciated? Those who defend an undebased coinage claim to establish no barrier against depreciation; they simply demand that the quantity of gold in each sovereign shall be held sacred from diminution. How does it invalidate that claim founded upon positive and clear law in the shape of an Act of Parliament to allege that during the continuance of the Bank Suspension Act, early in the century, a bank-note was legal tender to discharge debt? Because more than fifty years since creditors were cheated by an ignorant Legislature, are creditors now to be defrauded of what the law has declared them entitled to? A Bank of England note is at present legal tender, no doubt. Why? Because there is a statutory obligation on the Bank to convert it to gold. What a miserable quibble, then, is it to pretend to argue that Lord Overstone has stated an untruth in declaring that a debtor can discharge his obligation only in gold! The logic of the argument is on a par with the courteousness of the expression.

But in treating the proposals of Mr. Lowe and his friends, while keeping steadily in view the maintenance of the sovereign at its legal standard weight, persons considering this question should not lose sight of the fact that the reduction by a seigniorage asked for on the ground of defraying the charge of coinage, is a mere pretext, savouring somewhat of dishonesty. At any rate, it is not put forward candidly. The real object is to bring English gold coins down to a level with those of France, whereby they might be capable of circulation on the Continent in an international coinage. If England is to enter such a cosmopolitan convention, however, some other means must be devised than that of "tampering with our standard, and violating good faith" towards creditors.

THE OBSERVER.

(September 26, 1869.)

In our number of September 12, we noticed the discussion which was then going on in *The Times* with reference to the coinage question. This discussion still continues, and a new correspondent of the highest reputation as a currency economist has lately entered the field. Lord Overstone has addressed a letter to *The Times*, which we conceive solves the problem which was submitted by the Chancellor of the Exchequer for consideration during the recess of Parliament.

The international monetary conference held in Paris during the summer of 1867 had recommended that the international coin should be a gold piece of the value of 25 francs. This is about one per cent., or twopence, less in value than our sovereign; and it was suggested that we should coin a new piece, which should contain only 112 grains of fine gold in place of 113, which the sovereign at present contains, in order that it might be of the precise value of 25 francs, and that this new coin should be held to be a pound sterling. At first sight it naturally appeared to every one that this would be a debasement of the coin, a lowering of the standard of value, and a direct fraud upon the national as well as the private creditor. Those who recommended this step towards a universal international currency, however, undertook to prove that such would not be the case, provided there was a seigniory or mintage charge equal to the grain of gold subtracted from the sovereign. This, according to Colonel Smith, late Master of the Calcutta Mint, would increase the exchangeable value of the new sovereign, making it equal in purchasing power to the old one.

This was the proposal submitted by Mr. Lowe in his speech at the end of the parliamentary session, viz., " Can we, by placing a sufficient mintage charge, make a smaller amount of gold buy as much as a larger amount, and ought this to be done?" The letters of *The Times* have been chiefly directed to this point. One half of the correspondents maintain that by the process suggested 112 grains of fine gold would purchase as much as 113 at present do. The other half argue, on the contrary, that the mintage charge would not in any way change the intrinsic value of the gold, or add to its purchasing power.

In this state of the question Lord Overstone comes into the field. He points out, precisely as we did in our number of the 12th of September, that the pound sterling is a piece of money containing 113 grains of fine gold, and stamped by the State, to certify its quality; that this is the amount of gold which the State is bound to pay the national creditor in the name of the pound sterling, as also the amount of gold which the private debtor is bound to pay to his creditor. To pass a law to authorize the debtor to give less than this would be, therefore, a flagrant breach of faith, which could not be tolerated for a moment. The creditor would have the right to say, " I gave you so much gold when you contracted your debt to me, and I will not take less in return. I do not recognize your theories about making 112 equal to 113, and I demand exactly what I gave you, and what you bound yourself to return to me." Such was the purport of the letter of Lord Overstone, and we consider it settles the question. The Legislature could never pass a law which bears on the face of it so manifest an injustice as that suggested. We therefore consider the problem settled, and are convinced Mr. Lowe will admit as much.

Before concluding this article, we have a few remarks to make with respect to the theory of Colonel Smith and the other correspondents of *The Times,* who hold that, by adding expense to the production of an article, you will increase its exchangeable value. It is proposed by the advocates for the change of the weight of the sovereign from 113 grains of fine gold to 112 grains, that 113 grains should be handed by the importer to the Mint, which should return to him a piece containing only 112 grains, the Mint retaining the unemployed grain as seigniorage. "This new sovereign of 112 grains will be equal in exchangeable value to the one of 113 grains," maintain those gentlemen, "for the value of a commodity depends always upon the cost of its production." Persons who assert such a doctrine ignore one of the first, fully recognized, principles of political science, viz., "That the exchangeable value of commodities depends entirely upon the demand and supply, and the cost of production only affects the value in so far as it affects the demand and supply."

This is particularly the case with currency, whether that consist of metal or paper. If, for instance—let us suppose the case—the number of sovereigns and every other item of the circulating medium should be doubled, other things remaining the same, it is absolutely certain that the price of all commodities would be doubled, or that the purchasing power of every piece of money would only be the half of what it previously was. Again, if the currency was diminished by one-half, a result the very reverse would occur. Every piece of money would be doubled in value. If, by Colonel Smith's proposition, the amount of gold in circulation was diminished, then he would be right, for this would be a diminution in the supply. But this he must prove. It will not do to take

The Observer.

for granted that the value will be increased by merely levying a tax upon the coinage.

Let us examine more particularly this point. Why, we ask, should the amount of gold converted into sovereigns be diminished by the process suggested? The importer of the gold hands over to the Mint so much gold, and the Mint returns him 100 light sovereigns in place of 100 full weight sovereigns, as it previously did; that is to say, the Mint retains one per cent. of the gold given it. What does the Mint do with this? As a matter of course it converts it into another sovereign, which it disposes of as a profit for the establishment. There is thus 101 sovereigns instead of 100, which, according to the principle of demand and supply, will render the new sovereign just over one per cent. of less value in exchange than the old one. The International Coinage Commissioners, presided over by Lord Halifax, which held their sittings in 1868, came to the same conclusion which we have just announced, but by a different process. They reported as their opinion that the new sovereign of 112 grains of fine gold could not have the same purchasing power of the old one of 113, and that for the following reason:—" The subtraction of the grain of gold is for the express purpose of making the new sovereign exactly of the same value as 25 francs. Now the present sovereign exchanges for 25 francs and two pence. It therefore follows as certain that the new sovereign of merely 25 francs value must be two pence less value than the old sovereign."

We have entered into the discussion with regard to what determines the purchasing power of currency, merely as a matter of reasoning and investigation. This, however, is not at all necessary. As we have already stated, we consider the reason given by Lord Overstone as quite sufficient to deter the nation from making the alteration suggested. The national creditor and the private creditor have lent so much gold, and have stipulated that the same amount of gold should be paid back to them. We are, therefore, bound, as a nation, to keep good faith with both, and to see that they are not defrauded, which they would have a right to consider themselves, were we to countenance the paying them back in a smaller coin than that in which their engagements were contracted.

THE SOVEREIGN.
(The Times, September 28, 1869.—To the Editor.)

SIR,—Lord Overstone, notwithstanding the correction which I ventured to suggest to him, persists in saying that " Gold of *fixed weight and fineness*, and in the form of coin, is the medium in which every creditor is entitled to receive, and every debtor is bound to discharge, a debt. This is a plain, distinct right on one side, and obligation on the other side." This proposition has two aspects. It purports to state the law and the practice of this country. I assert that it greatly misstates both. Lord Overstone, in the very letter in which he reproduces this sweeping statement, admits that a bank-note, which is neither bullion nor coin, discharges a debt—that is, that when it is tendered in payment, the creditor cannot legally refuse it and ask for gold. " Oh, but," says Lord Overstone, " the note is a promise to pay, and so it discharges a debt." The proposition, then, is false on the showing of its author, and ought to be re-modelled thus in order to make it accord with the opinions of its author:—" Gold of fixed weight and fineness in the form of coin, *and promises to give the coin in exchange for the bank-note*, are the medium in which," &c. Lord Overstone takes up the position that a sovereign of the same value as the present sovereign, the value being made up of slightly different ingredients, cannot be substituted for the present sovereign without a breach of faith. His theory is that the standard of value is in the coin itself, and nowhere else, and so he omits the note in his account of legal tender.
Aliquis.

Now, whatever may be the imperfection of a sovereign having a grain less gold in it than the present sovereign is by Lord Overstone assumed to have, it surely is, on the theory which considers the circulating coin as the standard of value, a better payment than a piece of paper, which is, as far as material goes, worth nothing at all.

Lord Overstone's proposition assumes that all sovereigns, when issued, are required by law to be of the same weight and fineness. If this is not so, the circulating sovereign cannot be, as he asserts it is, the absolute standard of value, nor can the creditor be entitled to receive "gold of fixed weight and fineness." I alluded to the real state of the law of coinage in my former letter, of which, to judge by his reply, Lord Overstone has never heard. Sovereigns which do not exceed the Mint remedy for fineness of 1-16 carat, and which weigh $122\frac{1}{2}$ grains instead of 123·274, are legal tender, and such sovereigns fall short of the legal weight of the sovereign by 0·91 per cent. That is to say, between two sovereigns the law allows a difference of more than 2d. in the value of the gold, and compels the creditor to take either one or the other in payment of a debt. Which is the standard of value—the sovereign which, as bullion, is worth 238d., or the sovereign which, as bullion, is worth 240d.? Both cannot be, for that would be as absurd as to have two different lengths for a foot, or two different weights for a pound. The difference between one sovereign and another already allowed by law without any compensation is greater than the proposed change with the compensation of a Mint charge of corresponding amount. So that it appears that Lord Overstone's proposition must undergo a second modification, and that, instead of "gold of fixed weight and fineness," we ought to write "sovereigns the difference between the value of which does not exceed 2d."

Lord Overstone's proposition will then stand thus:—Sovereigns the difference between the value of which does not exceed 2d. and promises to pay them are the medium in which every creditor is entitled to receive, and every debtor is bound to discharge, a debt. What inference Lord Overstone may draw from this proposition I know not. To me it seems to establish one thing very clearly, and that is that we must look for the standard of value elsewhere than in the sovereign as defined by law.

As a statement of fact, the proposition I am considering is still less accurate. It appears from a statement of the late Master of the Mint that some 35 millions of our circulation are below the limit at which sovereigns cease to be legal tender, and that they continue to circulate, nevertheless. So that about half the gold coin is already lighter than the proposed new sovereign, and that without any compensation,—

> "And what is the oddest part of the curse,
> Nobody seems one penny the worse."

Do not these things teach us to look for the standard of value, not in the circulating sovereign which is by law allowed to vary so much in value, and by practice varies so much more, but in the terms on which alone the sovereign can be obtained? A sovereign is worth what it will cost to obtain a new one, and so is a note.

Lord Overstone asked, what is the limit to mintage? I answer, the point at which it will pay to counterfeit sovereigns—that is, to make them of the same fineness and weight as lawful coin in order to escape the tax or deduction levied or made by the Government.

I am, Sir, your obedient servant,

Sept. 27, 1869. ALIQUIS.

THE SOVEREIGN.
(The Times, September 28, 1869.—To the Editor.)

SIR,—It is constantly put forward as an argument to induce this country to join the International Coinage League that Belgium, Switzerland, and Italy saw the advantages of the system so clearly that, as soon as circumstances per-

Par.

mitted, they entered into it by converting their old currencies into coins of equal value with the franc. But it can be proved that neither of the three nations named threw aside their old systems for the sole purpose of joining the League; neither did they enter into it from mere admiration of its abstract or theoretical beauty. It can also be clearly shown that the circumstances which drove each of them into the measure are so totally different to our present position as to offer no valid ground for inducing us to follow their example.

The following were the real positions of each of these States:—

1. As soon as Belgium became separated from Holland it was requisite that she should prepare within a reasonable time to assert her sovereign rights by having a coinage of her own. There was also a political necessity that, whenever the change should be made, she should, as much as possible, separate her subjects from the former *régime*, and that for this cause the new currency should not be of the same denomination or value as the Dutch florin.

2. Switzerland, until she adopted her new currency, possessed several separate systems of coinage. In so small a country this was at all times an absurdity and inconvenience even among her own people; but when she became the main link of communication between the parts of Europe north and south of her, the necessity of some change which would insure uniformity of coin in their own country was quite evident.

3. Italy became one nation by the coalition of several smaller ones, nearly each of whom possessed a separate currency. The political motive of asserting her sovereignty by having a coinage of her own was, therefore, the same as in the case of Belgium. The necessity, also, of uniformity in the money of all her provinces was as urgent as in the case of Switzerland. Italy, therefore, was compelled to fix on some new standard of value for reasons compounded of those which influenced the other two.

Now, these considerations pointed out to each nation the absolute necessity of making *some* alteration in their currencies. Switzerland and Italy, so far as the internal trade of each was concerned, might adopt any standard or integer, whether it was of the same value as a coin already existing in some other country, or one entirely invented by themselves. Belgium had also the same range of choice, with the one exception, that the Dutch florin was not desirable on political grounds. But whatever standard of value each selected for the future, the great and inevitable inconvenience of the change itself must be endured.

It was natural, therefore, that, France being a near and conterminous neighbour to them all, they should select her coin, the franc, as the integer of value, and thus obtain by means of the trouble which *must* be endured in passing from one currency to another, the advantages, however slight they might be, of having a coin of equal value to the one just over the frontiers.

When nations actually touch each other this is certainly an advantage not to be despised, so far as regards small and daily transactions between the inhabitants on the borders. It is evidently of no importance in wholesale trade, the greater part of which is carried on by means of bills; and there must even under the new system be an exchange between Paris and Antwerp, or the other capitals and chief towns.

The motives in all the cases for *some* change being so urgent, each nation was right in endeavouring to obtain an advantage, however slight, which might even in a small degree compensate for the trouble of a change which was forced upon them by other considerations. A man will accept even three-halfpence in the pound in the winding-up of a bad business, rather than receive no dividend at all.

It will be observed that these arguments are based on the supposition that the choice the above three nations made was perfectly free. But with a too powerful ally like their great neighbour, it may be thought that a little

Par.

friendly advice was also given. France would readily perceive that the advantages of the League to her would at least be something, however small it might be, provided, as in these cases was the fact, she could not possibly suffer any inconvenience herself, as her own coinage would remain unaltered. The same kind and disinterested advice has been recently offered to us by foreign writers. The change on our part may give some very slight convenience to them; the inconvenience and risk must fall upon us, which, no doubt, they will be able to bear with stoical fortitude. If philosophy can do no more, it at least teaches us to bear with equanimity the misfortunes of others.

Now, if England possessed a different currency in each county, or even only as many as recently existed in Switzerland and Italy, the necessity of one uniform standard of value would force itself upon all commercial men; and, provided it was arranged so as to ensure the due performance of previous contracts, they would be willing to submit to the great temporary inconveniences of the change, in order to secure the future advantages of uniformity at home. But even then in our case the only argument which could be brought forward to persuade us to adopt the French system would be the possible advantage to tourists,—the itinerants who go over for the purpose of passing their time pleasantly (or otherwise) to themselves, and to get the occasional opportunity of "writing to *The Times*" on the subject of the extortionate charges in continental tavern bills.

The three nations above-mentioned must have changed their currencies even had the franc never existed. And had they each adopted a different integer of value, they would equally have accomplished the purpose which was forced upon them by the circumstances of their respective cases. Their motives, therefore, when fairly investigated, furnish no arguments in favour of an international coinage, taken as a mere abstract principle, nor prove in any degree that they altered their coins for the express purpose of joining the League.

One feature, however, which is common to the proceedings of all three nations is particularly deserving of attention. As soon as they had fixed upon the value of the coin which was in future to form the basis of their currency, they followed the example set them by France more than half a century back, and provided a tariff rate by which contracts still existing and expressed in the old money should be *honestly* discharged in the new. To English philosophers was left the unenviable task of proposing a plan in which that important condition was left out.

EXCHANGE BUILDINGS, PAR.
Sept. 27, 1869.

P.S.—Your paper of this day contains a letter, signed "J.," intended apparently to remind us that by the plan of the Chancellor of abstracting one grain of gold from the sovereign we should be enabled to provide for the constant loss in our coinage arising from wear. Now, the proposed plan of arriving at the reduction of the intrinsic value of our coin to that of a 25-franc piece has been already proved to be impracticable, because it has been shown that under the circumstances which would prevail, were the new scheme adopted, we should get no bullion to be coined.

But even supposing that the plan could be made to work, your new correspondent has merely given a fresh illustration of the old adage of "robbing Peter to pay Paul." The deterioration by wear is inevitable, and cannot be replaced, except at the expense of some one. By our present arrangements this loss is theoretically and frequently practically thrown upon the *last* holder of the light sovereign. Your correspondent "J." takes this unfortunate individual under his special care, and to relieve him he suggests the propriety of making the charge of all on the *first* owner of the sovereign.

If we were to grant the injustice of making any individual pay a loss which is incurred for the general benefit of all who employ the coin, it would be a difficult matter to decide upon abstract principles which of the two parties named (the first or the last possessor) should incur the penalty. Practically the question is decided by the consideration that the present plan is the only mode by which an unfair deterioration of the coin can be prevented.

THE GOLD COINAGE.
(The Daily Telegraph, September 29, 1869.—To the Editor.)

SIR,—Your correspondent, Mr. Leonard Bruton, of the Bristol Chamber of Commerce, asks a very important question—namely, whether the introduction of the contemplated change in the quantity of fine gold contained in the sovereign will not necessitate a re-coinage. As far as I can judge, it will be necessary to call in the present sovereigns, if for no other reasons than for the altered weight which the new coin will have, especially with 1-10th alloy, instead of 1-12th. The present sovereign, with 113·001 grains of fine gold, weighs 123·274 grains. The new sovereign, with 112·006 grains of fine gold, will weigh 124·452 grains. The Royal Commissioners were of opinion that a re-coinage would be necessary, but they admitted that a gradual re-coinage would be required under any circumstances, a large portion—about a third—of the gold coins in circulation being already below the legal weight. There is no reason, however, for apprehending the loss of 1,000,000l. by such re-coinage, as Mr. Bruton suggests. The holders of the present sovereigns will receive for them coins of precisely the same value, and will lose nothing. The Government will defray the cost of re-coinage, estimated at 150,000l., but they will be reimbursed by the mintage, thereafter to be imposed. This, of course, does not provide for the deficient weight of the gold in circulation; for, as it is, the holder of light coins loses the difference.

Mr. L. Levi.

The precise method for obtaining an international coinage is another question. I fully coincide with Mr. Bruton, that if the advantage were limited to getting rid of the decimal fraction between 25 f. and 25 f. 20 c., it would scarcely be worth the trouble of the change. The contemplated reduction, however, in the weight of the sovereign is most valuable, inasmuch as it will enable us, by another slight change, to obtain the best unit of accounts for international purposes, and the simplest and best decimal unit. If the new sovereign be divided into twenty-five shillings of tenpence each, accounts may then be kept either in sovereigns precisely worth 25 francs; or in ducats or Victorias, as they may be called, of a hundred pence each, or ten francs; two and a half of such Victorias being equivalent to one sovereign, and ten such to four sovereigns, or one hundred francs. If Mr. Bruton will consult my evidence before the Royal Commissioners on International Coinage (p. 26), my report on the International Monetary Conference presented to both Houses of Parliament, and my paper read at the Society of Arts (vol. xvi., p. 17), he will see that the friends of international coinage are not satisfied with a single international coin, but aim at one common unit of accounts, decimally subdivided or multiplied; the subordinate coins, as well as the principle units, being alike precisely identical and interchangeable.

I have the honour to be, Sir, your obedient servant,

TEMPLE,   LEONE LEVI.
Sept. 28, 1869.

THE ECHO.
(Sept. 30, 1869.)

THE SOVEREIGN.

IT is well known by this time that a conspiracy has been laid to tamper with the beautiful sovereign—to reduce the shining gold which it contains, and to alter its purity by increasing its alloy. The plot was concocted at Paris at the International Monetary Conference in 1867, but the scene of action has been since transferred to London, and the Chancellor of the Exchequer has placed himself at the head of the conspirators. In days gone by Kings and Queens could at pleasure alter the monetary standard of the country, and under the Edwards and the Henrys the pound sterling, from 407 grains, gradually fell to 113; but since it was fixed at that limit in 1817, no change has been allowed, and so it has remained unto this day, when with a view of bringing about an international coinage, and for the purpose of effecting some economy in the Mint, one grain of gold is proposed to be taken away from the weight of the sovereign, its value being replaced by a mintage charge of one per cent.

It could not be expected, however, that such a suggestion would be allowed to remain unchallenged. The pound sterling, it is said, is not a conventional coin—a token—but a specific quantity of gold. Every contract entered into for the last one hundred and fifty years and more, was based on that understanding. Alter the weight of the sovereign, and an open breach of faith will be publicly sanctioned. The holder of stock and the public creditor of every species of security will be defrauded of one pound in every hundred. The sovereign will no longer purchase the same quantity of other commodities; the exchanges will be affected; and it is a debasement of the standard which England ought never to allow. This and much more has been said for the last two months by a few warm partisans of things as they are, defenders of existing institutions.

But let us see how the matter does really stand? First of all, has a good reason been made out for the change? What interests will it subserve—what advantages are we to get? To our mind, an international and decimal coinage is a great desideratum. What annoyance would it cause if every county in England had its own moneys, weights, and measures? Would it not be worth while to make some sacrifices to bring about one general system? Well, that is precisely the state of Europe, or rather that of the civilized world, at this time, and a laudable effort has been made to blot out this inconvenience. Should we stand quite aloof, and say to other states, You may change, but we will not move? Surely it does not become us, nor is it consistent with our interest, to be so selfish and insulated. But how is it to be achieved? The proposal is this. Upon the bases of the coinage of the Convention, which includes France, Italy, Belgium, Switzerland, and several other countries, France might coin a twenty-franc piece containing 112·006 grains of fine gold. Let England lower the weight of her sovereign to the same extent, and they will be interchangeable. Nay, more: should the United States make at the same time a small change in her dollar, we should have a French five-franc piece and an United States dollar, each equal to four English shillings; four United States dollars and a French napoleon, equal to sixteen shillings; and five dollars equal to an English sovereign. We are not sure, indeed, whether this plan of equation will answer the object in view, and doubts may be raised as to the possibility of taking the sovereign as an international unit. It may be noticed that France does not possess such a coin, nor does she want it, seeing that the napoleon of twenty francs, which has a very extensive circulation, would differ very little in size and in weight from a twenty-five-franc piece. If an international currency is to be attempted, we should prefer one and the same money of accounts everywhere, with its divisions and subordinate coins perfectly alike. If, for instance, we could see our way to a ten-franc piece as the unit of one hundred pence for a universal coin, then we could understand each other perfectly at a glance, and both the principal unit and all the other coins would be the same throughout, the shilling of tenpence being like the franc, and the penny like the ten centimes.

In any case, however, the quantity of grains of fine gold in the twenty-five or the ten francs must first be settled,
The Echo.

and therefore it is proposed that 112·006 grains should be the future weight of the pound sterling, instead of 113·274 grains. Such being the point we have to reach, how can the reduction be made in the sovereign without unsettling all accounts? The sovereign of 112 grains will surely be a new and inferior unit to that of 113 grains, and the prices of all articles must rise in proportion to the diminished value of the coin received. But a plan has been found to remedy all this. At this moment the sovereign is coined for nothing, though the cost of making it and keeping it in full weight is nearly 1½ per cent. Charge one per cent. of seigniorage, and the value of the sovereign will be precisely the same as if no reduction of weight had taken place. No one can deny the perfect lawfulness of charging a mintage. The wonder is that any other plan should have been introduced. Gold is a commodity, like sugar, coffee, tea, or any other article. If the importer needs to have it assayed, manufactured, or stamped before he can give it currency, *he* ought to pay for that, and not the nation. The only difficulty is, whether the creditor of a sovereign of 113 grains of fine gold can be satisfied with a sovereign of 112 grains *plus* the rate of mintage. At first sight it would appear that he must be the loser. But the value of the new sovereign in the market will be the same as the old one, since no other sovereign of greater value will be in circulation. Nor does the creditor really get 113 grains of gold, pure and simple. If he is paid in bullion, he must change it at the Bank of England at 3*l.* 17*s.* 9*d.* per ounce, and thus lose 1½*d.* per ounce. If he is paid in sovereigns, we know that a very large number of them circulate much lighter in weight than they ought to be; so that, even as it is, a theoretical precision is not attained. What the creditor has a right to receive is twenty shillings' worth of pure gold, including the cost of manufacture, and that will exchange in England and everywhere within the range of the Convention for the same value as a sovereign of pure weight without that charge.

R

But let it not be thought that the realization of an international coinage depends in any way upon this particular plan. We may find it better to avoid this question altogether by fixing a tariff between the old and the new coinage. We may, as we said, set aside the sovereign, and adopt a new unit,—say, a ten-franc piece, or even a given number of grains of gold. There are other questions also open for consideration. The alloy is understood to be henceforth one-tenth instead of one-twelfth. What effect will that have on the weight of the sovereign, and how shall we compare the weight of the old with that of the new— would not this of itself necessitate a re-coinage, and a calling-in of all the existing sovereigns? " A Banker's Clerk " calls our attention to the fact that it would be impossible to test the accuracy of counting by weight if " Lowe " sovereigns were mixed with those now current. Steps must be taken to secure the mutual recognition on the part of all contracting nations of the same principle for the exchange of coin against bullion, and guarantees would have to be given for the purity of the coinage. Would it not be better, before we commit ourselves to any plan, to have an official International Conference, and see what mutual concessions may yet be made, on what points we are really agreed, and in what way the interests of all may be best preserved? The Royal Commissioners proposed such a course, and, with them, we are disposed to think that the various questions might be best considered, the various interests of different countries discussed, and their conflicting views reconciled, by authorized representatives of the different countries meeting in such a Conference.

The Echo.

THE GOLD COINAGE.

(The Daily Telegraph, October 5, 1869.—To the Editor.)

SIR,—I trust you will consider this question of sufficient importance to justify you in affording a little more of your valuable space for its discussion. With all due respect, however, to your correspondent, Professor Leone Levi, who commenced it in your columns, I must say that I consider his reply to me which appears in your issue of this day, to be so weak that, if I had not something to say, apart from my rejoinder to him, of paramount importance relative to the proposal of the Chancellor of the Exchequer to depreciate the English sovereign by 1 per cent., I should not now trouble you.

But to begin with Professor Levi. He now admits it will be necessary to call in our existing gold coinage. That is my first point. But the Professor says: " The holders of the present sovereigns will receive for them coins of precisely the same value, and will lose nothing." I beg you to observe, Sir, that this is mere assertion, not proof. I say, on the contrary, that every one who gives up 113 grains of fine gold, and is compelled to receive in exchange for them 112 grains, will lose one grain, or nearly 1 per cent., or 2*d*. on every sovereign, and that this on an issue of 800 millions will amount to 8,000,000*l*., or on 100 millions to one million; just as would happen if every holder of 100 sacks of flour (or any other article) were compelled to give up the one-hundredth part of every sack, and receive 99 parts of each in exchange, with a new stamp upon it merely, he would lose one sack (or other article) in every hundred. This too, it may be said, is mere assertion. But the difference is that in this latter case the assertion requires no demonstration, because it is self-evident. It might, however, be proved, if it were necessary; but as it is not, I may as well save your space. Not, however, to

Mr. L. Bruton. R 2

leave the matter quite so bald, I will refer to competent authorities, such as the Report of the Royal Commissioners and the evidence appended to it; amongst others, I may mention Professor Newmarch, The Right Hon. G. J. Göschen, M.P., Sir John Bowring, and—*mirabile dictu*—Professor Leone Levi himself! And, what is indeed passing strange, the Professor has actually, in his last letter, directed my attention to this evidence as well as to other productions of his, all of which I may say, in passing, I had previously read, and also that of other witnesses in the same cause, but not all on the same side. And what, then, is the evidence of the Professor, to which he himself refers me? Here it is, *verbatim et literatim*, at page 27 of the evidence appended to the Report of the Royal Commissioners on International Coinage, dated July 25, 1868.

Professor Leone Levi is giving evidence, and he says:

"It has been suggested we should declare the present pound to be worth 25 francs; but I cannot conceive how the pound, which is worth 25·20 francs, could by any method whatever be declared to be worth 25 francs. If you declare it to be of less value than it is it would be melted or exported."

"There is that difference?"—"There is, and you cannot touch it."

I think I need say no more on this point. "Out of thine own mouth, and at thine own request," &c.

But, Sir, I must ask your permission to say a word or two on another branch of this question—viz., that of creating a 25-franc piece for the purpose of promoting a system of international decimal coinage. And here, too, I am sorry to say, Professor Levi is equally inconsistent, as I shall prove in the same manner, and from the same evidence—*i.e.*, his own. That Professor Levi is now a most zealous advocate of the proposal for issuing a 25-franc piece for promoting this object, I suppose cannot be denied. It was one of my reasons for troubling you with my former letter. But in his evidence to which he refers me, what did he say? Why, the following, amongst a multiplicity of other things, against the very same proposal:

Mr. L. Bruton.

"Q. 368, page 27 (as before). On the whole you object to the 25-franc scheme?"—"A. Entirely."

"Q. 369, (the Astronomer-Royal). Would any part of your difficulty be in any way removed by giving a new name to the coin?"—"A. I do not think the adoption of a new name would settle it, because you would have a coin precisely equal in size, or perhaps larger and better-looking and newer, very much like another coin at the same time in circulation, yet of less value. I think that is fatal, and by no process that I can conceive of could you say that to be worth 25 francs which is worth 25·20 francs. But, as I said, I am not at all satisfied with the pound and mille scheme. I do not think that it would ever be tenable, and this would only introduce another item of difficulty. There is another difficulty with respect to the 25 francs—that after you have made the change, you will still have to make calculations and to multiply or to divide the accounts of other countries by 5 or 25. Thus we should not attain that which we wish to attain; and I think that when you do enter into a laborious, expensive, and troublesome change, you should endeavour to make the reform as perfect as possible, in a permanent manner, and not with a view of having to change it again in ten, fifteen, or twenty years afterwards. Upon all considerations, therefore, I [that is, Professor Leone Levi] reject the 25-franc scheme altogether."

Here, Sir, I propose to leave this question of the 25-franc piece, either for national or for international purposes, so far as the Professor and myself are concerned; for we are in perfect accord, and the objections could not possibly be more forcibly put.

And now I come to that much more important matter to which I alluded at the commencement of this letter. Before throwing out the suggestion he did for an alteration in our gold currency and the mode of issuing it and the payment of its cost, the Chancellor of the Exchequer procured a Report from the Master of the Mint and the late Master of the Calcutta Mint, which is now before me. It is "A Return Ordered by the House of Commons, June 28, 1869," and is entitled—

Copy "of REPORT addressed to the Chancellor of the Exchequer by the Master of the Mint and Colonel *Smith*, late Master of the Calcutta Mint, on the MINTAGE necessary to cover the Expenses of Establishing and Maintaining the GOLD CURRENCY."

You will be pleased to bear in mind that I am now endeavouring to be as brief as possible; but I pledge myself to the accuracy of the extracts I shall make from this document. In the result I shall show, as I think, incontrovertibly, that one of the grossest blunders has been committed that was ever sent forth in an official document, and upon which, as I believe, the Chancellor of the Exchequer has been misled into the suggestion he has thrown out for charging a mintage or seigniorage of 1 per cent. on all the gold coinage to be in future issued in this country.

The result of the Report, then, is this (in brief):

That for the purposes named in the head of the Report it would be necessary to provide for the coinage,—1st, of four millions of bullion for ordinary annual supply, at ½d., or 0·21 per cent. £8,400

2nd, For annual renewal of six millions of coinage, at ditto, ditto 12,870

And 3rd, For loss by wear and tear 35,000

Total £56,270

Total coinage (in round figures), ten millions per annum; and this sum of 56,270*l*., the Report says, would amount to 1*l*. 8*s*. 1½*d*. per cent.

These are the exact words of the paragraph which immediately follows the figures (set out more minutely than I have given them, and that is all) quoted above:

"12. What does this amount to on our estimated annual coinage of about ten millions, made up of four millions of first coinage, and six millions of renewal?"—" It is 1·40676 (1*l*. 8*s*. 1½*d*.) per cent."

And then there follows another much more elaborate calculation, worked out algebraically, which brings out 1*l*. 13*s*. 6*d*. per cent. from the same data. How that happens I am not mathematician enough to decide; but of this I feel perfectly assured, that both are grossly erroneous. Any one else may see the same at a glance. How to account for the blunder I know not.

According to my arithmetic, Sir, a sum of 56,270*l*. per annum on 10,000,000*l*. would be 11*s*. 1*d*. (eleven shillings and

Mr. L. Bruton.

one penny) per cent.* instead of 1l. 8s. 1½d. or 1l. 13s. 6d. And here, Sir, I shall conclude with this single remark, that, if I am right, I think that the Chancellor of the Exchequer's proposal or suggestion must fall to the ground, for no one could have the conscience to charge one per cent. for that which costs a little over one-half per cent.; and if I am wrong I am open to correction, for which I wait, and shall then, perhaps, have something more to say on the merits and demerits of this startling proposal.

I am, Sir, your obedient servant,

LEONARD BRUTON,
BRISTOL, *Secretary to the Bristol Chamber of Commerce.*
Oct. 1, 1869.

* THE GOLD COINAGE.—Mr. Leonard Bruton, whose letter we published yesterday, concluded his remarks on the gold coinage by stating that the sum of 56,270l. per annum on 10,000,000l. would be 11s. 1d. per cent. Our correspondent is incorrect—the per-centage being 11·254 shillings, or a trifle over 11s. 3d. per cent.—[*Ed. D. T.*, Oct. 6, 1869.]

GOLD COINAGE.

(The Daily Telegraph, October 7, 1869.—To the Editor.)

SIR,—I observe the paragraph in your columns of this day, in which you say that I am incorrect in my calculation to the extent of 2d. per cent.—and so I should be if the exact sum were 10,000,000l.; but that is not the case. I expressly stated that, to save your space, I left out details, and I took the round figures, as the paragraph I quoted from the Parliamentary Return did. The exact sum, however, is 10,177,777l., as you will see by the copy of the Parliamentary Paper referred to, which I take this opportunity of enclosing: 56,270l. upon this sum would be 11·057 shillings, or 11s. and rather more than two-thirds of a penny; so that I threw in nearly a third of a penny to avoid fractions.

But the difference I have now explained is very immaterial. The material question is the error in the Parlia-

Mr. L. Bruton.

mentary Return, which, from the same data, gives 1*l*. 8*s*. 1½*d*., or 1*l*. 13*s*. 6*d*. per cent. (which we please, I suppose); and I trust, Sir, you will keep that question before the public until some explanation or acknowledgment has been given by those who are responsible for what at present appears to be a gross mistake.

     I am, Sir, your obedient servant,
BRISTOL,   LEONARD BRUTON.
Oct. 6, 1869.

THE GOLD COINAGE.

(The Daily Telegraph, October 9, 1869.—To the Editor.)

SIR,—I see by the letter of Mr. Leonard Bruton, in your paper to-day, that no one has yet pointed out the very excusable misapprehension into which he has been led by the wording of the paragraph which he quotes from the "Report of the Master of the Mint and Colonel Smith," &c. A moment's consideration will show that the real meaning is, that 56,270*l*. is 1*l*. 8*s*. 1½*d*. per cent. on four millions, the assumed new coinage. It is clear that on the re-coinage of six millions of light sovereigns there is no one to bear the expense, and consequently the whole "mintage necessary to cover the expenses of establishing and maintaining the gold currency" must be borne by the four millions of bullion. I shall be glad if you will permit me to call attention to this point, as it gives me the opportunity of pointing out the utter absurdity of this scheme of the two Mint Masters. An experience of twenty years in the bullion trade leaves me totally unable to imagine where the patriotic individuals are to be found who will "import" bar gold into the Mint for coinage to the extent of four millions per annum, and submit to be mulcted of 1*l*. 8*s*. 1½*d*. per cent. thereon, when they have only to send their gold to Paris, and they will receive its value less 4*s*. per cent. Even if it were desirable that the State should maintain
H. M. H.

the weight of the sovereigns in circulation, on what principle should the importers of the four millions of bar gold, required for new coinage in each year, be called upon to pay, not only for the coinage of their own bullion, but for the re-coinage of six millions of light sovereigns, and the average loss by wear and tear of the whole circulation?

But·is it advisable that the State should be bound to maintain the weight of the coin? I should have thought that it was self-evident that such a rule would offer a premium on the "sweating" of sovereigns, of which a certain class would not be slow to avail itself; and the effect would be to swell indefinitely the average annual "loss by wear and tear." Under the present system, what individual loses one shilling in the year by light gold? I venture to answer, not one person in a thousand, except the bankers and merchants, who protect themselves against the loss in their calculations of profit. It would, however, be only just if the Mint were to pay for light sovereigns the price per oz. at which they are issued—viz., $3l.$ $17s.$ $10\frac{1}{2}d.$, instead of leaving the Bank of England to give only $3l.$ $17s.$ $6\frac{1}{2}d.$, which is all they will realize after melting into bars.

The impolicy of Mr. Lowe's suggestion of reducing the weight of the sovereign has been thoroughly illustrated by many practical writers in the press; but there is one point which I have not observed to have been dwelt upon. I refer to the fact that to alter the intrinsic *(pace, Mr. Lowe)* value of the sovereign, is to tamper with "the measure of value" of probably two-thirds of all the commercial and financial transactions in the world, for the hypothetical advantage of making it exchangeable with a proposed new coin, which, after all, would not be a unit, but a compound denomination—25 francs. It is consolatory to observe, that, if all the theorists are in favour of Mr. Lowe's idea, all the practical men are against it; and as there are surely more men of business than philosophers in the House, it may be assumed that there is not much chance of the perpetration of such a suicidal act. I am so much at a loss to understand how a man of such intellect as Mr. Lowe can be misled by a theory, that I can only think his faith in the scheme must be like that of the old father of the Church, and that if asked why he believed in it, he would answer, "*Credo quia impossibile est.*"

I am, Sir, yours, &c.,

Oct. 7, 1869.

H. M. H.

THE GOLD COINAGE.

(The Daily Telegraph, October 13, 1869.—To the Editor.)

SIR,—Your correspondent "H. M. H." may be right in assuming that the authors of the Report (285), when they say, as they do, "Our annual estimated coinage, amounting to about ten millions," meant four millions; but I cannot admit that the latter is "the real meaning," if any regard is to be paid to the facts, the figures, and words stated in that Report. Your correspondent, or any one else, may, by procuring the return from the printers to the House of Commons, Abingdon-street, at the cost of one halfpenny, satisfy himself on this point; or, if "H. M. H." will furnish me with his address, I will send him a copy of it. I cannot silently submit to bear the blunders of others. If the authors of the Report have taken the wrong datum for their calculation, that is their fault, not mine.

It is quite certain that the future annual coinage of gold is estimated in that Report at 10,177,777*l*. And, although it is true that the sum of 56,270*l*. would be 1*l*. 8*s*. 1½*d*. per cent. on 4,000,000*l*., it is not so stated anywhere in that document, and it is equally certain it would be but 11*s*. 1*d*. on the former sum, as I have proved. This point was not overlooked by me; but it was not my duty to alter official documents. I am bound to take them as they are sent forth.

Mr. L. Bruton.

But, putting this particular question aside for a moment, let us return to the proposal of the Chancellor of the Exchequer, to deduct from each future sovereign one grain of gold, or nearly 1 per cent. On 10,177,777*l.* this would amount to 101,777*l.* Now, the Report in question says that the cost of "the annual coinage of about ten millions, made up of four millions of first coinage and six millions of renewal," would be 56,270*l.*; so that the Chancellor of the Exchequer proposes to charge individuals who will be compelled to have gold coined for the use of the public to pay 45,507*l.* per annum more than the operation costs—that is, 80·87 per cent. profit on the outlay. And if the sum were but 4,000,000*l.*, the Chancellor would get but 40,000*l.* per annum, being 16,270*l.* less per annum than it costs, which is evidently not his intention. Moreover, the present annual coinage of gold is upwards of 5,000,000*l.* per annum, without providing for renewal or wear and tear. (*Vide* Report of the Royal Commissioners, p. 94.) Therefore 4,000,000*l.* could not suffice in future for both purposes.

But what benefit would individuals or this nation derive from the change? I can see many evils which would result in addition to those mentioned by your correspondent "H. M. H." (I wish, by-the-bye, the reply had come from "H. M. M.," *i.e.*, Her Majesty's Mint.)

I said in my former letter that I desired to abstain from entering on the wide field I have just hinted at until the question of the cost of the operation *per se* shall be disposed of. Keeping therefore, for the present, to this latter point, we must add to this sum of 101,777*l.* per annum, the other item of 1 per cent. to be deducted from all our gold coinage at present in circulation (in consequence of its being necessary to call it in), amounting, according to this Report, to 80,000,000*l.*, which gives, as I have shown before, 800,000*l.* of further loss to individuals or the State. It is said that about one-third of that amount is already below the legal standard. If so, it is liable to be called in, and will be, as fast as it reaches the Bank of England, and the unfortunate individuals who carry it to the Bank will have to bear the loss. But there is, in return, security by this arrangement against the wilful " sweating " or " clipping " of the Queen's coin. The statement in the Report that one-third of our present gold coinage is below the legal standard is based on a calculation of Professor Jevons; but even if that statement be correct, does it afford any sufficient reason for making this immediate, voluntary, and anticipatory sacrifice on the whole of the present gold coinage?

Again, why should particular individuals be compelled to pay this tax? Can any article be a fairer subject for a general tax than the cost of supplying the whole nation with the legal coin of the realm? And, as to the " tottle of the whole," we now know what it is. The evidence of the officers of the Mint, contained in the Report of the Royal Commissioners on International Coinage (page 94), tells us that " the annual coinage expenses amount to about 30,000*l*." The details are given, and it appears that one-half is fairly chargeable on the silver and copper coinage, which yields a profit, leaving 15,000*l*. as the present annual cost of coining 5,000,000*l*. of sovereigns and half-sovereigns, not including " wear and tear," which is paid for by individuals as the worn coins are brought into the Bank.

Is it worth while, then, apart from the question of cost, which alone I have previously dealt with, to debase our " standard of value," which has been the same now for more than fifty years, and to throw the whole of our currency arrangements, and all contracts between debtor and creditor into confusion, for the sake of saving this paltry sum of 15,000*l*. per annum? The mentioning of " contracts " reminds one of the National Debt of (say) 800,000,000*l*., which this scheme would also depreciate nearly 1 per cent.; for the nation has contracted to pay that debt in " pounds sterling," each pound containing 113 grains of fine gold; and the nation's creditors cannot honestly be compelled to accept instead 800 millions of

Mr. L. Bruton.

coins of the same name, but containing only 112 grains of fine gold, or nearly 1 per cent. less, nor can any other creditor. I never heard of any one in this country who was dissatisfied with the present English sovereign. If other nations desire an "international coin," it is much easier for them to create a new gold piece of equal value to the English sovereign than it is for us to depreciate ours (*vide* Report of the Royal Commission); and it should be known that the Americans prefer it, and that the Senate of the United States has decidedly repudiated the idea of depreciating their dollar for this purpose (*vide* Appendix to the Report of the Royal Commissioners, pp. 316 to 320).

Upon the whole, Sir, I think there can be no doubt that this scheme will never be sanctioned by the English Parliament; and, fortunately, without that sanction it cannot be carried into effect.

I am, Sir, yours, &c.,

BRISTOL, LEONARD BRUTON,
Oct. 9, 1869. *Secretary to the Bristol Chamber of Commerce.*

GOLD OR SILVER, OR GOLD AND SILVER.

(The Times, October 7, 1869.—To the Editor.)

SIR,—*L'Or et L'Argent* is the title of a treatise by M. Louis Wolowski, yet in the press, but of which the first part has, by the author's courtesy, been recently brought under my notice. The subject, whether in its abstract consideration or in its bearing upon the question of an international coin, is so interesting that I ask your leave to offer a few remarks upon this new work of M. Wolowski, the more earnestly because he will shortly publish the treatise in its completeness.

M. Wolowski regards with no approval the proceedings of the International Conference of Paris in 1867 convoked *Mr. J. G. Hubbard.*

by the efforts mainly of partisans of a gold standard. It afforded the opportunity of repairing by the aid of foreign auxiliaries the repeated defeats they had sustained in their attempts to subvert the monetary system of France. By an unanimous vote the Conference decided in favour of a single gold standard. Against this decision M. Wolowski energetically protests. I will endeavour briefly, with a sketch of the incidents affecting the proposal, to interweave his arguments against it.

"Until the present century silver had almost everywhere prevailed as the measure of value, although it had, as money, shared with gold the office of a medium of exchange. At the present time, with the exception of those countries which adopt the English sovereign, silver either rules alone as the measure of value, or holds that function concurrently with gold."

"Were the aspirations for a world-wide international gold coin to be realized, and were silver consequently deprived of its function as legal money, it would sink in value; and gold, on the other hand, with a widely-extended area to occupy, would be materially enhanced in value. Every debtor would be more heavily weighted in the discharge of his obligations, and a greater uncertainty would attend the estimation of money contracts having a distant maturity, depending, as it would, upon the variations of a single medium."

"There is no such thing as a standard of value; there can be none, for no standard can be found which is itself invariable. The law of Germinal, An. XI. (1803), did not pretend to establish a standard of value, it founded a "double legal money;" 100f. might be paid in coin containing either 29 grammes of gold or 450 grammes of silver. The option resting with the debtor gave him a certain advantage, but that advantage was in harmony with a wise and humane intention."

"The ratio of 1 to 15½ fixed in 1803 undervalued gold, which consequently bore a premium varying from time to time, but averaging about 1½ per cent. until 1850, when the increased supplies of gold reduced its relative superiority, and materially modified the ratio between gold and silver, as determined by the law. Commerce, always on the alert, found a profit in importing gold and in exporting silver, and this movement eventuated in emptying France of nearly the whole of her silver coin. The inconvenience inflicted on the country by the loss of its smaller coins was severe. However quickly fresh silver was coined, it vanished as quickly, and at last it became necessary to coin silver pieces of 2 francs and under at the reduced fineness of 835-1,000ths. The loss of the ecu of 5 francs as a medium of exchange has been compensated by the issue of quarter-napoleons; but the ecu when coined is still of the standard quality— 9-10ths fine. In despite of all attempts to supersede it, the silver franc has been thus far maintained, and the important principle of a double legal money, or double valuation, "*une monnaie bimetallique*," adopted by the States parties to the Convention of 1865 has been triumphantly supported up to the present time."

" The advocates of a single gold standard ignore alike the imperfections of a single medium and the merits of a double legal money, the superiority of the latter being more obvious if considered with a view to its incorporation in an international system than when viewed solely in its operation in any particular country. In framing the pendulum of a clock, steel and brass are combined, and the greater expansion or contraction in a variable temperature of one metal is corrected by the influence of the other, and the result of the combination is found in a more regular and equable movement; and so, to restrain the irregular oscillations of a measure of value, it should be compounded both of gold and silver, instead of employing for the purpose, one only of those metals. To establish, as by the law of 1803, gold and silver in a given ratio to each other is to have two legal moneys, but only one measure of value."

In this statement of the case, fairly I trust, however

inadequately, representing M. Wolowski's views, considerations are suggested well worthy of our attention, but which seem to have been little noticed in the general discussion of an international coinage.

It can hardly be questioned that a disarrangement of the measure of value either locally or generally would be a serious evil, or that to nullify the capacity of either gold or silver as a measure of value would have the effect of introducing a very sensible change in that which should, as far as possible, be unchangeable. Assuming for the argument that gold and silver now available in the commercial world for the purposes of money amount to 600 millions each, it is an aggregate of 1,200 millions that bears the disturbing influence of any extraordinary annual accession to the quantity of either metal. If gold alone were the legal money and standard of value, the increased production would be nearly twice as severe in its disturbing influence. If gold be substituted for silver as the standard coin of countries now employing a silver legal money to the amount of 300 millions, a portion, perhaps one-tenth, might be required for the subsidiary coins, but the residue, 270 millions, would lose its vocation as money, and, thrown back on the markets of the world, it would everywhere depress the value of silver and impair its stability as a standard. Gold, on the other hand, summoned to exercise its functions over a larger area, would be proportionably enhanced in comparison both with silver and with other commodities. If, then, equability is desirable in those materials which general consent has selected as the means of valuation, it would be unwise to affect the value by forcibly interfering with the functions of either of the precious metals.

M. Wolowski urges these reasons as arguments in favour of the retention of the double valuation in France; but the question arises—is this argument as strong now as it would have been in 1849, when the money of France was almost wholly silver, and when the adoption of an exclusive gold standard would have involved the entire
Mr. J. G. Hubbard.

change of her metallic currency? It would seem that the existence of a double valuation in France involved her in serious inconveniences during the period of transition from a silver to a gold coinage, arising in her case, not from direct legislation, but from the influx of Californian and Australian gold.

M. Wolowski makes light of these inconveniences—
" Silver, attracted by the higher price offered for the East, was exchanged abroad for a larger quantity of gold. France lost nothing in the exchange."—(*L'Or et L'Argent*, p. 185.) No doubt France received for her silver the equivalent she had herself fixed in 1803; but if, between 1850 and 1868, the proportionate value of gold to silver, instead of being 1 to 15·50, ranged at 1 to 15, and she was consequently drained of her silver, can it be accurate to say, "*La France n'y perdait pas?*" Japan had fixed the relative values of her gold and silver coin at 1 to 4; but the intrusion of commerce and the unscrupulous proceedings of foreign traders who hastened to relieve the Japanese of their gold at the stipulated rate of exchange for silver, brought on a reform of the currency of Japan only after a very extensive but unequal barter of the precious metals in which it could hardly be said, "*Le Japon n'y perdait pas.*"

France, it is true, has rarely been subject to the inconvenience she has recently experienced; but does not the reason of the unfrequency lie in this, that the coinage of France between 1803 and 1850 had virtually been a silver coinage with a silver valuation, and that gold had been, as an "*article de luxe*," occasionally desired by fastidious travellers, always at a premium? And would not the establishment in 1803 of a more exact equilibrium between gold and silver have entailed an intolerable uncertainty and inconvenience in all monetary transactions?

M. Wolowski, repudiating the name of a "double standard," illustrates his idea of the double valuation—
"*double monnaie legale*"—by the simile of the pendulum. The illustration admirably expresses the truth that the

s

average of the indications of several standards constitutes a better criterion of value than the indication of one alone. Thus, in the adjustment of the valuation of tythes, it was provided by the Act of Commutation that the amount of each commutation should yearly be adjusted by an average resulting from the combined prices of wheat, barley, and oats, and M. Wolowski's simile of the pendulum seems to require that every engagement should be discharged half in silver and half in gold. Perhaps M. Wolowski may, in the concluding portion of his work, explain how the discharge of obligations and debts of various kinds, public and private, could be effected partly in gold and partly in silver, or how, to avoid the inconvenience of using two media, the requisite sum in one medium could be ascertained.

But is the pendulum an accurate illustration of the system of double valuation as it existed in France? Would not the true illustration of the double valuation be found in two clocks, one with a steel, the other with a brass pendulum; the one going fastest in hot weather, the other in cold, but either available for the assessment of contracts for work by time at the volition of the employer of labour?

M. Wolowski has a tenderness for the debtor, whom he thinks entitled to any advantage arising from an uncertain contract. I do not perceive the justness or the sufficiency of this plea. In most countries the State is the strongest as well as the largest debtor, and could not safely be intrusted with the assessment of its own undefined liabilities, while, again, the existence of any uncertainty in the amount required for the satisfaction of a contract must be considered in itself as a most serious imperfection.

It would be difficult not to agree with M. Wolowski in desiring to preserve for both gold and silver the function of a measure of value as well as that of a medium of exchange, and in deprecating the positive evil of any forcible displacement of either metal. M. Wolowski's theory requires that, with a view to an international, or rather a universal, coinage, all countries should agree upon and adopt a double

Mr. J. G. Hubbard.

valuation, and he insists upon this condition with a generous solicitude for the wants and welfare of the whole civilized world; but it would greatly aid his argument if M. Wolowski would show that the interest which each particular country has in the continuance of the present distribution and engagement of the precious metals can be so strong as to induce it to abandon the system which is most immediately convenient to itself. Admitting that a double legal money in any country affords the readiest means for diffusing throughout the commercial world the fresh supplies of whichever metal may from time to time become overabundant, does it follow that it is to the interest of England to discard for a double valuation the single gold standard which she adopted more than half a century ago?

M. Wolowski is acquainted with the *Essay on Money and Coins* of Joseph Harris, Master of the Mint in 1757. Harris sturdily upheld silver rather than gold as the standard of value in this country, but he strongly insisted that " there can be but one standard of money." " Although," he says, " there may be good reasons for coining each of them (silver and gold), yet it is very certain that one only of these metals can be the money or standard measure of commerce in any country." . . . " It is impossible that both these metals can be a standard measure of the values of other things at the same time, and one of them must be a mere commodity with respect to the other."

Whatever may have been the motive for making gold our standard in 1816, the choice is made and cannot be reversed, nor does the experience of the past 50 years, including as they do the period of the new gold discoveries, suggest any misgivings as to the result of the decision. While France was being emptied of her silver coin, from the ecu down to the smallest fraction of a franc, England maintained her silver token coins, and encountered no other inconvenience from the vast influx of gold than having by her own needless generosity the task of coining some millions gratuitously.

The question at issue is truely and tersely solved by M. Leon Faucher in words which I transcribe from M. Wolowski's treatise (page 31):—

"Il est bon, il est necessaire, il est inevitable, que les peuples adoptent des mesures différentes pour la valeur. Les Etats se prêtent une mutuelle assistance quand le metal qui est marchandise en deça de la Manche est monnaie au delà, et réciproquement."

It is difficult to read M. Wolowski's pages and not conclude that the agitation for an international coinage has been conducted with more zeal than knowledge. An international coinage, meaning thereby a system under which every coin of all consenting nations should have an international legal currency, is upon an extended scale at the present time an impossibility. But an "international valuator," bringing into immediate relation the several national coinages, and harmonizing their meaning in the expression of value, would be a most important gain, and may be attainable even now over a very considerable area. A common valuator implies that a stipulated quantity of fine gold (if gold is chosen) should be incorporated in one of the coins of each national coinage. That coin might be the unit of account, or it might be a multiple, or a fraction of the unit; it might, or might not, be uniform in title; it might be 9-10ths fine in one case, and 11-12ths in another; it might be coined at the cost of the State in one country, and with a charge of mintage in another. Variations on these points would in no degree affect its efficiency and utility as a common valuator. A 25-franc piece assimilated to the sovereign would answer the purpose, and I have noticed as yet no response, favourable or unfavourable, to the suggestion of the sovereign by the International Coinage Commissioners, or to their remark that had the Paris Convention of December, 1865, taken as their basis the value of gold as measured by silver on the average of the ten preceding years, they might have adopted as a 25-franc piece the exact equivalent of the English sovereign.

Mr. J. G. Hubbard.

The general use of a gold coinage in France is comparatively recent, and although any change must occasion some inconvenience, there can be no comparison between the claims of the English system, which dates from 1816, and that of the Monetary Convention, which dates from December, 1865; the one is nearly 50 years older than the other.

I shall look with great interest for any further remarks from M. Wolowski upon the "double legal money," and especially upon the difficulties attending its operation, which I have challenged his ingenuity to solve; but I must warn him that it will require a very clear and very strong case to overthrow the prevailing impression in this country that the wisest course to pursue with our own coinage is—*to leave it alone.*

I remain, Sir, your obedient servant,

J. G. HUBBARD.

PRINCE'S GATE,
Oct. 1, 1869.

MR. LOWE AND THE COINAGE.

(The Economist, October 9, 1869.—To the Editor.)

SIR,—Mr. Hunt has failed to give the slightest proof or illustration of the House of Commons having kept either to the spirit or the letter of the Resolution of 20th October, 1696, quoted by him in the *Economist* of 18th inst. as so deserving of imitation next year, namely:—

"That this House will not alter the standard of the gold and silver coins of this kingdom in fineness, weight, or denomination."

And it becomes a matter of some interest to the public to investigate whether the promise and performance of this Resolution have coincided with each other, or if it has not shared the fate of other abstract propositions, affirmed by the House of Commons as opportune at the moment, but modified or set aside, and properly so, in altered times and circumstances.

Mr. F. Hendriks.

In 1696, the Resolution to the contrary notwithstanding, there was but one real standard of value, and that was silver. It was the sole metal on which debts or taxes could then be legally discharged. Guineas, or other gold coins, circulated only as commodities.

Sir William Petty, the most practical and able of the men of business who cultivated Political Economy at that period, remarks :—

"So there can be but one of the two metals of gold and silver to be a fit matter for money. Wherefore if silver be that one metal fit for money, then gold is but a commodity very like money. And as things now stand, silver only is the matter of money."—(*Political Anatomy*, p. 347. Dublin edition.)

Locke, in 1691 and 1695, and Mr. Lowndes in 1695, had, in their respective treatises and reports on the amendment of the coin, entirely concurred in viewing silver only as the matter or standard of the currency. Locke, indeed, had rather a strange theory of the positive unfitness of gold as a standard, for he wrote in 1695, that—

"Silver coins make the money of account or measure of commerce all throughout the world. . . . Gold is not the money of the world or measure of commerce, nor fit to be so; yet it may and ought to be coined to ascertain the weight and fineness."

The question of introducing a gold coinage as legal tender, side by side with the silver coinage, remained in fact in abeyance until 1717, when the Lord High Treasurer referred the matter to Sir Isaac Newton, then Master of the Mint. Newton made three representations or reports containing his views on the best method of preventing the melting down of the silver coin, by arranging a new scale of valuation of gold in proportion to silver. But Sir Robert Peel was wrong in stating (in his speech, of 1819, on the resumption of cash payments, as quoted by Lord Overstone, in to-day's *Times*) that—

"That great man, Sir Isaac Newton, came back at last to the old, the vulgar doctrine as it was called by some, that the true standard of value consisted in a definite quantity of *gold* bullion."

All that can be truly affirmed is that, acting upon Newton's advice, silver, in 1717, 3 Geo. I., ceased to be the sole

Mr. F. Hendriks.

standard, and the double or alternative standard of gold or silver, at the debtor's option, was adopted. This was change No. 1.

In 1774, we arrive at change No. 2. Silver was made legal tender only for sums under 25*l*. by tale and above 25*l*. by weight, and gold remained legal tender without restriction. In 1783 came change No. 3. Gold and silver, both without restriction, again became legal tender. In 1797, we have change No. 4, when bank-notes appeared on the scene as legal tender. In 1798, another change, No. 5, whereby silver was, as in change No. 2, made legal tender under 25*l*. by tale and above 25*l*. by weight. In 1817, change No. 6, to our present single gold standard, debasing our old silver standard upon the plan recommended 12 years before by Lord Liverpool, in his well-known letter to the King on the coins of the realm, and restricting its legal tender in a token form to 42 shillings by tale.

It is difficult indeed to see the justice of Sir Robert Peel's conclusions in 1819, notwithstanding Lord Overstone calls them memorable, that—

"Every sound writer on the subject came to the same conclusion—that a certain weight of gold bullion, with an impression on it, denoting it to be of that certain weight and of a certain fineness, constituted the only true, intelligible, and adequate standard of value."

Now, Mr. Harris, of the Mint, the sound author, according to Mr. Hubbard, who has so much lauded his "*Essay on Money and Coins,*" observes that—

"In these parts of the world silver is, and from time immemorial hath been, the money standard, and that it is the fittest material for a standard. . . . All other metals, gold as well as lead, are but commodities rateable by silver."

And with a prophetic inkling of what, a generation later, Lord Liverpool would carry out, Harris bewailed the chances of interference with the silver standard, and observed (in Part II., 8, of his *Essay*)—

"Others go yet farther and say that gold is our standard—that you may debase silver coins as you please, and treat them as mere tokens without giving any one a right to complain. This is making short work of it indeed, and with one stroke demolishing our poor old standard."

Lord Liverpool was, however, as positive that our working standard was gold as Harris was that it was silver. His lordship stated (in p. 173 of his treatise)—

"That in this kingdom the gold coins only have been for many years past and are now, in the practice and opinion of the people, the principal measure of property and instrument of commerce."

Again, he went so far as to observe, what is open to very grave doubt and question indeed, and is, to say the least, a great exaggeration—

"That all payments had been regulated in conformity to the gold coinage for almost a century."

And contended that—

"The change to a single gold standard would make no alteration in bargains, nor in the terms of all covenants and contracts."

If we are to be purists to the very grain, and sticklers to the utmost tittle of the law, we may well gaze with astonishment at seeing Lord Liverpool held up to the public in 1869, by the Bank of England Directors, as the guardian of the standard, instead of its destroyer and alterer from what it was, according to those maxims of Burleigh and of the Elizabethan age which Lord Overstone holds up in to-day's *Times* for reverential admiration. The equity is indisputable of that maxim of the Roman law affirming that the value of money is to be considered and regarded as at the time of contract of an obligation, and not as at the time of its discharge. For instance, the successors of all who, in the seventeenth or eighteenth centuries, had purchased, by payment in silver, a perpetual interest of (say) 3 per cent., derived from the funded stock of our Government, have had a right to receive their half-year's interest of 30s. if paid to them in silver, as it might have been for the last century and a half or more, at the legal tender rate, and according to the Mint Indentures of one pound troy of silver of standard fineness, for 62s. But from 1817 down to the present time, owing to the change then made in the fineness, and, in other words, to the debasement made in our standard, as recommended by Lord Liverpool,

Mr. F. Hendriks.

they have only received one pound troy of standard silver per sixty-*six* shillings instead of per sixty-*two*.

So much for the alleged permanency of our standard, which we are to be led to believe has remained intact through all the transformations of changes, Nos. 1 to 6, we have been considering. Marvellous that it should have passed unscathed through so many fires! Well might *The Times* remark in its leading article of 28th June, 1816, that—

"Queen Elizabeth's standard is estimated by Locke at $7\frac{1}{2}$ grains of pure silver to a penny, whereas Lord Liverpool's is only after the rate of $6\frac{4}{11}$ grains."

"Again and again," did that journal remark, "do we most urgently call on the Legislature to cause this subject to be inquired into by persons of science, and not sacrifice a million of money to the upholding the credit of the late Lord Liverpool's pamphlet."

One might imagine from Mr. Hunt's and Lord Overstone's way of referring to the ancient Elizabethan and other legislation on our standard that at least no change in the fineness of the gold coin can be discovered. But turn to the Mint Indentures before 1718, say for the period between 1670 and 1718, and it will be found that the current value of one pound troy weight of coined gold was 44*l.* 10*s.*, but that in 1718 it rose to 46*l.* 14*s.* 6*d.* of coined gold to the same weight of standard gold bullion. And this debasement from the old fineness has continued to the present date.

And yet in the face of all these legalized changes in fineness, in weight, and in denomination of our standard, those who are supporting the international coinage movement, as called for in these days by the altered state of commerce and intercommunication, and by the special effect of the gold discoveries and the consequent gradual entire resort to a gold standard, now in process of accomplishment by the leading nations of the old and new world, are erroneously supposed to have neither precedent nor prescription for any change or reform of our standard recommended for a great and sufficiently important object. This supposition should be protested against when we see how scanty is the foundation for the objection.

Even the quotation by Mr. Hubbard of Harris's opinion in 1757, as against a seigniorage, is by no means justified in the opinion of other equally competent and much more recent Mint authorities. For example, the late Mr. Robert Musket, of Her Majesty's Mint, in chapter xii. of his well-known work (pp. 68-78 of the second edition, 1812), strongly advocated a seigniorage of at least one-half per cent., whilst he reckoned the then expense of coinage at three-quarters per cent. Even Lord Liverpool, judging from what he states (at page 154 of his treatise), chiefly objects to seigniorage as not imposed upon the coin of foreign merchants. This objection of his would surely have been removed had he lived in times like these, when a seigniorage is levied by the United States, by Australia, by India, and by France and some other countries on the Continent, in the indirect form of the delay and consequent loss of interest in the delivery of coin in exchange for bullion. To this their legislative enactments expose the public, even although at the present time, from the large amount of recent coinage and the absence of any drain for warlike and other operations, the contrary to this rule, *i.e.*, immediate delivery of coin, exceptionally prevails.

I am, Sir, your obedient servant,

FREDK. HENDRIKS.

PALACE GARDENS TERRACE, KENSINGTON,
Sept. 20, 1869.

INTERNATIONAL COINAGE.

(The Times, October 19, 1869.—To the Editor.)

SIR,—The question of the permanent addition of the amount of a seigniorage to the value of the bullion in a coin is of sufficient importance to merit further investigation. A case which has occurred in the experience of the

Par.

French Mint appears to offer a fact which will serve as a test of the soundness of the abstract theory. It was mentioned in my letter published the 25th of September, but was there only employed for the object then in view—viz., to ascertain, if possible, the limit of the tax which could be imposed on the importer of gold.

In support of the theory of the seigniorage adding value to the bullion no example appears to have found more favour than the supposed parallel case of a tax on any commodity adding its amount to the original value of the article. Thus, putting the case that any foreign merchandise which can be delivered here at a total cost of (say) 20$s.$ per cwt., is suddenly taxed to the extent of 1$s.$ on that weight before it is allowed to be entered for consumption, it is naturally asserted that the importer must then sell at above 21$s.$ per cwt. before he can obtain a profit. This is generally followed by the usual explanation that, according to the abundant or short supply of the article then in the market, the last importer may lose, or the owner of the free goods may gain, but that it must all eventually be adjusted, either by the goods coming in at a lower price, the consumer consenting to pay the tax, or finally by his going without the article.

But before this example can be applied to the question now under discussion we must see if the conditions of the two cases are similar, and shall, therefore, have to inquire into the nature of taxes on foreign produce, and trace them to their source. In the earlier times all entrance dues were collected as a toll, receivable in kind. Thus the lord of the manor ordered his steward, or clerk of the market, to take (say) a handful from every sack of flour before it could be admitted for public sale. The Government above him would act in the same manner with foreign goods; and in the case above cited the importer of 21 cwt. would have to give up about 1 cwt. to the Customs, in order to be enabled to freely sell the remaining 20 cwt. Here the usual stereotyped paragraph about supply and demand in the market, &c.,

must be supposed to be introduced by the writer according to established usage.

But one important consideration must not be lost sight of. The abstraction of part of the goods does not alter the relative proportions between the quantity for sale and the average demand for it. The toll taken by the lord of the manor is used by himself and household, and up to its extent prevents him from bidding in the market against other purchasers, and thereby tending to enhance the price. Neither would the collectors of the Royal dues destroy the 1 cwt. received. It would either be employed for Government purposes, and thus, *pro tanto*, deprive the importer of a customer; or be sold in open market in competition with his remaining store. In neither case, therefore, would the remaining quantity be enhanced by what was taken away.

Now, if any juvenile currency doctor is preparing for a hearty laugh at the idea of any one in the nineteenth century illustrating present questions by examples drawn from the time of the Norman Conquest or Saxon Heptarchy, he is earnestly requested to restrain his mirth until he has time to recollect that, so far as relates to gold (the object of the present inquiry), our mode of collecting the tax is now identically the same as was in general use for all articles in those benighted times. As far as relates to gold we still exact our toll in kind. Every 480 ozs. gold entering the Mint is coined into 1,869 sovereigns, according to law and usage. Of these rather more than 1,865 revert to the owner of the bullion; the remainder is retained somewhere. Here, again, there is no loss of coin; the owner certainly has only 1,865 pieces to dispose of, but they are not enhanced in value by the abstraction of four from the actual quantity into which his gold was coined. The portion retained is not carted away with the cinders of the Mint furnace, but enters, although not through his hands, into the general money-market, to reduce the pretended increased value of his own. And thus the doctrine enunciated by all the really great authorities on the *Par*.

question that the sovereign, our standard of value, represents the 1-1869th part of 480 ozs. of gold is fully confirmed.

Suppose that our Government were suddenly to awake to the necessity of carrying out in practice their theoretical principle of coining gratis, and consequently paid a man *at once* the 1,869 sovereigns for the 480 ozs. bullion, the believers in the theory that a seigniorage permanently adds its amount to the value of the coin must adopt one of two courses :—

1. They must show that the old sovereign, which has paid a seigniorage, will purchase a bill for more francs to pay for wheat purchased (as in the example in my second letter) than the new sovereign of equal weight, but which has been coined free.

2. Or, failing in their attempts on the first case, they must frame a memorial fit to be presented by the holders of old sovereigns, and giving valid reasons for soliciting a return of the duty which they had heretofore paid.

Fortunately for this country the period is so remote since mere theorists were permitted to meddle with our real standard of value that we have thus been compelled to frame the case of Government suddenly coining gratis· to obtain our example to reason upon, since it would be difficult from our own stores to produce a specimen sufficiently "fresh" to be presentable. But a case from France may be brought forward which is not too stale for use. It was stated in my letter of the 25th of September that previous to 1835 the French Mint charged nearly 3-10ths per cent. for coining, but reduced it at that time to about 2-10ths per cent. Now, if among the advocates of the new plan there is any one better acquainted than the rest with the practical working of bullion operations in France, it would be conferring a kindness on their general body if he could point out an instance in which a full weight piece coined before 1835 (and therefore having paid 3-10ths per cent. tax) was on that account worth 1-10th per cent. more than one afterwards coined, and which had consequently paid only 2-10ths per cent. Or if he can show that the extra 1-10th per cent. was returned to the holders of money coined before 1835 the example will be equally satisfactory.

The gentlemen who boast that by the dexterity of their manipulation they can hide from the public any amount of seigniorage under the glitter of the gold in the coin are respectfully invited to explain how this little pea contrived to escape undetected from under the thimble.

Experience, therefore, as well as reasoning, points out that the fortunate possessor of an Australian nugget submits to the tax because he otherwise cannot pay his butcher and baker, they being unable to give him change. The universal custom of all civilized nations also forbids him to coin for himself. That the value of the coin he receives is not enhanced by the amount retained is evident from the fact that the whole of the 1,869 sovereigns produced from each 480 ozs. of bullion is eventually thrown into the money market.

Theories founded on pure abstract reasonings are expected to be of general application, and are usually put forward with that recommendation. They are, however, unfortunately, subject to two inconveniences. First, the professional doctors are prone to giving different prescriptions for the same case; and, secondly, it frequently happens that when we wish to apply them to actual facts some unpleasant discrepancies arise. The latter, of course, must be the fault of the facts, which are proverbially "stubborn things," and predisposed by the inherent perversity of their nature to give as much trouble as possible to the makers of systems.

For example, what can be more explicit than the dogma laid down by Sir John Lubbock, that the mere act of coining *gratis* adds a value to the coin beyond what was originally possessed by the bullion it contains?

On the contrary, the doctors who have been called in to consult on the case of the Chancellor of the Exchequer assert that coining *gratis* is an erroneous proceeding,
Par.

because we are thereby compelled to convert large quantities of gold into money which is not intended for circulation in this country, but to be exported and sold as bullion.

Now any one is, of course, at liberty to believe implicitly in either of these doctrines, but it seems difficult to accept both at the same time; because the man who has, according to the first dogma, gained an increase in the value of his gold is stated by the second theory to give up this advantage by immediately exporting it as mere bullion. Perhaps, however, this may be attempted to be explained on the "general principle" that a man values a thing freely given to him less than if it had cost him something to acquire it.

At this stage of the inquiry that troublesome fellow "facts" starts up and insists upon being heard. He proves, beyond the possibility of doubt or denial, that the importer of gold actually pays a tax here of somewhere about 2-10ths per cent. before he can get his bullion coined. In future editions of these plans of the International Coinage Committee the word "*gratis*" must, therefore, be expunged, and "2-10ths per cent. tax" inserted whenever they are referring to this country. The difficulty of comprehending how both the amended propositions could be true at the same time is, however, rather greater than in the former case, as we should then have to explain why the owner of the bullion should throw away an advantage which it has cost him 2-10ths per cent. to obtain.

Discarding, therefore, all theories founded on "general principles," as being more likely to lead us into danger than to guide us to a safer harbour, let us direct our course by well-ascertained facts. So far as regards the question of seigniorage, their results may be summed up in a very few words:—

1. Importers of gold are willing to pay about 2-10ths per cent. for having their bullion converted into coin.

This is shown by the example both of England and

France. The fact that the latter country saw the propriety of reducing their charge from about 3-10ths to 2-10ths per cent. also furnishes strong reasons for supposing that 2-10ths per cent. is about the *maximum* amount which can be levied.

2. The owner of the bullion pays this tax for his own convenience, and because he cannot help himself out of his difficulties by any other method. But he does it effectually, and "once for all." The tax does not adhere to the coin nor enhance its value, because the whole 1,869 sovereigns are thrown into the money-market, although through different channels. Can any of the adepts in the science assert that the sum retained (about 4l.) may act twice on the market—first, by enhancing the 1,865 coins delivered by 2-10ths per cent., and again when sent there directly themselves?

Your obedient servant,

EXCHANGE BUILDINGS,   PAR.
Oct. 6, 1869.

P.S.—In the above observations the sale of gold to the Bank is taken as our basis of calculations, because that is the usual and ordinary mode of disposing of it. The detailed calculations already given by two of your really practical correspondents confirm my own estimate of the amount of the tax, and justify me in putting it down roughly, and only for the sake of using a simple number, at about 2-10ths per cent. Exceptional cases may occasionally occur to alter this amount to a slight degree. Thus, when interest is very low here it might happen that submitting to the delays of the Mint was to a trifling extent cheaper than selling to the Bank at 77s. 9d.; but the difference is too unimportant to deserve the trouble of testing it by figures.

There is, however, one point accidentally omitted in the above letter. In *one* case it is true that coined gold is of more value than the amount of bullion contained in it, and that is when the transaction is confined to the purchase of gold bullion only, and during the continued existence of a seigniorage. Thus, taking the loss on sending gold to be coined at the rate already assumed of 2-10ths per cent., the man who has received only about 1,865 sovereigns for his 480 ozs. may reasonably be supposed to be able to buy the same quantity in the market for about that sum of 1,865*l.* But this is not on account of the value of the coin being increased, but because the seller of the bullion, who wants money for it, is aware that, under ordinary circumstances, he must lose nearly 4*l.*, whether he sends his gold to the Bank or the Mint; and he would, therefore, be willing to sell it to any one at the same price. The truth of this is immediately seen when we take the case of the Government suddenly determining to coin *gratis*. The owner of the 480 ozs. would then be able to obtain the whole 1,869 sovereigns immediately; and under these circumstances for him to sell his gold for 1,865*l.* would be evidence rather of his extreme liberality than of commercial acuteness.

Sir John Lubbock's doctrine of bullion gaining value by being coined must, therefore, be materially modified. Its increase in purchasing power must be restricted to dealings in gold only; and instead of using the expression of "*gratis* coinage," it must be limited to times when a seigniorage is exacted, and then only to the amount of the tax, and employed in the purchase of gold.

THE SOVEREIGN.

(The Times, October 20, 1869.—To the Editor.)

SIR,—Your correspondent "Par," in *The Times* of to-day, asks,—" What can be more explicit than the dogma laid down by Sir John Lubbock, that the mere act of coining gratis adds a value to the coin beyond what was originally possessed by the bullion it contains."

Sir J. Lubbock.

So far from having laid down any such dogma, I said exactly the reverse (see *The Times* of the 22nd of September),—namely, " It is obvious that the act of coining will *not* add to the value of the gold as long as the expense is defrayed by Government."

I am, Sir, your obedient servant,

15, LOMBARD ST., E.C.   JOHN LUBBOCK.
Oct. 19, 1869.

THE TIMES.

(October 19, 1869.)

IF we would be happy, we must ask no questions. Every new controversy only dissipates a remaining illusion. The great Conservative Premier left us at least one belief. When he asked triumphantly, " What is a sovereign ? " he answered correctly indeed, and in the terms of his art; but somehow he encouraged us all to feel ourselves resting on a very solid pecuniary basis. People still attach a rather transcendental idea to the pretty little bit of metal which performs so important a part in the affairs of English life. At least they never dream that its reign is threatened, and that what all Birmingham failed to shake may yet yield in time to the superior force of changed circumstances. Coins have their day, as the most ordinary collection will show, and the sovereign may become a thing of the past. What is it, in fact ?—to repeat the old question. The only true answer is that it is a piece of mixed metal certified by the Royal mark to contain 5 dwts. 3¼ grains of gold. When it issues from the Mint no doubt it is what it pretends to be; but " all that is bright must fade," and wear away too. By fair means or by foul, by continual contact with dirty palms and rougher coins and the miscellaneous contents of bags and pockets, the sovereign parts with surface after surface, and in process of time becomes an arrant impostor, like a discarded servant in the livery of an old master. The standard is as inexorable, and therefore as ideal, as the dramatic " pound of flesh." Less by a hair's breadth—by much less, indeed—the " sovereign " is no longer the "pound." The pound of account is the only reality in the matter. Tens of millions of sovereigns are in circulation, passing, happily, unquestioned in the wide and unsuspicious circle of English society, more or less under weight, and therefore no longer lawful coins of the realm. The Englishman is made to feel this when he passes into Ireland. After patiently receiving in exchange for a Bank of England note a mass of one-pound country notes that cannot be seen, touched, or smelt without an actual nausea, he is not a little indignant to find that no " George," or, indeed, any sovereign not of a very late issue, will pass for more than 19s. 6d. It will not even pass for its weight in gold, for there is the trouble of weighing it to be paid for. Of course the law is the same here. Nobody is bound to take a sovereign on its unsupported pretensions. What people must take is the pound of account—5 dwts. $3\frac{1}{4}$ grs. of gold. There are moneys of account which have disappeared in the body, or are only to be found in collections, though they remain in bills and ledgers. The actual ducat has long given place to the piastre. That is to be expected; but not that our enormous currency of sovereigns should be in truth only so many bits of metal to be measured and weighed before they need be taken for pounds sterling. A Nonconformist will respect a Bishop if he is a good man, and if he teaches the truth, and that is all the respect we are bound to pay to the bits of gold with Her Majesty's name and image, and accepted by confiding Englishmen for sovereigns.

We are all very proud of this solid foundation for our currency, trade, and finance. It is like the earth, which cannot be shaken at any time. In the direst collapse and difficulty we, most of us, revert with renewed homage to the pious formula which determines the immutable relation of the pound sterling to the ounce of gold. But we must

pay for our pride. The result is we have no coins of the good old kind that carried the values on their faces, and could not be gainsayed. For the very small affairs of life, and for very moderate reckonings, our shillings and pence have a little brief authority; but when we come to the scale of gold matter yields to mind, the solid, substance to the airy formula. The Queen's own officers need not take a sovereign in payment of taxes or customs unless they like it. Upon the whole, the confidence is great and the convenience incalculable. Our currency is very convenient indeed, and, of course, very sound, except that just now the shillings and sixpences are beginning to look rather washed out. If our sovereigns were for English use or abuse only, there need hardly be a question. But the Chancellor of the Exchequer tells us, what, indeed, had long before come to the knowledge of most of us in one way or another, that when our romantic honesty has made the new sovereign fully worth what it pretends to be, and, in fact, a very convenient shape for 5 dwts. $3\frac{1}{4}$ grains of gold, the speculators in bullion deal with the coins accordingly. It is convenient to have the gold in a perfectly guaranteed, separable, and negotiable form, and capable of being sold, circulated, or melted just as occasion may suggest. Many millions, we are assured, pass quick from the Mint to the melting pot—a capital offence in the days of our forefathers, and savouring of insult now. There is a sort of absurdity, like some of the penalties of the doomed in ancient mythologies, in the Mint, at no slight labour and cost, coining beautiful sovereigns, to be speedily melted down and re-cast in plain ingots. It is to be considered that this abuse, for such it is, has increased, and no doubt will increase. Every new sovereign is at once a piece of model currency and a most useful article of trade. The British Mint is a manufactory which produces for the benefit of all nations a commodity which is absolutely, instantly, and universally convertible at its alleged worth, and which has the great additional advantage of being worth sometimes
The Times.

even more than a pound of account at the place where it happens to be. Unfortunately, this often involves that, in order to realize the fortunate difference of value, the coin must be melted down. But the practice prevails, and must increase, for it is the special boast of the British Mint that it coins for the open 'Change of the whole world, and that a sovereign shall be at least what it professes to be everywhere. As the process is expensive to our Government, and rather ridiculous, it is impossible to suppress a misgiving that it may one day receive a check, though in what form it is not easy to divine.

Thus far the loss suffered by the British State through its exact fulfilment of its pecuniary contract is not out of proportion with its other losses by abuse, wear, and tear. We are annually forging iron plates and other fabrics to the amount of millions of pounds sterling, only to see them speedily worn away, spoilt, destroyed, sold for waste matter, superseded, cast in heaps, or cumbering dockyards for long terms of years, till the dockyards themselves perhaps have to be condemned. Wear, tear, and waste—the moth, rust, and thief—run through all materials and all institutions, and we must make up our minds that so costly and splendid a possession as our gold currency will not be secure from the universal law of depreciation, and even depredation and abuse. Everybody who in his private capacity happens to be more or less a pillar of the social State finds that he has to bear the burdens of many about him, and to pay for their waste, their dishonesties, their petty trickeries, and their follies. England must always expect to do the same. The occasion for change in the matter before us had not yet attained so intolerable a magnitude as to justify any palpable qualification of our perpetual engagement to pay a pound of gold—that is, a perfect sovereign, containing pure metal to the stipulated weight—to every one who presents himself with the promissory note. It has not yet been shown that the smallest fraction of a grain could be deducted from the proportion of gold in the composition of the sovereign without lowering its current value in the market of the world to exactly that amount. The British public at home are generous, easy, and confiding. They do not often ask how much a sovereign has lost by honest use, and they do not know how often the coin is really short of its proper value by several pence. But even we at home might become more particular and more sceptical if the State seriously attempted to pass upon us a coin which made no secret of a small deduction to pay for its manufacture, or rather to pay generally for the costs of the Mint. But, whatever we at home might please to do with the shortened sovereign, it is quite certain that abroad it would only change at its true value; and in all former controversies on the metallic currency it has always been maintained that there is one law for home and for foreign use in dealing with the standard coin of a country. It must be worth its weight in gold, and not a grain less upon any pretence. It is quite possible that the grievance, which is undeniable, may one day become intolerable. It may be possible to devise some way to make the world pay for the manufacture, or rather relieve the British public of a part of the cost. It is possible that some day the Bank of England may be permitted to give ingots in payment of bank-notes to a very large amount, unless a premium be paid for the more convenient form of coin. But we have not come to this pass yet, and need not yet attempt to anticipate the ingenuity, or other qualities, of our remote descendants.

THE BULLIONIST.

(October 23, 1869.)

OUR GOLD CURRENCY.

THE proposal to degrade the English standard of value, the sovereign, and thereby incidentally to cheat creditors, has been, as recently mentioned in these columns, pretty well thrashed out of existence. Its propounders seem to be aware that their scheme has failed to commend itself to the public mind; and, judging from a singularly characteristic article in a leading contemporary, they are preparing to beat a retreat. *The Times*, during the controversy, has given its columns freely enough to the advocates of both sides of the question; for its own pronouncements it obviously assumed to claim a judicial character. That it has been inclined to the opinions so rashly hazarded by the Chancellor of the Exchequer there can, however, be no doubt. And it is for this reason alone we feel bound to notice the latest deliverance of our contemporary on the subject, and to point out what appears to us to be the real significance of its rather hazy language.

It may be remembered that Mr. Lowe, when he made his now famous " suggestive " speech, spoke of the gold currency as an unnecessary and expensive luxury, a superstition—if we remember rightly—at any rate, as a crotchet. Now this is the theme which our contemporary, dropping any show of advocating the sweating or clipping proposal, works up into a lengthy, nebulous, and inconclusive article. " We must pay for our pride," we are told, in insisting upon having a gold currency; but that " so costly and splendid a possession will not be secure from the universal law of depreciation, and even depredation and abuse." Well, a metallic currency is liable to be worn by use, as all instruments are with which men work, and the cost of renewing them must, of course, be borne. But is that any reason for discarding good instruments, and adopting such as, being cheaper, are also less trustworthy? Are the enormous mass of the exchanges in the country to be carried on by means of one-pound notes, that " cannot be seen, touched, or smelt without an actual nausea ? " And if not, what is to be the substitute for the sovereign ? The writer in the leading journal fails to state.

But a radical misconception seems to run through whatever argument this article contains. The sovereign,

as the law prescribes, contains no doubt 5 dwts. 3¼ grains of standard gold, or, more accurately speaking, 123 $\tfrac{174}{623}$ grains, full weight. This is the standard, inexorable, within the limitations laid down by physical laws. By no possibility, even with all the refinements and approach to exactness in the modern minting machinery, can each coin be turned out precisely and mathematically equal in weight to every other. That is a recognized and necessarily accepted defect in all standards whether of weight, measure, or length; and that it should now be advanced as an objection to a gold currency, seems to savour of a foregone conclusion. Then we are gravely assured that a pound, according to Sir Robert Peel's definition, which is that of the law, is no longer a pound when the coin has been a short time in circulation, as, by trituration and abrasion, it loses a portion of its just weight. Here again we have a consideration submitted which can only escape the charge of puerility by being admitted to be a rather unadroit evasion of the real point advanced by the Chancellor of the Exchequer. We say that the law allows for this unavoidable deterioration of the coin;—otherwise a metallic currency would be reduced to an absurdity and an impossibility, since a sovereign of exact weight issued from the Mint to-day will, within a week's circulation, have lost a portion of its weight by wear. In order to meet this inevitable defect, by royal proclamation and universal usage, a deficiency in the weight of the sovereign of ¼ grain $\tfrac{171}{623}$ is tolerated in circulation; that is, if a sovereign does not weigh 122¾ grains, it is considered light. When the coins get below this weight they are sooner or later remarked upon, and the last holder loses the amount of the difference. What is there in all this to make a ground of for even the insinuation of a charge against the use of a gold currency? Is it true that "the Queen's own officers need not take a sovereign in payment of taxes or customs unless they like it?" We venture to say, and with some confidence, that these valuable officials possess no discretion of the sort.
The Bullionist.

Light coin they, like other creditors, may reject; but the Queen's officers are certainly bound to receive that which the law and the Queen herself have declared to constitute a legal tender.

The grounds upon which gold has been made the standard and current money of England stand firm and unshaken before the half-audacious half-hesitating assaults of Mr. Lowe and his friends. Its advantages are manifold and obvious, and the trifling loss by wear and tear, which is calculated to be about one in a thousand yearly, is a mere bagatelle compared with the convenience. But again: there is this bugbear of the new sovereigns going to the melting-pot—" many millions, we are assured," says the writer, "pass quick from the Mint" to that receptacle. We know not who it is that has assured our contemporary, but we have no hesitation in expressing our conviction that this assurance is substantially without any warrant in fact. When Alderman Lawrence, shortly before the close of last session, asked the Chancellor of the Exchequer what his authority was for the statement that English sovereigns were systematically melted down, in an establishment founded at Brussels specially for the purpose, what was the answer? A direct refusal to give any answer or explanation whatever. The allegation has been made; no authority is vouchsafed; explicit denial has been given on local and personal knowledge; and to whomsoever will be at the slight trouble to consider the conditions of the subject, it must become at once clear that this wholesale re-transformation of sovereigns into bullion cannot possibly be carried on at a profit, which is equivalent to saying it does not exist. That gold coin may be occasionally used in the arts by goldsmiths, as a convenient form of the metal, is probably true; but that owners of bullion should take it to the Mint—that is, really, to the Bank—pay the cost of assaying it, submit to the loss of any fraction less than the eighth of a carat grain in each pound troy so assayed, and to a further deduction of $1\frac{1}{2}d.$ an ounce; and that then, the bullion turned into coin at this cost should be quickly, and " by millions," converted again into bullion at a profit, is an assertion of which one might say *Credat Judæus*, only we are certain that our good friends of that nationality would be the last to believe it.

"It is not possible that the smallest fraction of a grain could be deducted from the proportion of the gold in the composition of a sovereign without lowering its current value in the market of the world to exactly that amount." So admits *The Times*, while bewailing the costly nature of our gratis coinage, which, however, is not gratis by any means. This is pretty obviously a forced conclusion, but it is a sound one. As to the suggestion of paying banknotes in ingots, it may be some relief to think that the consideration of that "ingenious" idea is left to "our remote descendants."

INTERNATIONAL COINAGE.

(The Times, October 26, 1869.—To the Editor.)

Sir,— On my return from the Continent my attention was called to Mr. Hubbard's letters on international coinage, addressed to *The Times* during my absence, and as there occurs frequent mention of my name, may I request the favour of a small space for a reply?

Mr. Hubbard commences his letter by warning the Chancellor of the Exchequer against "relying upon the arguments and conclusions propounded by" those dangerous men, "Professor Jevons, Mr. J. B. Smith, Member for Stockport, and Colonel Smith, late Master of the Calcutta Mint." "As connected with their advocacy of an international coinage (he says), it will be my duty to show that Mr. Lowe's reliance has been misplaced."

Professor Jevons and my namesake, Colonel Smith, may be safely left to defend their own opinions. As a

Mr. J. B. Smith.

member of the Royal Commission on International Coinage I ventured to differ from some of my colleagues—of whom Mr. Hubbard was one—on the question of the effects of a mintage charge, and I am obliged to avow that neither Mr. Hubbard's arguments nor those of your other correspondents have led me to doubt the soundness of the views I then advocated.

Strange notions exist as to this question of an international coinage. I have heard it called "one of Mr. Lowe's crotchets," and as the letters addressed to you tend rather to favour that impression, allow me to give a short sketch of its history.

The idea of uniformity of weights, measures, and coins, and the possibility of one general system for use by all nations, was the dream of far-seeing men more than three centuries ago, and, like other dreams of great minds, we may, before long, see it realized. But, according to the Report of the Royal Commission on International Coinage, public attention was forcibly called to the subject in our own day at the time of the first International Exhibition in 1851, by the difficulty which was then experienced in comparing the value of the manufactures of different countries, on each article of which tickets were affixed in the weights, measures, and moneys of their respective countries. The jury, composed of all nations, were so impressed with this difficulty, and the advantages to all countries of an international system of moneys, weights, and measures, that they unanimously passed resolutions recommending its adoption by all nations, which resolutions have been repeated by the juries of every international exhibition since held. At the same time associations were formed in the principal cities of Europe and America, and International Congresses have been held from time to time to discuss and promote this great object.

The movement gathered strength by France in 1865 entering into a Convention with Belgium, Switzerland, and Italy for an international coinage. The use of the same moneys, weights, and measures throughout these countries which has resulted from this Convention has been attended with so many benefits that in 1867 France invited a Congress of nations for the purpose of deliberating upon the best means of securing a common basis for the adoption of a general international coinage. The Congress was attended by thirty-three delegates, representing twenty different nations, the Master of the Mint and Mr. Rivers Wilson being appointed to represent England.

The Congress unanimously agreed upon the adoption of a single gold standard, and that a gold coin of the value of 25 francs should be struck by such countries as prefer it, and be admitted as an international coin.

France having requested an answer as soon as possible whether England was inclined to associate her efforts with those of other nations in the endeavour to establish an international coinage, the Government of Mr. Disraeli, before replying to this request, very properly referred the proceedings of the Congress and the report of the English representatives to the examination of a Royal Commission.

The inquiries of the Commission revealed the fact that most countries impose a charge (mintage) upon the coinage of gold. The United States and our own possessions in Australia and India impose a mintage of 1 per cent.

It is obvious that it will be indispensable in the adoption of an international coinage that the charge for mintage should be identical. This and other requisite changes will, no doubt, cause considerable temporary inconvenience to some countries in the adoption of an international coinage; but it is a singular circumstance that England can join the Convention with scarcely any inconvenience at all; for it so happens that, by adopting a mintage of 1 per cent., an English sovereign would be of the exact weight of 25f. of French money. If, therefore, those countries could agree upon an identical mintage, an international coinage might be immediately adopted between England, France, Belgium, Switzerland, Italy, Greece, Roumania, and Rome.

Mr. J. B. Smith.

Then arose the question whether if England, which now coins gold for nothing, were to charge a mintage of 1 per cent., a new sovereign weighing 112 grains of fine gold, *plus* one grain for mintage, would be of equal current value, and possess the same purchasing power with the existing sovereign, containing 113 grains, on which no mintage has been charged.

I maintained the affirmative. There was no novelty in these views. Adam Smith a hundred years ago said in his singularly pithy style—

" If a seigniorage (mintage) were levied the coin would increase the value of the metal in proportion to the charge for seigniorage. Abroad such coin would sell only for its weight in bullion; at home it would buy more than that weight."

These views have been confirmed by every eminent economist from that time to John Stuart Mill of the present day, and they are so consistent with common sense and our daily experience that it is surprising sensible men can be found to acknowledge that the cost of manufacture adds to the exchangeable value of all raw materials, while they doubt that the value of the raw material, bar gold, is increased by its being manufactured into coin.

The State charges postage for the service of delivering people's letters, but if it ventures to charge mintage for the service of turning their gold into coin Mr. Hubbard prognosticates the most direful consequences. He says :—

" Parliament is omnipotent to legislate, but legislation is not omnipotent. Parliament might be persuaded by the Member for Stockport to enact that a sovereign with 122 grains of gold should be equivalent to a sovereign with 123 grains, but such legislation would be as futile as that which earlier in the century affirmed that the shilling and the one-pound bank-note, then at 20 per cent. discount, were equivalent to a guinea. The pound sterling is at once the unit of our money of account, the medium of exchange, and the standard of value, and its legal embodiment is a coin containing 123 grains of standard gold, neither more nor less, and it could not be varied without entailing mischief far exceeding any possible advantages."

I admit Mr. Hubbard's standard of value to be a sovereign of 123 grains of standard gold, which quantity of bar gold was given for it to the Mint. No charge, however, was made by the Mint for manufacturing it into coin. The Mint returned in coin the same weight that it received in bar gold. It is proposed in future that, instead of coining sovereigns gratis as heretofore, a mintage charge shall be made of 1 per cent. by abstracting one grain from each sovereign. Will Mr. Hubbard or anybody else give 123 grains of gold to the Mint for a new sovereign unless he can obtain as much as he gave for it? Inasmuch, then, as the same weight of gold must be given to the Mint for the new sovereign as was given for the existing sovereign, and as no sovereigns could in future be obtained from the Mint except by paying 123 grains of gold for them as heretofore, a sovereign of 122 grains *plus* one grain paid by the owner of the bullion for mintage must be of equal current value with a sovereign of 123 grains *plus* nothing for mintage, that being paid by the State.

A sovereign, then, is worth what it will cost to obtain it, and that is 123 grains of standard gold.

When Parliament voted " that a shilling and the 1*l*. bank-note, then at 20 per cent. discount, were equivalent to a guinea," the fraud and absurdity were patent, because the guinea was a coin of intrinsic value and had cost 126 grains of standard gold, while the bank-note, having cost nothing but the value of the ink and paper on which it was printed, and merely bore on its face a promise which could not be fulfilled, had only a conventional value.

Mr. Hubbard says, "abroad our coins are appreciated, not by what we call them, but by what they are." This is precisely Adam Smith's doctrine. But Mr. Hubbard adds, " and so we should need to send 123 new sovereigns to pay for goods which we could have bought with 122 old sovereigns ; while, on the other hand, our foreign debtors might take us at our word, and save 1 per cent. by discharging in our new standard obligations contracted in the old."

Now, every country coins money for the purpose of providing a convenient currency for the exchange of com-
Mr. J. B. Smith.

modities, and not for the purpose of export to a foreign country, and if any simpleton were to export new sovereigns of 122 grains for the payment of a debt of 123 grains of gold in a foreign country he would deservedly suffer for his folly. But Mr. Hubbard is a less shrewd merchant than I take him to be if he were guilty of a like folly. No, Mr. Hubbard knows better than to carry out such notions into his daily mercantile transactions. Instead of exporting new sovereigns of 122 grains each to pay a foreign debt of 123 grains of gold, he would, if he could not buy a foreign bill, buy with his new sovereigns 123 grains of bullion and export that for the payment of his foreign debt. As for our foreign debtors paying us in new sovereigns, has Mr. Hubbard ever asked himself the question, how can foreigners obtain these new sovereigns? Can they obtain them for 122 grains of gold?

If they export produce to this country and order it to be sold for new sovereigns, and direct these sovereigns to be paid to their English creditors, they are paying their debts in sovereigns which have cost 123 grains of gold. If they send bullion and order that to be converted into new sovereigns, it could only be done by paying the Mint 123 grains of gold for each, so that in either case the English creditors, so far from complaining of the payment to them of sovereigns which cost 123 grains of gold, would only be too glad to extend their dealings on the same terms.

Mr. Hubbard, although he sees fearful consequences would follow the imposition of a mintage of 1 per cent., strange to say, once advocated a mintage charge himself. " So long ago as 1843," he says, " I recommended in a pamphlet a mintage charge of $1\frac{1}{2}d$. an ounce." Again, he says, " A mintage charge cannot be safely carried beyond the cost of mintage." A mintage charge, then, of $1\frac{1}{2}d$. per ounce, or one not exceeding the cost of mintage, according to Mr. Hubbard, would do no mischief; it is only when the charge is raised to 1 per cent. that calamity begins.

But supposing that it should turn out that the expenses

of our coinage cost 1 per cent. on every sovereign coined; that, including the outlay upon buildings and machinery, the wear and tear, and the cost of the establishment, which cannot be dispensed with, whether fully employed or not, it should in the whole amount to 1 per cent.; then that, being the cost of our coinage, according to Mr. Hubbard, would be a legitimate charge for mintage, and should according to his own doctrine calm his fears.

The time is arrived when it becomes necessary that Government should decide what answer is to be given to France. What shall be done? The Royal Commission reported :—

"We entertain no doubt that an uniform system of coins, bringing into harmony the various standards of value and moneys of account, alike in their higher denominations and their lower subdivisions, as well as an uniform system of weights and measures, would be productive of great general advantage."

They were also of opinion that the idea of international uniformity should not be abandoned, but that renewed attempts should be made to render it feasible, and concluded their Report as follows :—

"The assembling of some general International Conference on the subject seems to have been looked forward to by many members of the Conference at Paris, and we are disposed to think that all the various questions might be best considered, the various interests of different countries discussed, and their conflicting views reconciled, by authorized representatives of the different countries meeting in such a Conference."

I have already in my addenda to the Report of the Royal Commission expressed the opinion, which I repeat, that "the Government of England will incur a great responsibility if it let slip the opportunity of heartily responding to the unmistakable desire the world expresses for uniformity. Railways and electric telegraphs, free trade and the abolition of passports, have in a remarkable way brought nations into personal contact with each other, and different nations have now become something like what the different provinces of an empire were to each other in times past."

Already, by means of international signals, the ships of

Mr. J. B. Smith.

all nations are beginning to talk to each other at sea, and the adoption of an international money of account such as that suggested by the Master of the Mint and Mr. Rivers Wilson would, in a similar manner, be understood, like musical writing, all the world over, and be an era in the world's history.

Among the countries which look with most interest on this question are the United States of America, the largest gold-producing country in the world, and which, taking a wide view of this subject, are prepared to suffer great temporary inconvenience to attain so great a triumph of civilization as an international system of moneys, weights, and measures. It will be necessary for them soon to reconstruct their monetary system, and, if we do not soon decide, they will probably found a system of their own. Let us, then, sweep aside petty difficulties, and go hand-in-hand with our brethren across the Atlantic, and with all nations, in bringing about another and the greatest triumph civilization has yet achieved.

I remain, Sir, yours obediently,
JOHN BENJAMIN SMITH.

KING'S RIDE, ASCOT,
Oct. 8, 1869.

MR. LOWE ON THE COINAGE.

(The Economist, Nov. 13, 1869.—To the Editor.)

SIR,—Most of the opponents of the reform of our gold coinage, advocated by the Chancellor of the Exchequer, appear to consider the advantages to be gained by the establishment of an international system, common to all the chief commercial nations, as greatly subordinate to the importance of settling various theories of intrinsic value, and of the special perfection of the present pound sterling over all foreign coins. Some, indeed, have gone so far as

Mr. F. Hendriks. U

to deny altogether the advantages of such a system, and have favoured the eccentric view that they are appreciable only by the "inexperienced traveller,"—to use the phraseology of one of the Royal Commissioners,—and that they are of no consequence to the commercial public. But the same Commissioner, if we may judge from his more recent letters, has so far relented from his original sweeping condemnation of the plan as positively to patronize its leading principles, *provided* his notion, and that of the majority of the Commission presided over in 1868 by Lord Halifax respecting the fitness of the sovereign in its present weight and fineness to be the model for the international coin of the world, can be carried into effect.

It may be observed that this Commission, the majority of whose members were, from their antecedents, known to be opposed to any change, had, in their Report of July 25, 1868, come to the remarkable conclusion that they "had felt it" (see p. xviii. of Report) "to be their duty to state the grounds on which, with a view to the general interest of the commerce of the world, the English sovereign *and* pound *(sic)* might form a convenient basis for an international currency." No one, however, would bite at this bait. It was at once seen to have been thrown out to choke the scheme. The able writers who have taken an interest in it abroad received this alternative with studied coldness, and the newspapers of Paris, Bordeaux, Bremen, Florence, and of other places, had most intelligent articles showing how inadmissible is the proposition under the actual circumstances of the day.

At the International Monetary Conferences in Paris in 1865 and 1867, the consent of the representatives, upwards of thirty in number, of various nations, was obtained to an international combination, on a well-defined threefold basis —(1.) Of a single gold standard: (2.) Of a common fineness of gold in the coin, nine-tenths pure metal and one-tenth alloy: (3.) Of weights of the coin, bearing a metrical relation to the kilogram of gold, taking as the unit or units

Mr. F. Hendriks.

of coinage either the 5-franc gold piece (the $\frac{1}{620}$th part of a kilogram of gold nine-tenths fine), or else any of the multiples of this weight of 5 francs. In this category of alternative and contemporaneously circulating units is included the 10-franc piece, such as has since been coined by Sweden, and is there called a carolin, and such as will be the 10-florin piece intended to be coined by Austria, equal in weight, fineness, and form, to the 25-franc piece of France it has been resolved to coin, and of which a few pattern pieces have already been struck by the Paris Mint. This latter coin of 25 francs weighs the $\frac{1}{124}$th part of a kilogram of gold, nine-tenths fine, is 24 millimètres in diameter, and is doubtless the coin destined to become the international pound or 5-dollar piece of the future. It is the coin advocated in the plan of the Chancellor of the Exchequer. The difference between it and the present pound sterling of England is so small that it naturally seemed incredible to M. de Parieu, the accomplished statesman who has mainly directed the international movement abroad, and to Prince Napoleon, who assisted at the Conferences and presided over some of them, that England should hesitate to abandon routine and improve her system of metallic circulation. No nation indeed is more interested than herself in promoting every improvement in the tools or machinery by which freedom of trade and facility of inter-communication are facilitated and encouraged. And an international coinage is, in these respects, an important adjunct to the network of railway, postal, telegraph, and money-order systems, with which the trade and well-being of separate nations are so closely allied and bound together by one common bond of usefulness to all.

It is at once evident that to the greater part of the conditions of common joint action our country need interpose no difficulty. To the first, the single gold standard, we have pointed the way, and the rest of the world are gladly following our good example, notwithstanding the writings of those who, like M. Wolowski, in France, and Mr. Ernest Seyd, in England, are preaching up a crusade against it, and in favour of the now obsolete and used-up theory of a double standard. To the second condition, of a uniform fineness of gold, nine-tenths instead of eleven-twelfths, there is not the slightest difficulty in our conforming. It is a purely immaterial question of common convenience, and entails no discussion upon theoretical or politico-economical grounds. To the third, the all-important question of a reduction of the pure gold weight of our sovereign to that contained in 25 francs of gold, there is more than one liberal statesman in England, and many a one abroad, who consider that once for all, and to aid a great and liberal measure, interesting to the world at large, we should approach the question with a desire rather to profit by its manifold advantages than with fear of the trifling inconveniences entailed by this, as by any other, change of system. These inconveniences are, both in theory and in practice, reduced to a minimum by the plan which Mr. Lowe has submitted to the judgment of a public who will doubtless, sooner or later, see fair play given to its consideration by the Legislature.

So far from the adoption of the plan of the Chancellor of the Exchequer imposing a sacrifice upon us, it may be turned to a saving of the taxation of the country, as it will provide a fund for defraying the cost of the next coinage and of future re-coinages also. It entails, however, the addition of a fourth general condition to the three conditions we have already referred to as constituting the basis of the agreement of the nations represented at the Paris Monetary Conferences. All other nations parties to the Convention of December, 1865, or hereafter joining it, would have to adopt identical Mint regulations, *i.e.*, a moderate and uniform rate of seigniorage, amounting to 1 per cent., combined with the English plan of immediate delivery of coin in exchange for bullion, instead of the power still possessed by the French Mint legislation of delaying such delivery. It is probable also that some

Mr. F. Hendriks.

general arrangement must be come to for agreement upon the prescriptive obligation of our English system being extended to foreign countries as to the delivery of a weight of standard bullion, equal to the full original weight of the coin, whenever bullion is demanded of the Bank in exchange for coin representing the Mint value of a bar of gold. To this original weight would have to be added, in the new system, the weight represented by the seigniorage.

This *quid pro quo*, that provided England reduce the weight of her sovereign, foreign nations must some of them give up their alternative gold and silver standard, and others their single silver standard, and must adhere rigidly to a strict and common definition of Mint regulations both as to seigniorage, as to reimbursement for regular reintegration of the coinage, and as to immediate delivery of coin in exchange for bullion, and of bullion, *plus* seigniorage value, in exchange for coin, is a sufficient trouble for us to call upon them to face, without our turning the flank of the movement and saying—" Take our non-metrical sovereign of 123·274 grains, eleven-twelfths pure, as the basis of an international currency, and adjust your own coinages in conformity to it." This is an ingenious device of the friends of immobility, as pleasing to those who wish nothing to be changed, as it is incomprehensible to those who understand the desirableness of advancing rather than of hindering a good movement.

If there be any meaning plainer than another in the letters of an anonymous writer who has recently largely availed himself of the columns of *The Times*, it appears to be an object to persuade the public against Mr. Lowe's scheme on the very narrow ground that the international coinage movement is something essentially French, palmed by the Empire on weak, subservient, and helpless neighbours, and which it behoves us Britons to resist. Such an argument might have passed muster in the days of our grandfathers, when everything not intensely English was looked upon as immoderately bad, and when it was sung of the French, at a period too when their metallic currency was far superior to our own, that—

"Our glory they envy, and happiness too,
And would change our old gold for their tinsel so new."

But what are the foundations upon which the Commissioners base their opinion that the interests of the commerce of the world makes the present sovereign so convenient as the best basis for international coinage, and deserving of adoption by all other countries? All that we can find by way of argument on their behalf is the alleged greater diffusion, in the commerce of the world and in contracts relating to the distribution of property in general, of the pound sterling as compared with the dollar and the franc. Strangely enough, in this view is found concurring Sir John Bowring, the staunch advocate of a decimalization of the pound, with Mr. Hubbard, the inveterate foe to that scheme. What the real facts of the case are it is proposed to examine in a subsequent letter.

I am, Sir, your obedient servant,
FREDK. HENDRIKS.

November, 1869.

MR. LOWE ON THE COINAGE.

(The Economist, Nov. 20, 1869.—To the Editor.)

SIR,—Resuming the subjects touched upon in the last letter (*Economist*, Nov. 13), we may observe that the pound sterling is everywhere familiar it is true, but so also are the dollar, the napoleon, and the kilogram of gold, nine-tenths fine, containing 155 napoleons exactly. And we need have no hesitation in concluding that the new pound sterling, according to Mr. Lowe's plan, exactly equivalent to the 25-franc piece, or to 10 florins, or to half an eagle, or 5 dollars, and the kilogram of gold, containing 124 exactly of *any of these coins*, would be more welcome internationally, *Mr. F. Hendriks.*

and would become more familiar to the world at large than the present pound sterling, which is not a given proportion of the kilogram of gold without fractions of an inconvenient character.

The object of the parties to the Convention of December, 1865, is quite misunderstood, if it be construed as desiring the positive supremacy of any one particular coin. It is distinctly confined to obtaining, in the first instance, a common measure for all the leading coins of the chief commercial nations, and to the establishment, by means of a reciprocity in concessions between them, of perfectly accurate, well-defined, and easily calculable proportions, free from fractions, between the values of their own coins, as compared with those of all other countries. Under such conditions alone can international interchange, and protection against waste by needless re-meltings and re-coinage, be established. The coins must, if such an expression can be used, speak a common language, or their utility is impaired.

It is a great mistake too, on the part of the Royal Commission, to ignore the fact that other coins besides the sovereign, particularly the napoleon and dollar, are already as widely diffused through the commerce of the world. The united export and import trade of the European countries alone who have·already joined the Monetary Convention, or have signed preliminary treaties of adherence thereto, amounts to no less than 500 million pounds sterling per annum at the present time, or to nearly one-fourth more than the aggregate exports and imports of the United Kingdom.

Then again, the circulation in gold 20-franc and 10-franc pieces is much larger on the Continent than the circulation of sovereigns in the United Kingdom and elsewhere. Our total gold coinage from 1817 to the present date amounts to about 195 millions, of which not much more than one-half, or say 100 millions at the outside, is in present circulation. But the corresponding total of the gold coinage of France down to the present time amounts to about 270 million pounds sterling, and that of Italy and Belgium to about 20 millions—altogether to 290 million pounds sterling in value, or to about half as much again as the gold coined in England. The gold 20-franc and 10-franc pieces in actual circulation may be reckoned as at least 2½ times as valuable as the total current sovereigns and half-sovereigns, for whilst it is pretty well established that from 90 to 100 millions sterling of the English coinage have been melted or re-coined, or have disappeared from circulation since 1817, it is certain that out of the 270 million pounds worth of French gold coined since 1792, more than 205 million pounds worth has been coined subsequently to the gold discoveries, *i.e.*, between 1851 and the present date. Very little of this recent coinage is believed to have been demonetized or lost from circulation. And there are reasonable grounds for assuming that not far short of 250 million pounds sterling worth of what may be called the napoleon coinage is current in the world.

We now have a basis to estimate the comparative cost of making the reduction in the English pound sterling required to render it conformable with the provisions of the Convention of December, 1865, and of the cost of bringing the coinage of the countries now included in that Convention into agreement with our sovereign.

The Chancellor of the Exchequer's proposition amounts to this:—We should have to reduce the weight of pure gold in our currency from 113·0016051 grains in each pound sterling (its present full weight) to 112·0089343 grains (the present full weight of pure gold in 25 francs). This reduction upon 100 millions sterling—assumed as the maximum amount remaining in circulation in Great Britain and other parts of the world—would leave a gross profit of 1,398,314*l*. on the operation of re-coinage of gold, which it will be absolutely requisite to undertake within the next few years. In other words, instead of the next general re-coinage costing the nation 631,925*l*. to reintegrate the

Mr. F. Hendriks.

legal tender weight that the 100 millions of existing gold currency will have lost in their circulation, there would be an ultimate receipt in money by the Exchequer amounting to 766,389*l.* by carrying out the new coinage on the basis of the equation—one new pound sterling equal to 25 francs exactly. And the 631,925*l.* saved, added to the 766,389*l.* gained, make up the total of 1,398,314*l.* of gross gain.

But to call on foreign countries to level up their coin to English standard on the basis of the alternative equation—25 francs equal to one present pound sterling—would entail a positive loss of nearly 3½ millions sterling. It may be said that comparing the loss to the foreign Exchequers with the gain upon the converse operation to the British Exchequer, there is a loss of about 5 million sterling, besides which the operation would take nearly twelve years to accomplish in the foreign Mints, being 2½ times as extensive as what would be required from the British Mints, where it might probably be finished in five years of continuous working.

It is not only as regards the comparative extra costliness of the operation that the proposed scheme for adopting the present pound sterling instead of the 25-franc piece, or new international pound, would be unacceptable. The number of persons interested in the gold franc circulation amounts to 70 millions for France, Italy, Switzerland, and Belgium, as against 30 millions, the population of the United Kingdom. If we add to this the population of countries which have joined the Monetary Convention since December, 1865, we get a total of about 130 millions, or more than four times that of the United Kingdom. That of our Indian Empire may be excluded, as, contrary to what any other nation in the world but ourselves would have done under like circumstances, we have hitherto refrained from introducing there the same currency as that of the mother country.

The Monetary Convention of December, 1865, has already conferred the great advantage of a common and compact coinage as between France, Italy, Switzerland, and Belgium. But it has not perhaps been sufficiently brought to the notice of your readers that the Convention is rapidly attaining a very much wider range. The two oldest nationalities, Greece and Rome, have passed laws to assimilate their currencies to it, and to establish tariffs of adjustment between old and new debts. The youngest member of the family of nations, Roumania, has been glad to associate herself with the plan. Spain, even before the recent revolution, had adopted the principles of the Monetary Convention, and her Provisional Government has ratified them. Austria, after mature consideration and the appointment of a large mixed Commission of Inquiry, added her name to the roll of adherents by signing a provisional treaty in 1867.

In North Germany, where no less than six different systems of complicated currency are still in force, and in the South German States, where there is another system, there is the strongest possible disposition to comply with the conditions of the Convention, as soon as some agreement can be arrived at, upon the principles by which a transition to a gold standard can be regulated, the present silver standard dominating all their systems, however various may be the coins and their subdivisions.

In Northern Europe we find that Sweden has given a welcome to the principles of the Convention. That country was represented at the Paris Conference of 1867 by Mr. Wallenburg, a Director of the Bank of Stockholm, and an unflinching and able advocate for the 25-franc piece or new international pound. Denmark and Norway will almost as a matter of course follow in the wake of Sweden, and it is believed that opinions in Russia are also very favourable to the change.

The foregoing may suffice perhaps to prove that the anticipations in *The Times* leading article of the 8th September, 1866, that the movement would be confined to the Latin race, have not been realized, for we find the Teutonic
Mr. F. Hendriks.

and Scandinavian races and the mixed races of America quite as willing to take a share in it, and all disposed to make some sacrifice to further an object which, as has been observed by one of the most influential Presidents of an English Chamber of Commerce, is of much more value to the world at large than would be the introduction of the English tariff into the laws of all European countries.

It is mere partisanship to object that English commercial men take little interest in the subject, when we find so many Chambers of Commerce throughout the United Kingdom have resolved to support an international coinage ; and several of their presidents gave valuable evidence on this side to the Royal Commission. As to the commercial feeling upon it abroad, it may be noted that the " Handelstag " of Berlin are quite favourable to international coinage on the plan of the Convention of Dec., 1865, and, in June of the present year, the German Customs' Parliament arrived at a decision to invite the allied Governments to enter as soon as possible into negotiations with the view of leading to the establishment of a new decimal coinage, and of taking care to frame it on principles offering guarantees for its ultimate extension to such a general monetary system as will be of service to all civilized nations. The Customs' Parliament also adopted the petition of the permanent committee of the German Chambers of Commerce in favour of a single gold standard.

It is also understood that, at the International Congress which sat last month at the Hague, a resolution was adopted "to move all Governments to take immediate further action in obtaining improved coinage." The progress of the movement and the deep interest taken in it by the United States, and by other countries of the new and old world beyond the limits of Europe, will be reserved for another communication. Some observations may also be offered on the extent of the daily loss we suffer in England from the want of an international coinage, and on the further losses we shall be liable to if through supineness we allow ourselves ultimately to be "left out in the cold," and adopt the measure at some distant period when larger inconveniences than at present will arise and probably some real sacrifices have to be made.

When, as in the present instance, we perceive a principle independently advocated by almost all civilized nations, we may feel tolerably confident that good is at the bottom of it. This remarkable consent of foreign nations in favour of an international coinage may well outweigh in the balance those imaginary difficulties and impediments which certain writers in *The Times* have been given such ample space to dilate upon. The truest friends of commercial progress will not however fail to discern that the circumstances of the present day are propitious for a reform of our coinage, like the one Mr. Lowe has had the boldness and public spirit to advocate. Such a reform is called for to meet the requirements and the inevitable results of an altered and modern state of things in respect of the metallic circulation of the world, as affected, and, to a certain extent, revolutionized, by the Californian and Australian gold discoveries.

I am, Sir, your obedient servant,

FREDK. HENDRIKS.

Nov. 17, 1869.

THE BRITISH COINAGE.

APPENDIX NO. XI. TO REPORT OF THE ROYAL COMMISSION ON INTERNATIONAL COINAGE.

IN Great Britain the weight of gold is now expressed in ounces troy and decimal parts of an ounce, and the metal is always taken to be of standard fineness (11 gold and 1 alloy), unless otherwise described. The weight of the sovereign is oz. 0·2568 of standard gold. The divisions of the troy pound, however, continue still to be likewise used. One pound troy contains 5760 grains, and is divided into 12 ounces of 480 grains each; one ounce into 20 pennyweights of 24 grains each. The pound troy being to the pound avoirdupois as 5760 to 7000, is 0·8527 pound avoirdupois. One ounce troy is equal to 31·104 French grams; one gram to 15·43235 grains.

The degree of fineness of gold, as ascertained by assay, is expressed decimally, fine pure gold being taken as unity, or 1·000. Thus gold of British standard is said to be 0·9166 fine; of French standard, 0·900 fine. Another method of expressing fineness is still in pretty general use, founded on an ideal pound, "the carat pound," which is divided into 24 parts, called carats. When the gold is entirely fine it is said to be gold of 24 carats. British standard gold contains two carats of alloy, and is said therefore to be gold of 22 carats. Jewellery gold may be of 22, 18, 15, 12, or 9 carats fine. For smaller divisions, the carat is subdivided into four parts, termed carat grains; and the carat grain into eight parts, or "eighths." Thus gold of 0·900 decimal fineness is reported as of 21 carats, 2⅜ grains; or, more usually, as 1⅝ carat grain *worse* than standard (22 carats). The smallest subdivision of the carat scale is $\frac{1}{768}$ part; that is, $24 \times 4 \times 8 = 768$. When the fineness of the gold is required to be expressed to a still greater degree of minuteness, the following course is pursued. It will be observed that if one pound troy, containing 5760 grains, were to be divided into 768 parts, like the carat pound, each part would amount to 7·5 grains. An "eighth" is accordingly subdivided into 7·5 parts; and any excess of gold, remaining to be expressed, over and above the last eighth, is awkwardly annexed as "surplus grains of gold on the pound," as a sort of supplement to the Assay report. Gold of 900 fineness on the decimal scale, becomes, when exactly expressed on the carat scale, worse $1\frac{5}{8}$ grains + 1·5 excess grains. The obscurity of such expressions is to be ascribed to a departure from the decimal method of calculation.

In the British Mint 15 pounds troy of standard gold are coined into 701 sovereigns nearly (15 lbs. = 700*l*. 17*s*. 6*d*.); which quantity is called a *journey* or journey-weight of sovereigns, from having at one time been a day's work. Gold coin still continues to be returned from the Mint to the importer of bullion, in bags containing 701 pieces, the transaction being one of weight. One pound troy is coined into $46\frac{29}{40}l.$, or 1,869 sovereigns per 40 lbs. troy. These gold coins are legal tender to any amount, provided that the weight of each piece does not fall below 122·5 grains in the case of a sovereign, or 61·125 in the case of a half-sovereign, which are the "least current" weights of the coins. The margin allowed for error in coining, known as the remedy or tolerance, is calculated upon the pound troy of coin, and amounts to 15 grains for the fineness, plus or minus, or $\frac{1}{16}$ of a carat, and 12 grains for the weight. The tolerance of fineness is therefore $\frac{1}{384}$ part, or $0·002\frac{29}{48}$. The tolerance of weight is $\frac{1}{480}$ part, or $0·00208\frac{1}{3}$. The last amounts to 0·257 grain on a sovereign. On the French gold 20 and 10 franc pieces, the tolerance is $\frac{1}{500}$ part, or 0·002, both in fineness and weight, 0·003 in weight upon the 5 franc. The gold coins of the Monetary Convention cease to be current when reduced by wear $\frac{1}{2}$ per cent. below the tolerances indicated. One sovereign is equal in value to 25 francs 21 $\frac{89}{100}$ centimes. Twenty-five francs are equal in value to 19s. 9$\frac{912}{1000}$d.

One pound troy of standard silver is coined into 66 shillings, of which the metal is worth from 3l. to 3l. 2s., according to the market price of silver. The remedy in fineness of British silver coin is one pennyweight (24 grains) per lb.; $\frac{1}{240}$ part, or 0·00417. In weight, the same. In French silver coin, the remedy in fineness is 0·002, or the same as for gold; in weight, 0·003 for 5 franc, 0·005 for 2 and 1 franc, 0·007 for ½ franc, and 0·010 for ¼ franc. According to the Monetary Convention of December, 1865, it is required that the silver pieces shall be re-coined when reduced by wear 5 per cent. below the tolerances indicated.

The standard fineness of silver is $\frac{37}{40}$; 3 alloy in 40, or 0·925. The fineness of the French standard silver is 0·900 in the five-franc piece; but an inferior alloy of 0·835 is used for the lower denominations. The single franc piece composed of the latter alloy is still made to weigh 5 grams, the weight originally chosen for the franc as the unit of the monetary scale, when the fineness of the coin was 0·900. It has now become a token, like the British shilling, of which the nominal value exceeds the metallic value.

The legal weight of the sovereign (123·274 grains) is derived from that of the guinea (129·438 grains), by deducting $\frac{1}{21}$ part. The weight of the guinea, on the other hand, came from one pound of standard gold (5760 grains) being coined into forty-four and a half guineas.

The British silver coins are a legal tender in payments to the amount of forty shillings only.

The material of the copper coinage is now a bronze mixture composed in 100 parts by weight of 95 copper, 4 tin, and 1 zinc, the same as in the copper coinage of France.

The shilling is represented by 12 pence in copper, and the pound by 240 pence. The penny is coined at the rate of 48 pence in one pound avoirdupois of 7000 grains or 453·59 grams.

The halfpenny, which is of half the nominal value of the penny, is coined at a different rate, namely, at 80 halfpence in the pound avoirdupois, and the farthing, which is one-fourth of the nominal value of the penny, is coined at the rate of 160 farthings in the pound avoirdupois, that is, at the same proportional rate as the halfpenny.

Copper pence are a legal tender in payments to the amount of one shilling only, half-pence and farthings to the amount of sixpence only.

SCHEME OF CURRENT BRITISH COINS.

			Pounds.	Shillings.	Pence.	Farthings.
In gold	Sovereign	= 1		20	240	960
	Half do.	= $\frac{1}{2}$		10	120	480
In silver	Crown	= $\frac{1}{4}$		5	60	240
	Half-crown	= $\frac{1}{8}$		$2\frac{1}{2}$	30	120
	Florin	= $\frac{1}{10}$		2	24	96
	Shilling	= $\frac{1}{20}$		1	12	48
	Sixpence	= $\frac{1}{40}$		$\frac{1}{2}$	6	24
	Groat	= $\frac{1}{60}$		$\frac{1}{3}$	4	16
	Threepence	= $\frac{1}{80}$		$\frac{1}{4}$	3	12
In copper	Penny	= $\frac{1}{240}$	$\frac{1}{12}$	1	4
	Half do.	= $\frac{1}{480}$	$\frac{1}{24}$	$\frac{1}{2}$	2
	Farthing	= $\frac{1}{960}$	$\frac{1}{48}$	$\frac{1}{4}$	1

EXTRACTS from an Act to provide for a new silver coinage, and to regulate the currency of the gold and silver coin of this realm. 56 Geo. III. cap. 68 (22nd June 1816.)

IV. And be it further enacted that from and after the passing of this Act, it shall and may be lawful for His Majesty's master and worker of the Mint, at His Majesty's Mint in London, to coin or cause to be coined any silver bullion, which at any time before or after the passing of this Act shall have been deposited at the said Mint, into silver coins of a standard and fineness of eleven ounces two pennyweights of fine silver and eighteen pennyweights of alloy in the pound troy, and in weight after the rate of sixty-six shillings to every pound troy, whether the same be coined in crowns, half-crowns, shillings, or sixpences, or pieces of a lower denomination, anything in any Act or Acts of Parliament in force in Great Britain or Ireland respectively, immediately before the passing of this Act, or anything in any indenture with His Majesty's master or worker of the said Mint for the time being, or any law, usage, or custom whatsoever to the contrary thereof in anywise notwithstanding.

XI. And whereas at various times heretofore the coins of this realm of gold and silver have been equally a legal tender for payments to any amount, and great inconvenience has arisen from both those precious metals being concurrently the standard measure of value, and equivalent for property, and it is expedient that the gold coin made according to the indentures of the Mint should henceforth be the sole standard measure of value and legal tender for payment, without any limitation of amount, and that the silver coin should be a legal tender to a limited amount only, for the facility of exchange and commerce; be it therefore enacted, that from and after the passing of this Act the gold coin of this realm shall be and shall be considered and is hereby declared to be the only legal tender for payments (except as hereinafter provided) within the United Kingdom of Great Britain and Ireland, and that the said gold coin shall hold such weight and fineness as are prescribed by the present indenture with His Majesty's master and worker of the Mint for making gold monies at His Majesty's Mint in London, and with such allowance, called the remedy, as is given to the said master by the said indenture, which weight and fineness are hereby declared to be and shall remain to be the standard of and for the lawful gold coin of the realm, so far as relates to gold coins of the denominations at present in use, and specified in the said indenture; and in case any gold coin

x

or coins of any other denomination shall hereafter be coined at the said Mint under any future indenture, such gold coin and coins shall hold the like standard in fineness, as the gold coins of the present denominations, and shall hold such weight as shall be proportionate to the weight of the present gold coins, according to the value for which such gold coin or coins of any new denomination shall be declared to be current.

XII. And whereas it is expedient that the silver coin of the realm should be a legal tender by tale according to its denomination to any amount, not exceeding the sum of forty shillings; be it therefore enacted, that from and after such day as shall be for that purpose named in any proclamation, which at any time after the passing of this Act shall be made and issued by or on behalf of His Majesty, with the advice of His Majesty's privy council, so much and such parts of the Act made in the fourteenth year of his present Majesty's reign, intituled " An Act to prohibit the importation of light silver coin of this realm from foreign countries into Great Britain or Ireland, and to restrain the tender thereof beyond a certain sum," as enacts or provides, or may be construed to enact or provide, that any tender in silver coin of the realm shall be legal to the amount of twenty-five pounds, or a tender for any greater sum, according to its value by weight, and also so much of any Act and Acts whereby the said last recited Act is continued, revived, or made perpetual, shall be and the same is and are hereby repealed accordingly; and that from· and after such day as shall be for that purpose named in any such declaration to be made and issued as aforesaid no tender of payment of money made in the silver coin of this realm of any sum exceeding the sum of forty shillings at any one time, shall be reputed a tender in law, or allowed to be a legal tender within the United Kingdom of Great Britain and Ireland, either by tale or weight of such silver coin or otherwise howsoever, anything in the said recited Act of the fourteenth year of his present Majesty's reign, or in any other Act or Acts in force immediately before the passing of this Act, or any usage or custom to the contrary in anywise notwithstanding.

EXTRACT from Mint Indenture (referred to in Sec. XI.) as to fineness of the Gold Coin.

Every pound weight troy of all the monies of gold aforesaid shall be in value forty-six pounds fourteen shillings and sixpence, and shall be in fineness at the trial of the same twenty-two carats of fine gold and two carats of alloy in the pound weight troy, which standard aforesaid of twenty-two carats of fine gold and two carats of alloy in every pound weight troy our Sovereign lord the King doth will and ordain and establish by these presents to be the right standard of crown gold.

THOMAS GRAHAM.

ROYAL MINT.

HALF A DOZEN PROPOSITIONS

RESPECTING

THE GOLD COINAGE.

Prop. I.—Our money of account is the pound sterling. All British commercial transactions throughout the world are based on this as their fundamental unit. It is therefore a cosmopolitan unit, and ought to be kept invariable. Moreover, the actual amount of our gold circulation is quite insignificant in comparison with the enormous sums which are transferred from account to account in pounds sterling: and these it is which that circulation represents; and on which the current, or retail, prices of commodities in general ultimately depend.

Prop. II.—The great and avowed object of our legislation on the subject of the Currency, from 1819 down to the present time, has been to establish an invariable relation between this unit of account and gold, to the effect, namely, that any amount of pounds sterling shall, practically, *and as a matter of legal right*, be convertible by their holder into gold, at the rate of 113 grains of pure gold to the pound sterling. And a process has been provided, and a system established, by which, through the instrumentality of the Bank, this shall be effected, viz.—by the conversion of good bills of exchange, or other valid claims for pounds sterling, into bank-notes, and presentation of those notes at the Bank for payment in *gold coin*.

For—

(*a*) The Bank is legally bound to redeem its notes in gold coin.

(*b*) The Bank *never* re-issues *light coin* (*i.e.* below the legal tolerance in weight).

(*c*) The Bank *does* issue (in payment of demands for pounds sterling) *every individual new coin coined at the Mint* (all of which contain their full legal weight of gold), amounting in value during the last fifteen years only to £90,000,000, from which it follows that the loss *from wear and tear*, to a presenter of bank-notes for payment to any considerable amount, may be regarded as infinitesimal, and *would be equally incident on a similar conversion of banknotes into the proposed " new sovereigns."*

PROP. III.—The substitution of Mr. Lowe's " new " sovereign, of 112 grains, for the present of 113, retaining the existing obligation of the Bank to redeem its notes in their nominal amount of " sovereigns," and without any legislative provision for compensating the holder of the notes for the diminished weight of the coin so called, would defeat this arrangement, and be tantamount to a lowering of the gold value of the pound sterling in the proportion of 112 to 113.

PROP. IV.—A light sovereign *is not a coin*, though, as a token voluntarily accepted as the equivalent of a legal one, it may, and does, continue for a very long time to perform satisfactorily all the offices of one, as a conventional medium of exchange within the United Kingdom. Whatever be the system of coinage adopted, there will always be light coins in circulation, so long as every individual does not weigh every sovereign that passes through his hands.

PROP. V.—The Government, having issued gold coin of its full legal weight and fineness, cannot be held answerable for its subsequent diminution, any more than for illegal coinage of base metal. If, for general commercial reasons, it take on itself the task of calling in and replacing light (*i.e. fairly worn*) coin, and cutting unduly worn or forged ones, the cost is properly chargeable on the general expenditure of the nation; and ought not to be levied, at all events, *on the material coin itself* to the subversion of the principle laid down as paramount in Prop. II.

PROP. VI.—The discussions that have taken place on this point show that a seigniorage, or a mint charge, has a tendency to introduce confusion and misunderstanding in the estimation of " value " (in the sense of purchasing power) of the coin, and to give the same coin different estimates of value in Britain and abroad. About the proposition, that a pound means 113 grains of gold, there can be no misunderstanding.

J. F. W. H.

www.ingramcontent.com/pod-product-compliance
Lightning Source LLC
ambersburg PA
030754230426

B00007B/969